Material Design
Informing Architecture by Materiality

Thomas Schröpfer

Material Design
Informing Architecture by Materiality

erial
gn

With a Foreword by
Erwin Viray

and Contributions by
James Carpenter
Justin Fowler
Sheila Kennedy
Elizabeth Lovett
Liat Margolis
Toshiko Mori
Nader Tehrani
Peter Yeadon

Birkhäuser
Basel

Layout, Cover Design, and Typography: Yoshiki Waterhouse, Cambridge/New York

We would like to thank the Harvard University Graduate School of Design
for the generous support of this publication.

Bibliographic information published by the German National Library.
The German National Library lists this publication in the Deutsche Nationalbibliografie;
detailed bibliographic data are available on the Internet at http://dnb.d-nb.de.

A CIP catalogue record for this book is available from the Library of Congress, Washington, D.C., USA

This book is also available in a German language edition (ISBN 978-3-0346-0034-7).

© 2011 Birkhäuser GmbH
Basel
P.O. Box 133, CH-4010 Basel, Switzerland
Part of ActarBirkhäuser

Printed on acid-free paper produced from chlorine-free pulp. TCF ∞
Printed in Spain
ISBN 978-3-0346-0035-4
9 8 7 6 5 4 3 2 1

www.birkhauser.com

Contents

Why Material Design?

Foreword by Erwin Viray

Phenomena exist in the material world.
Material makes thoughts tangible.
Materials manifest the world.

Architecture is defined by physical components that are materials. Materials are the substance of things. And there is no way to convey oneself except by language – language created by means of an impression in a particular medium. Expression is possible only by using specific materials.

We perceive reality through materiality, in the reality of matter.

Illuminating on the powers of the mind, Paul Valéry, the French poet and philosopher, wrote in his "Introduction to the Method of Leonardo da Vinci":

"Constructing takes place between a project or a particular vision and the materials that one has chosen. For one order of things, which is initial, we substitute another order, whatever may be the objects rearranged: stones, colors, words, concepts, men, etc. Their specific nature does not change the general conditions of that sort of music in which at this point, the chosen material serves only as the timbre, if we pursue the metaphor. The wonder is that we sometimes receive an impression of accuracy and consistency from human constructions made of agglomeration of seemingly incompatible elements, as though the mind that arranged them had recognized their secret affinities." [1]

"The monument (which composes the city, which in turn is almost the whole of civilization) is such a complex entity that our understanding of it passes through several successive phases. First we grasp a changeable background that merges with the sky, then a rich texture of motifs in height, breadth, and depth, infinitely varied by perspective, then something solid, bold, resistant, with certain animal characteristics – organs, members – then finally a machine having gravity for its motive force, one that carries us in thought from geometry to dynamics and thence to the most tenuous speculations of molecular physics, suggesting as it does not only the theories of that science but the models used to represent molecular structures. It is through the monument or, one might rather say, among such imaginary scaffoldings as might be conceived to harmonize its conditions one with another – its purpose with its stability, its proportions with its size, its form with its matter, and harmonizing each of these conditions with itself, its millions of aspects among themselves, its three dimensions with one another – that we are best able to reconstitute the clear intelligence of a Leonardo. Such a mind can play at imagining the future sensations of the man who will make a circuit of the edifice, draw near, appear at a window, and by picturing what the man will see …" [2]

Materiality is closely associated with the architectural space: "The monument, the creature of stone exists in space. What we call space is relative to the existence of whatever structures we may choose to conceive. The architectural structure interprets space, and leads to hypotheses on the nature of space, in a quite special manner; for it is an equilibrium of materials, with respect to gravity, a visible static whole, and at the same time, within each of its materials, another equilibrium – molecular, in this case, and imperfectly understood. He who designs a monument speculates on the nature of gravity and then immediately penetrates into the obscure atomic realm." [3]

And thus, an architect can be described as a person who cannot relinquish materials[4] – materials understood as an interest in an extension of body and flesh. In basic terms, an architect is unable to give up on materials. If he did, he wouldn't be an architect.

The task of an architect then, as Rafael Moneo put it, is to have a consciousness of materials, "accept techniques and use building systems for starting a process of the formal invention that ends in architecture; to be an architect, therefore, traditionally implied being a builder; that is explaining to others how to build. The knowledge (when not the mastery) of the building techniques was always implicit in the idea of producing architecture… The invention of form is also the invention of its construction." [5]

Being an architect means being an intermediary, the connecting link between ideas and materials. This role of a go-between requires more than simple enquiry, it requires solid investigation and research: an exploration of what can be coaxed out of materials, what can be added, what the materials can support, what they can hide, what they can emit, what they can keep, what they can simulate, and in the final instance, what they can create and what they can destroy.

The juxtaposition of the infinite world of imagination with a multiplicity of substances and materials can cause accents to be displaced, a balance to be upset, the same scene all throughout disrupted in order to find the possibilities that lie in the materials, and consequently it can allow the emergence of a materiality of possibility.

Material Design, thinking design materially, is a method that traces a route, a way, a path; capturing transitory phenomena, state of flux, constant change through materials; raising questions that must be asked if we are to know and live in theory and practice, in tribulations and in love, in thinking design and making architecture.

The skin is the material layer where soul and world commingle; the immutable milieu of the "changing, shimmering, fleeting soul, the blazing, striated, tinted, streaked, striped, many-colored, mottled, cloudy, star-studded, bedizened, variegated, torrential, swirling soul": [6] the skin, to one desire pure touch, gives access to information; it is a soft correlate of what was once called the intellect. Material and design thinking manifest in the touch of the skin.

Material design is a frame of mind. A deeper education unlearning one's first education. An attitude. Questioning. Inspiring: thinking, doing, and making. This book intends to open that frame of mind.

Erwin Viray
Singapore, July 2010

Notes

1. Valéry, Paul. "Introduction to the Method of Leonardo da Vinci" in Paul Valéry, *An Anthology*. Bollingen Series. Princeton, New Jersey: Princeton University Press, 1977. pp. 71-72.
2. *Ibid.* pp. 79-80.
3. *Ibid.* p. 82.
4. Tøjner, Poul Erik. "Struggle Against Style" in *Sigmar Polke – Alchimist*. Humlebæk: Louisiana Museum of Modern Art, 2001. p. 38.
5. Moneo, Rafael. "The Solitude of Buildings", Kenzo Tange Lecture, a commemorative lecture sponsored by Harvard University Graduate School of Design, given by Rafael Moneo when he accepted the post of Chair of the Department of Architecture, March 9, 1985. Casamonti, Marco. *Rafael Moneo*. Minimum Series. Milan: Motta, 2009. p. 90.
6. Serres, Michel. *The Five Senses: A Philosophy of Commingled Bodies*. London: Continuum, 2009. p. 23.

The Alternative Approach
Observation, Speculation, Experimentation

Thomas Schröpfer

Renzo Piano Building Workshop
in association with FXFOWLE Architects,
New York Times Building,
New York, New York, USA, 2007,
facade detail.

Architects rarely have the privilege of working directly with the object of their imagination. While other artists work immediately with their materials, architects work abstractly. They draw and direct materials, but they do not physically put the bricks and mortar into place. However, all of the experiential qualities an architect strives to convey in his or her designs hinge on their manifestation in built form. This manifestation is both limited and enhanced by the material properties the design deploys. However abstract and removed an architect may wish to be from the practicalities of material properties, it is through these means that the architectural concept ultimately justifies itself. A sensitive understanding of materials provides more than just a builder's means to a designer's end. Studies in materials inspire new understandings of part-to-whole relationships, organizational configurations, and phenomenological effects. Studies in material properties, at several scales ranging from details to the urban context, lead to a contemporary understanding of the built environment in relation to its components and the fabric into which they are inserted.

Throughout the discourse of architecture, the question of materials has often been entangled in a form-versus-tectonic framework. Should the material conform itself to the desired formal idea, or should the material properties themselves be celebrated in a manner "true to their inherent nature"? The role of materials in design tends to be questioned even more during periods of new material development and changing technological capabilities. We now find ourselves in such a time.

Rather than entering into hackneyed arguments and cornering ourselves as designers into the formal or the tectonic camp, this book argues for an alternative approach to exploring and implementing the material-design relationship. A 1:1 experiential and exploratory look into the inherent nature of material properties prompts new insights into the formal, conceptual, and expressive potential of these materials for designers. In developing a personal relationship with specific materials and their properties, a student of materials in architecture begins to formulate an argument for their use. The attitude that the designer develops during tangible material explorations is the unique combination of the material's potential and the designer's

intentions. The architectural discourse arising from these new attitudes lies outside of the jaded form-versus-tectonic exchange and transcends the fashionable but fleeting hype over the next "new" material. A combination of observation, speculation, and hands-on experimentation furthers an architect's ability to realize the design intent and equally informs the intent itself. Material studies not only push the boundaries of what and how an idea can be built, but they move the discourse as a whole into fresh territories. The division between materials and theory is no longer valid, if in fact it ever was.

The Material-Design Connection

Neither stone nor glass possesses any essence or 'truth,' nor is one or the other singularly apposite to our time. The whole matter rests on the ways the materials are shaped and transformed, the ways they become what they had not been before, the ways they exceed themselves.
– David Leatherbarrow[1]

Architects' opinions toward materials as a whole are a reflection of their perception of the world and their place as designers within it. These attitudes should be developed with intention. Often designers' attitudes change over time as their relationship with a material develops. The concepts of a material-sensitive designer are not necessarily based within the materials itself, but often concern other societal observations and are given resonance in a material as the concept is translated from abstract to built form. We observe a material's ability to both give conceptual meaning and to absorb it. A mere cataloguing of material products and their applications is only a shallow study into materials' role in fulfilling design intent. In his essay, "Materials Matter,"[2] David Leatherbarrow suggests that an investigation into materials at an urban scale is the key to seeing our cities in terms beyond the typical categories of history and future. For Leatherbarrow, the choice of materials gives evidence to the designers' views of society and their position within it. However, he emphasizes that it is not just the choice of materials that matters, but the ways and means in which they are worked to achieve the design intention. Leatherbarrow uses Jean Nouvel's remark in 1998 as an example

of an architect's material choice being wholly wrapped up in his greater understanding of society. Nouvel argues for a "non-image," in the sense of a continuity between the built world and the natural world. For Nouvel, glass is immaterial and useful in dissolving previously unavoidable barriers. The new manufacturing processes that allow for greater spans and the use of larger expanses of glass not only make the dissolution of barriers possible, they are evidence that a dissolution is desired at a societal level.

Glass is a case in point in that it possesses the potential for a wide range of phenomenological effects and is highly sensitive to the way in which it is handled. Its potential for transparency is dependent on the manner of its exposure to light, the angle from which it is being seen, and the chemical and physical characteristics given to it in its manufacturing. Its eventual appearance (or disappearance) is dependent on factors beginning with its initial chemical recipe, through parameters of its installation, and finally in the temporal conditions at the moment at which it is being viewed. While glass has existed as a material since the Bronze Age, its difficulty in production and transport, and its fragility kept it from becoming a major architectural material until the late 19th century. Its architectural use then became tied closely to that of a "new" architectural material: iron. Paxton's exhibition hall became a seminal display of glass's potential for ephemerality. The development of float glass in 1959 led to even greater production of glass. As its uses within architectural contexts increased, developments were made to make glass less fragile, more or less reflective, less brittle, etc.

Transparency is perhaps the quality that has captured architects' imaginations the most. Glass's embodiment of clarity, openness, and honesty has an almost polemical character. It gives glass its modern, democratic, and progressive nature. The conceptual desire for a transparent city is epitomized in Mies van der Rohe's 1922 design for a curvilinear glass skyscraper in Berlin. While never built, this much-published image became the phenomenological goal for many skyscrapers, though its realization proved problematic.[3] Mies argued that masonry walls typically used on skyscrapers of the time were an inappropriate material choice, in that they exhibited heaviness, with the

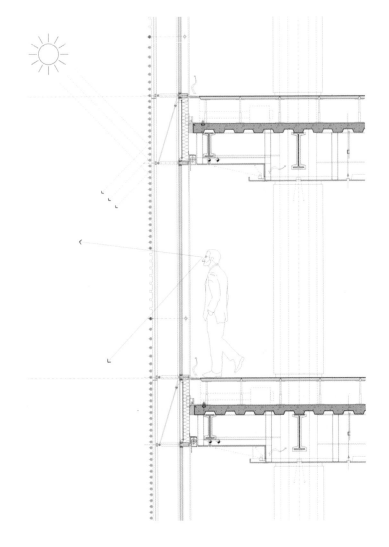

implication that they were load-bearing. "The structural principle of these buildings becomes clear when one uses glass for the non-load-bearing walls. The use of glass forces us to new ways."[4]

The glass skyscraper proved to be anything but transparent. Applied as a curtain wall, glass generally is highly reflective. No architect understood that better than Henry N. Cobb while designing the Hancock Tower in Boston, Massachusetts. Its reflectivity was manipulated and enhanced by the tall thin form to the point that it did disappear, not through transparency, but through sharp reflection. The blue tint of the glass allows it to fade into the sky while its sharp profile outlines the building's volumetric form (ill. p. 12).

Material Studies in Practice

Renzo Piano took up the challenge to create the ultimate transparent skyscraper in his competition entry and subsequent project for the New York Times Building (ills. pp. 11, 13–16). In describing the design intent, the project architect Erik Volz states: "Skyscrapers are often symbols of arrogance and power. With the New York Times Building we wanted to counter this with a light, more restrained and accessible tower."[5] It was important to the New York Times that the building embodies the characteristics to which it holds as a company and inspires those qualities in its writers. The ethical implications of a transparent environment that also reflects local conditions fit the goals of the media company perfectly. The metaphorical link of transparency with honesty and openness combined with the literal portrayal of the city made the Times Building a physical symbol for the paper. The success of the project as a whole hinges on achieving the physical realization of the phenomenological effects of transparency and reflection. The design team at Renzo Piano Building Workshop put forward the untested combination of untinted glass with a screen of offwhite ceramic tubes or "baguettes" hung on aluminum frames. While other materials were also considered, aluminum being the most likely alternative, the firm advocated heavily for ceramics because of the special qualities of the material. Renzo Piano himself had an attachment to the material, having developed a relationship with it over the course of his career.

Renzo Piano Building Workshop
in association with FXFOWLE Architects,
New York Times Building, ground floor plan.

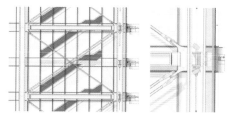

Renzo Piano Building Workshop
in association with FXFOWLE Architects,
New York Times Building, facade details.

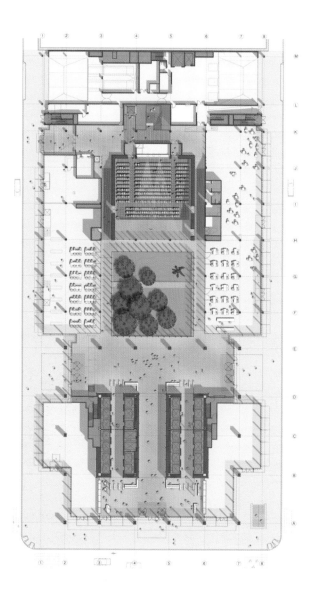

Volz comments: "The use of ceramics has a certain tradition in our office. Renzo likes the image of burnt earth hanging in the sky."[6] Volz goes on to describe the ceramics' irregular shape and texture along with its unique qualities of reflection as determinant in the material choice. While the office had experience in working with ceramics as a building material, they took no chances on it achieving the desired phenomenological effect. Several small models followed by full-scale mock-ups were created to test the appearance of the system and to make adjustments in order to achieve the desired balance of reflection and transparency.

Despite experience in building in ceramics, the design parameters for a skyscraper facade required the firm to research further into the potentials of the material. The tubes had to meet standards in structure, water absorption, and frost resistance. They did not even know a manufacturer who was producing long round ceramic tubes.[7] On a tour of Germany, the client noticed ceramic rollers being used to roll sewer pipes into kiln. The ability for the ceramic to withstand the heat of the kiln when other materials would have exploded or melted led the team to investigate their properties further. The final tube was an adaption of these rollers and the design team worked with their manufacturer to create the 196,000 ceramic rods for the New York Times Building that consist of a high-grade aluminum silicate.[8] In working directly with a manufacturer, the team was able to obtain the material with all the required properties at an achievable cost. While it was the Renzo Piano Building Workshop that forwarded the concept of a clear glass and ceramic "baguette" facade system, it took the combined efforts of their design partner FXFOWLE and the client team (The New York Times and their development partner Forest City Ratner) to realize the previously untested material at the scale of a skyscraper. Few projects had been completed with a similar use of ceramics, and none of them at a large scale or within the US. The client-design team was faced with a problem common to projects that aspire to invent new material applications. Few contractors are willing to take on the risk of building an unconventional system without adding a significant cost. There were too many unknowns involved in obtaining and delivering the unfamiliar building component to give an

Renzo Piano Building Workshop
in association with FXFOWLE Architects,
New York Times Building,
view from southwest.

Renzo Piano Building Workshop
in association with FXFOWLE Architects,
New York Times Building, detail roof isometric.

Shigeru Ban Architects,
Carta Paper Tube furniture, 1999.

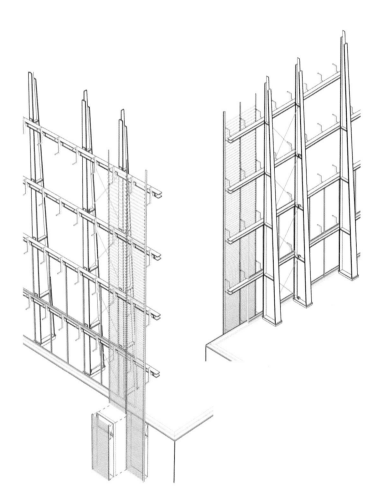

estimate at a price the clients could even consider. The solution to this problem came in foregoing the typical design-bid process for the facade contractor. The New York Times and Forest City Ratner paid four different curtain wall manufacturers that were likely to bid for the project to develop a wall section unit. The 5 x 13.5 ft (152,4 x 411,48 cm) unit was given specific parameters that included the ceramic rod system and an insulated window component. All four companies were able to realize the desired unit at an affordable cost. Once much of the guesswork had been taken out of estimating the facade costs, overall bids fell significantly to a realizable cost.[9]

While the innovative use of materials in architecture often stems from a personal investigation into a material, the implementation as a building component lies in the design and development team's ability to think creatively and work outside of their prescribed roles. As a practice, architects and developers need to be unsatisfied with building components as they are packaged and be willing to invest in the development of applications specific to their needs. The active involvement of architects at the material level becomes critical when we as architects begin to investigate new materials as they are developed by chemists and material scientists.

Another designer with a life-long commitment to material studies is Shigeru Ban. While Piano's studies focused on reinventing very traditional architectural materials, ceramics and glass, Ban came across a non-architectural material almost accidentally, and became intrigued by its potential. His dedication to the study and structure of paper tubes began very early in his career as a result of his unwillingness to waste spare materials (ill.). This initial investigation led to a successful string of projects, most notably the Japan Pavilion at the Hanover Expo in 2000 (ills. p. 17). Ban first began to experiment with paper tubes after he discovered them as a waste material that was used to deliver fabric for an exhibition installation. The extra waste product bothered Ban, who strives to be as economic and light-handed as possible. Instead of throwing them away, he took them back to his office. In 1986, he was able to incorporate them successfully as part of another installation, an exhibit celebrating Alvar Aalto's work

Shigeru Ban Architects, Japan Pavilion,
Expo 2000, Hanover, Germany, 2000,
exterior and interior.

Shigeru Ban Architects, Japan Pavilion,
exploded axonometric.

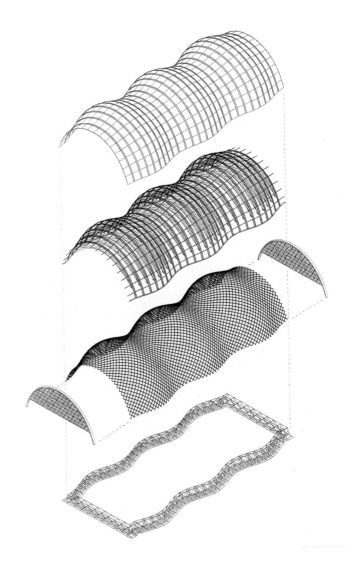

in furniture and glass. Ban wanted to capture the essence of Aalto's techniques and aesthetic, but budget constraints prevented him from using the finer woods commonly found in Aalto's designs. Additionally, Ban's resistance to use such a durable material in a temporary exhibit also inspired a nonwood alternative. Instead of wood, he employed paper tubes, which were inexpensive, made of recycled paper, and re-usable after the exhibit was dismantled. Thus began Shigeru Ban's career-long investigation in the structural potential of paper and a never-ending search for new ways to build with a mind for an economy of materials.[10]

Ban's dedication to paper tubes goes beyond experimentation with a material. It is connected to his broader interest in sustainable building practices, using the bare minimum, and the architect's role as a solver of greater societal problems. His experiments have not only been sporadic and client-project specific, but have been performed with the greater goal of ushering paper tubes into the lexicon of building materials. Despite the tubes' meek beginnings in exhibition and furniture design, they have been proven at the scale of exhibition halls and standardized to the level of emergency housing. Ban's first tube experiment, the Alvar Aalto exhibition at the MoMA, led him to a corrugated paper tube factory. There he learned that they were made of recycled material, that they could be produced at any length, diameter, and thickness, and that they were very inexpensive. While he used them in a non-structural capacity for the exhibit, their inherent strength sparked his curiosity. Three years later, Ban submitted a design for the Hiroshima Exposition utilizing a low-tech design with structural paper tubes. The entry was rejected due to the material's untested nature, but the submission led to a smaller commission, the Paper Arbor for the 1989 Nagoya Design Exposition. While the Arbor was small in scale, it was an important milestone for the material as it was the first time the tubes had been used structurally. After it was dismantled, Ban conducted strength tests on the tubes and found them to be stronger after exposure to the elements than they had been at the time of installation. Ban's dedication to testing and further experimentation led to larger-scale projects, each one building a case for the material to potential clients and to material regulators.[11]

In 1990, Ban got the opportunity to build his first permanent structure with paper tubes, the Library of a Poet. He was not yet permitted by Japanese building code to use them as primary structure, however he used prefabricated bookshelves instead to absorb the lateral loads and to provide insulation and exterior walls. This innovation would also be redeveloped and advanced in his Furniture House series. The success of this project eventually led to the authorization by the Minister of Construction of paper tubes under the Building Standard law in 1993, and the subsequent building of the Paper House as the first authorized building with structural paper tubes.[12] Once authorized as a viable structural material, Ban pushed the limits of the scale at which it could be deployed. The Paper Dome, Arch, and Expo Pavilion all pushed the boundaries of the perceivable strength of paper. Each however required a reinvention of connection details, more material testing, and subsequent reassurance to the building regulatory community that the structures were sound. Close collaboration with Frei Otto and engineer Gengo Matsui led Ban to a greater understanding of how to forward design with minimal materials. Meanwhile, Ban had also been pushing the smaller scale potentials of the lightweight, inexpensive material. While working with the United Nations High Commission for Refugees (UNHCR), Ban developed temporary housing for Rwandan refugees. The apparent worthlessness was one of the qualities that recommended paper tubes to the organization as a potential building material. Materials considered more valuable were often dismantled and sold by the refugees and replaced by local wood. This led to deforestation in the area. The ability to be made on site and easily assembled also made paper tubes an ideal material.[13]

Shigeru Ban's investigations into paper tubes stem from his greater views on architects' responsibilities to the earth and society. Just as David Leatherbarrow points out, the relationship between a designer and a material is a reflection of his or her greater understanding of the role of an architect. The experimentation in paper tubes has also enhanced and informed Ban's perception of architecture. After working to develop paper emergency shelters for earthquake victims in Japan, Turkey, and India, Ban commented: "Anyone who participated in the construction of a paper log house in that situation could not find himself spiritually untouched... Even if the paper log houses themselves were pulled down after several years, they will remain in the minds of the people who built and lived in them."[14]

New Materials: The Architect's Role

But in the blink of an eye, if a mass-production state of mind came into being, everything would soon be underway. In effect, in all the branches of building, industry, as powerful as a natural force, invading like a river that rolls to its destiny, tends more and more to transform raw natural materials and to produce what are called "new materials".
– Le Corbusier[15]

It is estimated that more new materials have been developed in the last 20 years than in the rest of history combined.[16] The development of different families of materials will reflect the concepts and desires of architects and also the structural and phenomenological desires of contemporary society. The way in which architects begin to consider new materials will determine the value with which society views them, and the longevity they will ultimately have as construction components.

As more materials are being engineered today, it is useful to look back at the emergence of an engineered material that is now ubiquitous in its architectural application. The beginnings of experimentation in reinforced concrete are linked to early modernist design and ambition. As the desire for non-traditional forms arose and the ambition to quickly construct more expansive architectural endeavors tied to industrialization, concrete re-emerged as a material with potential. However, concrete had many of the same structural characteristics as stone and was inadequate in tensile properties. Iron had been used to strengthen stone structures since the 17th century, therefore it was not a leap for architects and builders to begin to experiment with the combination of concrete and iron. Smallscale experimentation occurred throughout Europe and the US, but little significant progress was made until 1848. A French gardener, Joseph Monier, submitted a patent for concrete flowerpots and tubs embedded with a two-way grid

of iron mesh. While he did not understand the tensile properties that the iron reinforcing had on the concrete, he noted the increased inner cohesiveness of the combined material. Monier did not leave his invention to the realm of gardening, but continued experimenting with its potential applications. Ten years later he submitted patents for reinforced columns and girders, which he recommended for use in the construction of railway bridges.[17]

While Monier's work was the spark that set off the domino effect of development, reinforced concrete could not be systematically used as a building material because of its untested nature. Much like Shigeru Ban's paper tubes, the material needed further experimentation and documentation to be entered into the lexicon of architectural building materials. In 1877, Thaddeus Hyatt, an American inventor, teamed up with David Kirkaldy who was building a business of industrial testing machines. Together, they systematically tested the properties of reinforced concrete, therefore eliminating the dangerous process of trial and error from using the material in practice. In testing they discovered two important properties that launched reinforced concrete as one of the primary materials of the 20th century. The first was the discovery of the almost identical coefficients of thermal expansion of steel and concrete. Secondly, they discovered that their elongations under load were also very similar.[18] Soon after, the German builder G.A. Wayss bought the rights to Monier's patents and began developing a company building and experimenting with reinforced concrete. The company began documenting the material's behavior under various loads and its resistance to fire and corrosion. Results were published widely and soon *Das System Monier* was exported throughout Europe and America.[19]

While inventors and engineers were busy systematizing the material, architects were struggling to marry it to their new, "modern" way of building. Each school of thought experimented with the material and came to different conclusions. Reinforced concrete posed a particularly difficult problem to those trying to find the inherent "nature" of it. Frank Lloyd Wright's initial impression of concrete was that it was a sloppy material with very little inherent value because

Le Corbusier, Sainte Marie de La Tourette,
Éveux-sur-Arbresle, France, 1960.

a designer could mold anything into it without resistance. Obviously, Wright continued to consider the material and eventually celebrated it, using it extensively in both the Unity Temple and the Guggenheim Museum projects. Le Corbusier on the other hand, embraced the emergence of engineered materials as a whole. In his seminal publication, *Vers une architecture*, Le Corbusier wrote that "Standardized materials should replace natural materials, which are infinitely variable."[20] However high his enthusiasm, he, too, struggled to find an expression for concrete. His first attempts at using the Ingersoll-Rand Company's concrete cannon failed to achieve the machine-age sophistication for which he had hoped, ending in a somewhat sloppy finish he was forced to cover. The Villa Savoye represented the overall effect he dreamed possible with the advent of materials (though it was itself a hodge-podge of additive construction techniques), but his post-war period of work began to express concrete's potentials as a surface material. Sainte Marie de la Tourette and the Unité d'Habitation expressed the material at its most rough, and forced the architectural community to consider the engineered material's ability to exude a natural wildness that drew from the process of its formation (ills. pp. 18, 20).[21] Le Corbusier led the way in celebrating the rough finish and expressed formwork that would come to characterize concrete's modernist identity. Architects of this time period, such as Le Corbusier, Wright, Nervi, and Kahn were pushing the envelope to develop the character and range of expression we now associate with concrete as a material.

Reinforced concrete is a perfect example of a material development that began outside of architecture and was grafted in to solve an architectural need, both formal and structural. This is perhaps the most common way in which new materials find their way into our buildings. Architecture, unlike many other design professions, does not have a structured and well-funded means of conducting material development and testing. Innovations within architecture come from singular architecture firms with a dedication to material studies or out of educational institutions that prioritize these experiments. Clients are rarely willing to fund in-depth studies that are not directly related to the outcome of their commission, therefore research is often episodic and singularly focused. It is important

therefore for architects to have an awareness and a collaborative relationship with professionals outside of their discipline.

While new materials born in the early 20th century came from engineers, inventors, and scientists, later developments after the Second World War were often funded by large companies and governments for aerospace or military applications. This trend, often referred to as the "NASA effect" led to many material applications, e.g. in the realm of polymers. As interest in new materials heightened, new professions in the interdisciplinary realm of material science emerged in tandem with the goals of large industries and governments. The types of materials being developed reflect the excitements and concerns of society at large. The 1980s saw many new metal combinations and Super Alloys as a result of a quest for better commercial jets.[22] The most recent decade has seen the development of materials around concerns of sustainability.[23]

Often the delay in transfer between two industries is that a new material made specifically for a detailed use is not manufactured in a manner conducive to large-scale production. Until a larger building application and need is found, it will remain too expensive for architectural use. By contrast, materials developed by product designers at the forefront of material innovation often transfer more easily into architectural applications because they are already being produced in a manner meant for mass consumption and also because failed applications can be disposed of and replaced. However, as an architectural product, usually a building, is meant to last an average minimum of 30 years, the stakes are higher in initial material selection and a failed material application cannot be as easily replaced, thus requiring a greater burden of proof prior to implementation. Small-scale architectural projects, such as pavilions, exhibition stands, and installations are therefore critical to architectural innovation, as their small scale and temporal nature allow for more freedom of architectural experimentation (ills. pp. 35, 41, 85, 98, 122-124, 130, 148, 156, 157, 160, 165, 171, 172, 174-176, 183, 184).

The time lag between new material development and useful architectural applications results also from the way in which architects as a profession categorize materials. In most countries, building codes and standards list materials by their component (and thus assumedly appropriate) use. These are most often not even lists of basic materials but of already packaged and standardized building units of which the architect has little control over, other than brand selection. While this reduces liability and facilitates quick material selection, the architect's relationship with the material has been reduced to that of an informed shopper of a predesigned product. As long as the professional architect is not equipped to browse materials by anything other than basic classifications and prescribed applications, working along the lines of material properties, phenomenological effects, or dynamic potentials is difficult. The current architectural classification also inhibits the easy transfer of new materials into architecture: as new materials comprise increasingly more hybrid systems and dynamic qualities, they do not fit neatly under a label of *what* they are or even *how* they are used.[24]

Architects need to establish an alternative classification system that enables them to make material selections along several lines of criteria, thus facilitating the admission of new materials with undetermined architectural application. A quick look into the classification systems of engineers and material scientists is helpful to understand how these professions evaluate and integrate new materials. Different engineering professions employ different classification systems, but most systems operate by mapping material properties in a way that they can be matched with others in order to engineer a desired result. Emphasis is placed on what materials can *do* and how they behave under specific conditions. This type of classification is not oriented toward the selection of an application, but instead to help meet a specific performative need and hence facilitates experimentation in the potential application of materials.[25] Material scientists typically choose a different approach. They tend to classify materials hierarchically along the lines of their chemical composition. The focus is placed on their bonding structures and tendencies of molecular aggregation. Because these compositional characteristics are determinant of the overall material properties, this method of classification is useful to those looking to design a new material with a desired set of attributes. The material scientists' classification system facilitates

the invention of new materials with a desired set of properties.[26] Many members of the architectural professions have already begun to reclassify materials in an effort to spur innovation and as a result of their own frustration in attempting to enter into material experimentation. Some of these efforts are discussed in this book. Architecture has a great deal to contribute to the field of material science, beyond simply adapting the inventions of other professions for building purposes. Architects become the agents between material researchers and scientists and the clients. They contribute to the advancement of material studies in their own quest for materials that will express the contemporary formal desires of their concepts and their clients. Mohsen Mostafavi, Dean of Harvard University's Graduate School of Design, predicts the new interest of architects in malleable, dynamic surfaces will spur the development of materials that can accommodate these needs. "Right now there's a lot of interest and research into the role of the perceptual surface, so this could turn out to be an area of design where innovative materials will be generated... New materials are also responding to the increasing interest in complex geometries in architecture…"[27]

Quality, Craft, and Culture in Material Design

Materials embody the values and characteristics of their fabrication processes. Much of the potential innovation in material studies lies in the realm of fabrication techniques rather than in the advent of new materials. Many typical architectural materials embody meaning that stems from the ways in which they have traditionally been worked within a culture. The perceived value of a material is not always inherent within itself, but in the care, difficulty, and craft of its treatment within a culture. Taking a material outside of its established architectural application and studying its properties helps to reconsider its perceived value. Similar to Shigeru Ban's repurposing of paper tubes, an architect can find architectural value in a material where there was none.

The craftsmanship that a material requires in order to be used architecturally is a culturally specific knowledge that arises equally out of environmental parameters and social values.

Wood construction is an excellent material to compare across cultures because of its widespread use and long-term status as an architectural material. The constructional logic of wood leads many wood-based structures throughout the world to be strikingly similar. The general use of the material for structural support based in post-and-beam systems stems from wood's initial condition as tree trunks. While the myth of Laugier's primitive hut is a naive idealization of early construction techniques, it does reflect the existence of an inherent logic based in wood construction. A striking example of this lies in the traditional grain storehouses of Sweden and Japan. Early post-and-beam storehouses with thatched roofs were discovered on the Swedish island of Gotland; in form and structural logic they are identical to the Japanese tradition exemplified in the Ise Shrine (ill. p. 23).[28]

The Ise Shrine represents a tradition of preserving social values within the discipline of construction. Dating as far back as the 7th century, the Ise Shrine has since been reconstructed every 20 years, with few exceptions. The form and construction technique is based on the *kura*, or storehouses, of the Yayoi people during the Bronze Age.[29] The now well-codified practice of obtaining, treating, storing, and finally constructing with the timber pieces is conducted with a reverence rooted in the religious and ruling elite of Japan as well as in the great value of the large cypress members required. Up until the 13th century, it was possible to build the timber-heavy structures of the Ise Shrine from locally grown cypress. Since then, the timber has to be imported from ever-increasing distances at a price that reflects growing deforestation. The rebuilding of the Shrine requires 11,000 m³ of timber, traditionally of cypress. Of this, one third of the timber members must have a minimum diameter of 60 cm, allowing the primary structural elements to be cut from a single member. The largest of these are the columns that support the ridge beams of the main temples, measuring 76 cm in diameter and of 11 m in length.[30]

The sheer amount of timber needed to build these shrines makes the 20-year rebuilding cycle a costly event, especially considering the temporary nature of the materials and construction techniques. Great care is taken in obtaining and treating the wood so that maximum use is achieved out of each member. Trees are cut during the winter and brought near the site where they are stored for three years in ponds to treat the wood and to prevent over-drying. When they reach the sawmill, they are carefully inspected for flaws and the master carpenter marks cut lines that ensure the most efficient use of each timber. To prevent cracking, the ends are then waxed and braced to prevent splitting while the centers have wedges intentionally driven into them. The entire process is performed efficiently and cleanly by white-uniformed carpenters.[31] The difficulty, expense, and extensive labor required in constructing the shrine out of cypress lends the structure its nobility. The rebuilding of the shrine by the society is a truly sacrificial act in that the form could be achieved in other materials more easily.

Wood framing in America has a completely different value system attached to it. Unlike Europe and Japan, which had been logging their forests for centuries, Americans had an abundance of local timber. As settlers moved west during the 1830s to 1890s, heavy timber construction was gradually replaced or grafted with methods of light frame systems. While many initially considered light frame constructions flimsy in comparison to their timber siblings, the quickness with which structures could be built fit the fast pace of American development. As industrialization allowed for timber and nails to be mass-produced in standard members, hand-made joints began to be replaced with nails. Even as architects and engineers were debating the appropriateness of balloon frame systems, local contractors and carpenters were experimenting and incorporating framing into older types of domestic construction. While other cultures treated wood as a precious material, America used wood to fulfill a vital role in a society that valued speed, simplicity, and the ability to do more with less.[32] In no way was this more exemplified than in the early 1900s when Sears & Roebuck published "Modern Home No. 105," a precut balloon frame home in which every member was standardized. Sears & Roebuck, along with other large companies, owned and controlled means to manufacture the standardized members and hardware, transport them, and sell them to middle-income American families.[33]

Ise Shrine, Ise, Japan,
ritually reconstructed every 20 years,
690-current.

The mechanized and wholly efficient process of housing delivery appealed to Americans that at the time valued economy over individual craftsmanship. The difference in the process of timber framing in America compared to that of the Ise Shrine in Japan allows us to see that the value wood embodied was not a precious extravagance, but an accessible utilitarianism. Across the globe, wood was both rare and pedestrian. When the then prominent American architect Ralph Adams Cram visited the Ise Shrine in 1898, he was unable to understand the value in the shrine, which to him was merely a wood-framed structure. He described it as "sufficiently ugly and barbarous."[34] It was not until the Modernist period that the value of the Ise Shrine became celebrated among western architects, who saw it as an eminent example of the form-function paradigm.[35]

Technology, Representation, Communication

By dramatically altering the processes by which materials are worked, the material itself changes its characteristics, not simply in its appearance and function, but also in its cultural meaning and significance. Much material innovation emerges not in the making of new materials but in transforming the way in which we handle them. The recent surge in digital modeling and fabrication techniques has opened new possibilities in the handling of established materials, and allowed us to utilize previously unmanageable elements (ills. pp. 24, 25, 28, 29, 35, 41, 56, 57, 63, 67, 72-74, 90-98, 102, 103, 149, 156, 157, 165, 171-177, 179, 183, 184).

As architects, our ability to work with materials has as much to do with our ability to describe them as with the physical manipulations enabled by fabrication technology. Since the establishment of the architectural profession, orthographic projection has been the predominant means by which we design and communicate architectural space. While this technology is directly related to constructional logic, flatness and straight edges being the hallmark of successful building components, it is also rooted in a Cartesian descriptive system universally understood across the different professions involved in building. The plan, section, and elevation have stood as

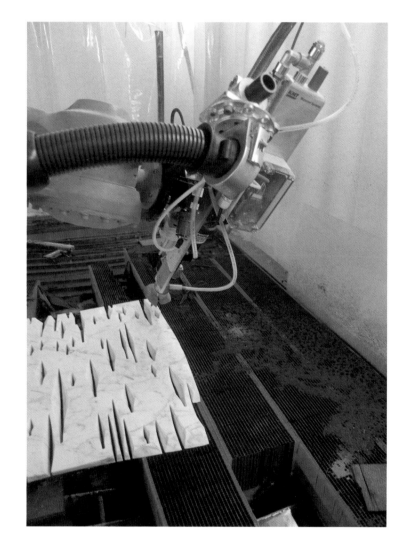

Martin Bechthold, Wes McGee,
Monica Ponce de Leon (Instructors),
Surfacing Stone: Digital Explorations
in Masonry Curtain Wall Design,
robotically controlled abrasive waterjet cutting,
Harvard University Graduate School of Design,
2008.

the primary means by which buildings are understood and built. In their book, *Smart Materials and New Technologies*,[36] Michelle Addington and Daniel Schodek argue that this overtly planar method of description has led to an understanding of building components that privileges the surface and that building components have been developed according to planar predispositions. This planarity also reduces phenomenological considerations to a prevailingly visual experience. Contemporary design is calling for a more subtle, softer intimacy with materials and consequently is developing more varied means of architectural communication.

The advances made in computer modeling are part of this new set of communicative means, and architects, engineers, and contractors are beginning to conduct business through threedimensional virtual models in order to obtain results with the desired complexity. Building Information Modeling (BIM) has developed and become standard in many areas of construction in response to an overarching desire to live in buildings in which materials are given back their third dimension. Computer modeling has also allowed materials to be considered in regard to their temporal properties. Much of the smart materials' intelligence lies in their ability to change properties over the course of time or under changing conditions. These types of behavior would have been impossible to describe in the traditional plan, section, and elevation logic. The ability to simulate and respond in time to changing properties is one of the greatest opportunities new technology holds for the future of material development. Exploiting these newly found dimensions lends new structural properties to thin materials, adds richness to surface materials, and allows better applications for smart materials.[37]

In a similar vein, new technology is also making large-scale three-dimensional forms more constructible. This, too, is directly linked to the ability to describe these curves in communication between professionals. Little can be said about these developments without mentioning the advances made by Gehry Technologies. Gehry Tech has pioneered BIM and parametric modeling in pursuit of finding buildable solutions to complex shapes. While these advances do not necessarily deal with material properties

Anish Kapoor, Cloud Gate,
Chicago, Illinois, USA, 2006.

specifically, they allow designers to apply materials in a manner that before was systematically indescribable, and therefore unbuildable. Frank Gehry proves this in his exuberant use of metal, a material normally conformed to planarity, in forms that contain complex curvature (ills. pp. 63, 67, 72-74).

Developments in architects' abilities to describe forms in three dimensions with greater sophistication result in material applications that reflect greater depth. Computer Numerically Controlled (CNC) 5-axis milling, stereo lithography (SLA), Selective Laser Sintering (SLS), and other forms of rapid prototyping are increasingly available to the design community, allowing for new or different operational logics to be applied to materials (ills. pp. 24, 40, 56).[38] These new technologies also reduce the emphasis on planar geometries in building units. While metals, glass, plastics, stone, and wood are all available as products with industrially produced form, in largely orthogonal geometries that makes products inexpensive to the building trade, these preformed orthogonal geometries can now easily be manipulated to create non-orthogonal geometries. The use of precision CNC fabrication, for example, allows a precise rolling-to-curve of metal panels over structural skeletons producing continuous curvatures of surfaces that can be found, for example, in works such as Anish Kapoor's Cloud Gate (ills. pp. 25, 94).

Inherent Expression: A Greater Understanding of Materials' Potential for Expression

When you are designing in brick, you must ask brick what it wants or what it can do. Brick will say, I like an arch.
You say, but arches are difficult to make, they cost more money. I think you could use concrete across your opening equally well. But the brick says, I know you're right, but if you ask me what I like, I like an arch.
– Louis I. Kahn[39]

A scale-less investigation into the qualities that define materials, both physically and conceptually, leads to a sophistication of their use within a greater design concept. A personal understanding of materials prevents an architect from applying them to his or her concepts in a way that is prosaic or an acquiescence to the latest

material trend. Hands-on experimentation and research into their physical and chemical make-up lead to an understanding of the potential expression and personality of a material. Louis I. Kahn's often-quoted conversation with a brick is somewhat vague in application and a bit naive, yet no one can argue with the results. Kahn's lifelong explorations into the character and potential expressiveness of brick are one of his most enduring contributions to architecture. Kahn was interested not just in the physical qualities of brick, but also in its inherent meaning within different combinations. Characteristics include brick's humbleness when compared to its stone sibling, its propensity for additive design operations, its readiness to be expressed as an individual or as a choral unit. The brick's heaviness and yet its ability to soar in the form of an arch were for Kahn very poetic. To him these aspects of the material would differentiate his use of brick from other masters of the material, such as Wright and Aalto. All three of these architects would work 1:1 with the material, yet they would each come to a unique attitude about its character and potential. While they all made innovations to the use of brick as a material, they also allowed the material to inform their design concepts. For Kahn, the humbleness of the construction unit led to a greater sobriety when used in large-scale public structures. The use of brick instead of stone kept the concept noble rather than elitist. The brick embodied the idea that a humble individual could aspire to greater feats.

In what is arguably one of the best examples, the Indian Institute of Management, Kahn wanted to architecturally connect three programs: institutional classrooms, faculty housing, and student dormitories. These vary drastically in scale. The main building itself had variously sized components including classrooms, meeting areas, and spaces for larger congregation. To connect these elements, Kahn employed the same system of load-bearing brick walls with concrete floor slabs. Kahn had already established a reputation for using brick within the United States, but in most of his previous applications had used brick as a veneer, not as a load-bearing element. Here, his structural explorations in brick created a consistent material language across the campus while also highlighting the differences in program through comparison. Greater loads were given higher arches, with the most extreme of these requiring a reverse arch.

The reverse arches in brick are, simultaneously, a reflection of India's seismically active environment and Kahn's historical links back to Roman brick construction techniques.[40]

Kengo Kuma has also developed an architect-material relationship. His is with stone. Stone is one of the most ancient and solid building materials, yet in his work Kengo Kuma has often contradicted this tradition in his search to create "non-monumental and transparent ways of building with stone." Although today most stone is applied as a cladding in a layering of wall components, society still considers the material as solid, representative of heaviness and stability. Kuma, in his work, challenges us to look at stone in a way that is truer to its new life as a wall component. Although in practice stone shifted away from the classical *poché* (carved voids from solids) our attitudes about stone have not. Kuma gives us a new perspective about stone that is not old, solid, and monumental, but modern, transparent, and personal.

Kuma designed his Stone Museum using Ashino stone, a lightcolored volcanic stone, which was also the stone chosen by Frank Lloyd Wright for the Imperial Hotel in Tokyo. In designing the three new buildings for the museum, Kuma employed primarily two different facade techniques, both aimed at achieving a dissolved yet crisp effect, in contrast to the heavy, rustic existing stone fabric (ills. pp. 26, 27). The first technique used a steel load-bearing system with horizontal stone louvers. The second technique uses a stone load-bearing system in which slots of stone have been replaced with thin strips of translucent white Italian marble, which allows a filtered light to enter while still achieving enclosure. The paving stone, both internal and external, is Shirakawa stone.

We have seen in what way a material investigation can inspire and enhance an architectural concept. Similarly, an architect's design concept can spur a quest for the most expressive material application in which to embody it. An architect that is always pressing the boundary of material expression is Dutch architect Lars Spuybroek. Spuybroek, principal of NOX, actively seeks material applications to accomplish both his progressive forms and specific phenomenological effects. NOX has realized many

Kengo Kuma, Stone Museum,
floor plan, elevations, and detail of stone wall.

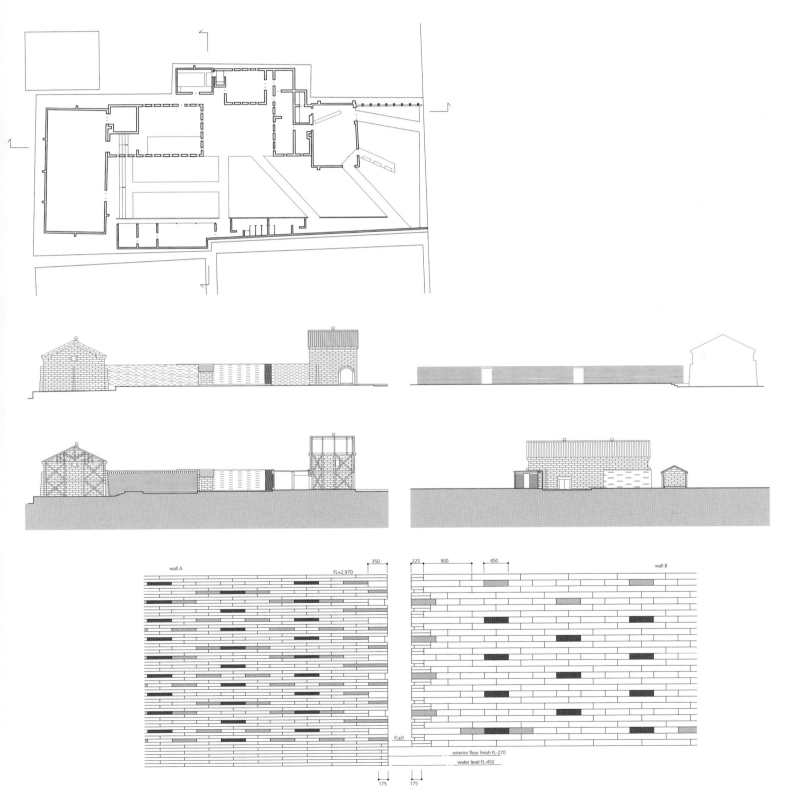

Lars Spuybroek/NOX, Maison Folie,
Lille, France, 2004, view and detail.

Lars Spuybroek/NOX, Maison Folie,
view at night.

Lars Spuybroek/NOX, D-Tower,
Doetinchem, The Netherlands, 2004,
view at night.

examples of experimental material use, which arise
from an integration of digital and interactive pursuits in order
to reinvigorate architectural design. Two built works, the
Maison Folie in Lille and the D-tower in Doetinchem, both
exhibit Spuybroek's original use of materials to accomplish his
desired effects (ills. pp. 28, 29).

The D-Tower is a piece of public art that interacts with data from
a website measuring the overall mood of the city in which it
stands, Doetinchem. In the evening, the tower will glow Green,
Red, Blue, or Yellow, corresponding to the feelings of Hate,
Love, Happiness, and Fear.[41] The material used had to be able
to be shaped into Spuybroek's curvilinear abstract forms, be
structurally sufficient, while being translucent enough for the
colored lights to glow evenly throughout the sculpture. NOX
used CNC-milled styrene foam covered with an epoxy. The
combination is a lightweight, rigid, and translucent structure.[42]

The collaboration of design intent, digital fabrication, digital
interaction, and creative material choice pushes the boundaries
of architectural design to new frontiers. The Maison Folie is a
cultural center in the center of Lille. Its facade was conceived
to achieve a soft, dynamic condition all in metal. NOX worked
with GKD Metal Fabrics to construct a facade made of Escale,
a stainless pliable mesh that becomes rigid only after locking
into its supporting steel structures.[43] The attractive visual
quality of the meshes were what first led the company to
consider servicing the architectural sector, however, product
development has shown many other attributes that make metal
fabrics a productive architectural material.

In a similar manner, Preston Scott Cohen has often had to
look beyond standard material components to accomplish
his unconventionally shaped forms. For Cohen, the material
needs not only to make construction of his highly defined
curves possible, but also to achieve them with a high degree
of surface resolution. In his Nanjing Performing Arts Center,
the concrete construction is covered with small-grained tiles
(ills. pp. 30-32). At the onset of the design, no tile could be found
with the correct shape and dimensions to achieve the desired
effect. However, the scale of the project created enough need

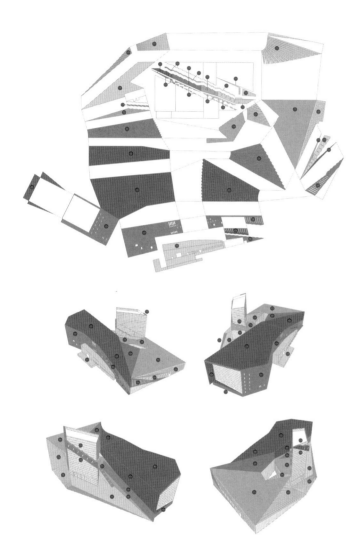

for tiles that the design team was able to custom-design a size and cut, allowing the final layer of the outer surface to become formally connected to the origins of its geometry. The resultant herringbone pattern is a formfitted finish for the arts center. China's economic circumstances allowed for the tile to be hand-placed, with the overall effect of a completely integrated and controlled system.[44]

Scale-less Design and Material Processes

A detailed look at the inherent qualities of a material lends itself to questions of operational logic. Properties such as such texture, elasticity, transparency, fluidity, and fragility indicate a range of opportunities and limitations of working with a material. Experimentation allows an understanding of a material's ability to bend, stretch, hold its shape, and withstand external forces. This leads to a proclivity toward certain types of operation: aggregation, weaving, modulation, and any other action that can be taken on a material to accomplish a designer's ends. For example, an operational logic such as modulation, applied to a material such as concrete, acknowledges its material properties such as malleability. Similarly, material processes such as casting refer to a fundamental operational logic. Like the material itself, this operational logic has no inherent scale, it is scale-less and hence can be envisioned for applications ranging from the detail to the building scale and beyond. For example, in Zaha Hadid's use of concrete, the same modulated continuity – a concept that reads as an order to subjugate the marks of the formwork – can be found across all building scales, ranging from furniture to building facades (ills. pp. 96, 97, 102, 103).

While individual acts of experimentation by students and practitioners push the boundaries of the profession, a more collective effort needs to be made to advance 1:1 material studies throughout the discipline. Architectural education systems should take their role more seriously as the frontier and disseminators of material properties: manufacturing companies and chemical engineers are encouraged, for obvious reasons, to keep a material's potential secret. Educational institutions need to fund and support large-scale investigations. While the emphasis that educational institutions place on materials ebbs

Preston Scott Cohen,
Nanjing Performing Arts Center,
tower and facade detail.

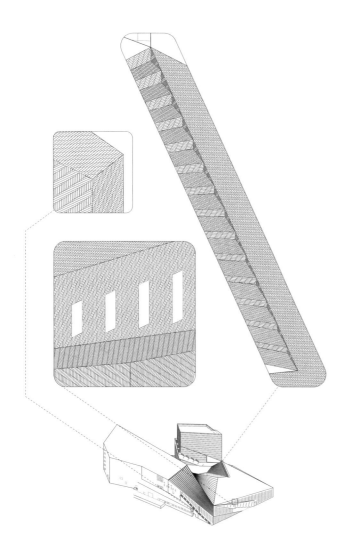

and flows over time, the history of 1:1 material investigations has existed since the days of early modernism. Johannes Itten felt material studies to be vital to an architect's education. As an educator at the Bauhaus, Itten established a Basic Course requiring all students to experience and demonstrate the character of materials. Contrasts such as smooth-rough, hardsoft, light-heavy, had not only to be seen, but also felt.[45] His courses within the school led a whole generation of architects to reconsider materials for architectural purposes.

Currently, there are many efforts to further integrate a more comprehensive study of materials within basic architectural education. Harvard University's Graduate School of Design maintains a unique material library, which is accessible online to the general public (ills. pp. 150-152). The GSD Materials Collection is an active and constantly updated library of materials and material applications, not simply a running catalogue of products. The library also keeps records of material experimentation and active explorations that are performed by students within the school (ills. pp. 87, 149, 156, 157, 160). In this way, students can build on the work of their predecessors, and a lineage of material studies can be developed. The database is organized in such a way as to promote an understanding of materials that goes beyond divisions by material type: materials are presented in the context of properties and not in terms of prescribed applications. As a result, students and professionals who browse the database may find, for example, that a film traditionally used to reduce reflectance in computer screens is applicable to building facades. The library also works in tandem with the core curriculum, requiring all students to contribute to the school of material experimentation. This not only gives students experience in handling materials in a form that is not already packaged as a building component, it also promotes material experimentation within their future practices. Other efforts outside the universities have recognized the need for more comprehensive material catalogues. These include the New York-based material library Material ConneXion, a "global resource of new and innovative materials for architects, artists, and designers," the Paris-based matériO, and the Swiss Material Archiv, to name just a few (ills. pp. 153, 154).

The architectural ambitions of today stem from a contemporary desire for more complexity, subtle and softer experiences, and increasingly tailored architectural experiences. The push for material innovation is not simply a search for the next fashionable facade but for desperately needed updates in building components to express 21st-century desires. It is little wonder that the material applications standardized and codified 50 years ago are insufficient for our time. As a profession our material palette has been limited by our simple classification system and by a lack of integrated disciplinary exploration. This book argues to re-emphasize the importance of the scaleless material experience and highlight explorations underway that are bringing our discipline into greater realms of expression.

Notes

1. Leatherbarrow, David. "Material Matters" in *Architecture Oriented Otherwise*, pp. 69-94. New York: Princeton Architectural Press, 2009. p. 91.
2. *Ibid.*
3. Dietrich Neumann. "Three Early Designs by Mies van der Rohe" in *Perspecta* 27 (1992). pp. 77-97.
4. See "Frühlicht" (1922), cited from Franz Schulze, *Mies van der Rohe, A Critical Biography.* Chicago: University of Chicago Press, 1986. p. 100.
5. Kaplan, David. "New York Times Building" in *Detail* 47, n. 9 (2007). p. 990.
6. *Ibid.* p. 991.
7. *Ibid.* p. 992.
8. *Ibid.* p. 997.
9. Stephens, Suzanne. "Renzo Piano Building Workshop and FXFOWLE present a quietly luminous addition to the Manhattan skyline with the New York Times Building" in *Architectural Record* 196, n. 2 (February 2008). pp. 102-103.
10. Ban, Shigeru. *Shigeru Ban.* New York: Princeton Architectural Press, 2001.
11. McQuaid, Matilda. *Shigeru Ban.* London: Phaidon, 2003. p. 14.
12. Ban, Shigeru. *Shigeru Ban* ... p. 111.
13. McQuaid, Matilda. *Shigeru Ban* ... p. 29.
14. *Ibid.* pp. 14-15.
15. Le Corbusier, *Toward an Architecture.* Introduction by Jean-Louis Cohen, Translation by John Goodman. Los Angeles: Getty Research Institute, 2007, p. 255.
16. Brownell, Blaine. *Transmaterial.* New York: Princeton Architectural Press, 2006.
17. Condit, Carl W. "The First Reinforced-Concrete Skyscraper: The Ingalls Building in Cincinnati and Its Place in Structural History" in *Technology and Culture,* v. 9, n. 1 (Jan. 1968). pp. 1-3.
18. *Ibid.* pp. 3-4.
19. *Ibid.* pp. 4-6.
20. Le Corbusier, *Toward an Architecture* ..., p. 258.
21. Weston, Richard. *Materials, Form and Architecture.* New Haven: Yale University Press, 2003. p. 88.
22. Beylerian, George M., and Andrew Dent. *Ultra Materials.* Bradley Quinn, ed. Hoboken, NJ: John Wiley & Sons, 2005. p. 24.
23. *Ibid.* pp. 6-7.
24. Addington, Michelle, and Daniel Schodek. *Smart Materials and New Technologies for the Architecture and Design Professions.* Amsterdam: Elsevier/Boston: Architectural Press, 2005. p. 27.
25. *Ibid.* p. 23.
26. *Ibid.* pp. 22-23.
27. Beylerian, George M., and Andrew Dent. *Ultra Materials* ... p. 149.
28. Weston, Richard. Materials ... p. 16.
29. *Ibid.*
30. Henrichsen, Christoph. "The Workshops at the Grand Shrine of Ise" in *Detail,* v. 42, n. 10 (October, 2002). pp. 1289-1290.
31. *Ibid.*
32. Peterson, Fred W. "Anglo-American Wooden Frame Farmhouses in the Midwest, 1830-1900: Origins of Balloon Frame Construction" in *Perspectives in Vernacular Architecture* 8 (2000). pp. 3-16.
33. *Ibid.* p. 13.
34. Chamberlain, Basil Hall. *A Handbook for Travelers in Japan.* Rutland, VT: Charles E. Tuttle, 1981. p. 92.
35. Reynolds, Jonathan M. "Ise Shrine and a Modernist Construction of Japanese Tradition" in *Art Bulletin* 83 (June, 2001). p. 321.
36. Addington, Michelle, and Daniel Schodek. *Smart Materials* ... p. 5.
37. Brownell, Blaine. *Transmaterial.* New York: Princeton Architectural Press, 2006. p. 8.
38. Beylerian, George M., and Andrew Dent. *Ultra Materials* ... p. 14.
39. Kahn, Louis. "Space and Inspirations," in *Louis I. Kahn, Writings, Lectures, Interviews.* Alessandra Latour, ed. New York: Rizzoli, 1991. p. 228.
40. McCarter, Robert. *Louis I. Kahn.* London; New York: Phaidon, 2005. pp. 250-251.
41. http://www.nox-art-architecture.com/ August 15, 2009.
42. Beylerian, George M., and Andrew Dent. *Ultra Materials* ... p. 261.
43. *Ibid.* p. 48.
44. Personal correspondence, Yair Keshet, Scott Cohen Architects.
45. "Bauhaus und Bauhauswoche zu Weimar" in *Das Werk* n. 9 (1923). p. 233.

Difficult Synthesis

Nader Tehrani

Office dA, Voromuro, installation, Boston, Massachusetts, USA, 2007, detail.

Introduction: Language and Surplus

Any and all architectural materializations can be argued to be the result of a form of surplus, an excess that is not to be misinterpreted as a vice, but rather an essential part of the structure of tectonic thought: that all architectures negotiate technical and communicative interests as an artifice, not as natural fact. Even the most technical of architectural requirements can rarely, if ever, determine a singular outcome, overcoming any possibility of structural, functional, or formal determinism. Part of the allure of the Classical reference in architecture is its systematic nature as a language, the relationship of its parts to the whole, and the idea that in its time, it was the result of a social contract of sorts; it was a shared system of construction as much as a shared system of communication, and thus enabled a range of manipulation from prose to poetics and from use to abuse.[1] For this reason, the vicissitudes of the Classical language, its details, and its joinery form a narrative that tells of its orthodoxies and transgressions, from the ideals of Andrea Palladio to the heresies of Giulio Romano. With the cultural changes of the past century, we have also witnessed the demise of Classicism in its central authority. Modernity, and what happens post-modernity brings with it forms of heterogeneity and cultural plurality that render obsolete the kind of hegemony once enjoyed by Classicism, and with it is lost the social order that not only brought forth its details but also their legibility. Notwithstanding these historic changes, the detail of contemporary architecture still enjoys a paradigmatic role in its account of current debates, predicaments, and our cultural condition. However, without the monocular lens of Classicism, we require multiple vantage points to make visible certain relationships that would otherwise get submerged by the indifference of relativism. This introduction attempts to chart some of these tendencies, along with the polemics, arguments, and debates that travel with them.

With the multitude of formal projects, theoretical platforms, and cultural differences, the theme of "performance" has somehow come to characterize a renewed thirst for an alibi of certainty. Performance has come to stand in for functionalism and this ambiguous umbrella has been posited as a response to a range of cultural phenomena, among them the grand narrative of ecological deterioration. In this context, performance offers redemption in light of architectural conceits, and as such serves both to eliminate and justify play. At the same time, in light of unprecedented technological advancement, from digital fabrication techniques to smart material applications, performance has offered a new technical culture with its own protocols, employing quantification to give moral absolution for its desire for formal innovation. In a parallel mode, renewed theoretical interest has emerged around themes such as ornament, pitting morality against performance and adopting the production of affect as an unquantifiable metric against which to judge formal maneuvers.

A Discipline in Search of a Medium

Notwithstanding the evident contradictions between the technical mandates of architecture and their requisite expression, the launching point of this discussion, beyond theories of tectonics, needs to address the techniques that guide the various disciplines, trades, construction guilds, and sub-contractors. Consider the myriad of details: the mortise and tenon connection for wood, the plug weld for steel, the butt-joint for glass, the stacked bond for masonry, a Soss hinge for paneling, or fabric forming for concrete. All of these details and procedures produce irreducible conditions by which the means and methods of an architecture – and its effects – are calibrated. It is one of today's ironies that design contracts, e.g. in the USA, specify that the architect is responsible for design intent, while the contractor is responsible for – and ultimately in charge of – the means and methods of construction. This legal detail sets up an adversarial relationship between these protagonists, divorcing the architect from the very techniques that help determine budget, scope, and implementation, while also distancing the contractor from the conceptual, theoretical, and organizational underpinnings of a design intent; in one simple act, it neuters the architect as a builder while lobotomizing the builder as thinker. Overcoming this legal loophole, one would need to imagine the necessity of the architect's role within the means and methods of production, not only from a practical point of view, but also to re-establish a platform of

Herzog & de Meuron, Signal Box - Auf dem Wolf,
Basel, Switzerland, 1995, facade detail.

empowerment: to create reciprocity between ideas and matter, conceptual strategies and implementation, or between process and product. What also seems to be at stake is the definition of what constitutes the medium of architecture. It is rarely challenged that architecture brings to building a certain level of self-consciousness – elevating it to an intellectual project, but the role of materiality and its precise dependence on the detail has not always been paired up as a conceptual investment. Of course, historically this emphasis has waxed and waned. Ludwig Mies van der Rohe's allegiance to the detail is well recorded in his by now infamous quotes: "Architecture starts when you carefully put two bricks together" or "God is in the details." At the same time, the discipline witnessed the demise of the detail after Brutalism with the ascendance of post-modernism and its emphasis on representation, iconography, and semantics; this was mostly documented in paper architecture initially, but then subsequently followed by its implementation through a building industry that had, by then, taken the reigns from the architectural profession. In that context, the detail was seen either as the "natural" consequence of process, an end-game bonus, or the fulfillment of a final phase – but it was never treated as the generator of a project, and hence central to the medium. Thus, for this discussion, I will try to bind the material detail to the very definition of the medium in the same way we may tie oils to painting or clay to pottery – the joint being the precursor or microscopic evidence of architectural thought at work. Returning back to the techniques then, it is hard to imagine the conceptual contributions of the Gamble House outside of the mortise and tenon joint inasmuch as we would miss the radical silence of Farnsworth House without the presence of the plug weld – the absence of a joint. Arguably, the Gamble House would be a debased intellectual investment if it were balloon-framed as much as if the Farnsworth House were to be assembled with exposed nuts, bolts, and washers. The precondition of the detail as the generator of ideas, inventions, and disciplinary advancement is at the core of this investment.

From a theoretical perspective, Gottfried Semper's charac-terization of the "Four Elements" – mound, hearth, roof, and enclosure – has helped guide the discipline towards an understanding of the connection between architectural elements and their materio-technical counterparts, thus linking the mound to masonry, the hearth to clay, the roof to carpentry, and the enclosure to weaving. If the performative aspects of each media are not obvious enough, the mere identification of "difference" between the elements is an important act of codification, because it instills in the architectural mindset an ideology of appropriateness to the use of materials. Thus, the use of wooden foundations in Venice actually reinforces the spirit of Semper's argument even if it refutes it in fact. At the same time, the performative interpretation falls short of explaining the ideological aspects of appropriateness, especially when confronted with aesthetic acts of surplus or resistance: if all the wooden piers under Venice – in their invisibility – help float the city, it does little to explain the tectonic peculiarities of the Venetian Palazzo. The patterned elaborations on the facade of the Palazzo Ducale, for instance, require a rhetorical reading of Semper's theory to underline the difference between a facade woven out of reeds and a facade that extracts out of the bonding pattern of masonry block construction an iconographic relationship with textiles. The mediation, negotiation, and ultimate fusion between material behavior and visual performance is thus at the root of this tectonic appeal to the detail.

Beyond Paper: Reclaiming Material Agency

In the landscape of contemporary architecture, various protagonists have played a critical role in advancing certain propositions within this debate. To start, it would be hard to imagine the kinds of material research and speculations of the last decade – in both practice and academia – without the presence of Herzog & de Meuron. Their systematic assault on the architectural culture of the 1980s, by way of material investigations, came with such a clear didactic dimension, that it challenged many methodological debates that dominated the times – to name a few, the stability of typology (Aldo Rossi), the emphasis on process (Peter Eisenman), or the indulgence of composition (Coop Himmelblau). All such procedures were to be examined through the lens of material operations with the detail as interlocutor. Their portfolio expanded one building at a time, with each one examining architecture not so much through their authorship, but rather through a deliberate radicalization of propositions about joinery, material behavior, and their requisite effects on long-standing traditions. Their Signal Box in Basel was one such testing ground, and it underlined the freedom of the skin from the contents of the building, while using copper's innate malleability as the vehicle by which the seamless operability of its apertures became possible (ill. p. 36). If that project produced one of the most salient icons of its time, it also displayed a certain orthodoxy with respect to the latency of material behavior, something all architects would look at with awe, or jealousy, for its obviousness. However, Herzog & de Meuron's focus on phenomena is not to be understated, and maybe it is their emphasis on effect that helps understand the perverse, if precise, calculations of their experiments. The levity of the Madrid CaixaForum, for instance, acquires its significance precisely because of its irreverence to gravity and the logic of brick construction, cutting the building at its ankles and objectifying it as a curated artifact, much like the contents of the building. Robbed of its original tectonic logic, the building instead acquires a new relationship with the public at the ground level, something that the original power plant's load-bearing walls could not impart. Perhaps more importantly, the building also engages a broader discursive battle with preceding mythologies, making brick, as it were, do precisely what it does not want to do; through an act of inversion (or negation), its arches, vaults, and thick walls now truncated from their conventional duties, can finally display the kind of weight and girth intended for masonry construction.

As a foil to those practices that have advanced material consciousness, Eisenman's admission of disinterest in construction, material research, and the building industry, serves as a good polemical alternative. His buildings are both the victim and benefactor of this bias towards the rigors of formal operations. Rarefied a discourse though it may be, his interiors – built out fully in gypsum board – help to retain a focus on immateriality, geometry, and the indexicality of his process, an abstraction so pure that it challenges the very tenets on which conventional tectonics is founded: gravity, differentiation of functional attributes, and tactility, among

other factors. At the same time, his eventual and inevitable engagement with the world of construction products and conventions – expansion/construction joints on the one hand, or baseboards, window sills, and door jambs on the other – remain so passive that they are devastating to his very cause, undermining the argument about form in which he is so invested. Consider Eisenman's iterative engagement with the Derridean fold; the search for the constitution of a trace in its most universal sense lead him, not so surprisingly, to a series of projects that, as architectural figures, appeared "folded," but also renditions that leave procedural traces of the folding process in the final account. If one cannot tolerate the literalness of this response, one should be reminded that architecture remains, despite all conceptual claims, devoted to spatialization and figuration as a central vocation, and by extension material agency as its medium. In this sense, Eisenman can hardly be faulted for extending this age-old dedication to the métier, even if there are fundamental problems in using architecture as an illustration of conceptual claims. But given that the fold has such vast implications and potentials from the viewpoint of construction, the corollary challenge would be to determine how one could interrogate the medium of architecture to conceptualize the fold – not so much as a metaphor for a theory, but rather as a procedural device to advance the discipline itself; implicit in this challenge is the burden of examining the "seam" of the fold, the "continuity of matter" over the fold, the "thickness" of the fold, among a host of questions which cannot escape material thinking. Lest this be misunderstood as an advocacy for pragmatism, feasibility, or construction management, then the relationship between constructive logics and theoretical possibilities must be underlined to understand the conceptual stakes within this debate: the notion that buildings themselves contain embodied knowledge, polemical stances, and theoretical advancement.

Extending this preoccupation with the fold towards more sophisticated ends, the roof of the Kyneton House by John Wardle lends a more precise eye towards disciplinary invention by way of engaging the details of its conception (ills. pp. 38, 39). Researched through the process of scoring and folding paper, the roof establishes an extended covering that protects

John Wardle Architects, Kyneton House,
country Victoria, Australia, 2008.

John Wardle Architects, Kyneton House
interiors.

the Australian house from the sweltering heat, while also using
its folds to create apertures to bring in southern light. Working
with the rigor of origami, the geometry of the roof is folded
out of a pure rectangle, making each facet the result of a clear
rotation from this primary figure. In turn, acknowledging the
innate complexity of the roof as a composite system – fabricated
in zinc, sheathing, structural steel, and gypsum board – the
project is layered in such a way as to expose the various
strata as independent laminates. These laminations point to
a phenomenon so endemic of contemporary construction:
that mass, despite its volume, is gauged and fabricated by
sheet material; concealing the volume of the roof through the
displacement of the various strata, the articulation of these
laminations exposes this tectonic current to surreal ends.
While each strata plays on its own material logic, the thinness
and levity of each layer makes the roof appear to hover,
disengaged from the very house it protects, assuming a
relationship with the horizon; its razor-like folds speak to the
distant topographies while the flatness of the overall figure to
the expanse of the plains. The pedigree of this thinking is, of
course, quite different from the preoccupations of Deleuzian
thinking, and yet the fold is an indispensible device that speaks
to the manifold tectonic imperatives the roof has to engage:
from water drainage to lighting apertures, from structural forces
to layers of skins, and from applications of metal sheathing
to plastering processes. Though highly crafted, Wardle is
carefully waging a struggle against the individual technical
feats of the building's components, while framing the broader
conceptual readings that are unleashed by the building as a
whole – escaping as it were the simple fascination with craft,
and instead placing his investment in the intellectual paybacks
of material operations. Wardle's separation of materials and
their subsequent re-joining acknowledges the literal movement
of a building – the varied rates of expansion and contraction of
different materials – but more importantly helps to conceptualize
this fact as the basis for a spatial and tectonic layering. If his
theoretical claims are restrained, the building's effects, instead,
are quite startling, de-familiarizing the very conventions on
which each craft is based.

Inputs, Constraints, and Intents

The fold, taken more literally, is a staple of technical culture;
no one knows this better than Frank Gehry, who effectively
radicalized the metal sheathing industry over the past 20 years
with his wide adaptations of metal skins (ills. pp. 63, 67, 71-74).
Blurring the traditional seams between roofs, facades, and
socles, Gehry's predisposition towards figuration required a
technology that could navigate the most extreme hydrological
mandates. Working with conventional standing and flat
seam detailing, he advanced the geometric possibilities of
panel construction one shingle, or seam, at a time. Despite
the sophistication of the complex curvatures he enables – or
maybe precisely because of them – his paneling systems remain
indifferent to the very figures they adorn – inattentive to the
differences between coping or corner conditions, as much
as perhaps irreverent to the syntactic demands of tectonic
differentiation. Extended as wallpaper over the elevations, the
metal panels become part
of an extended monolithic field that wraps the architectural
figure. Even if left untransformed, the flat seam detail is a crucial
detail that makes this broader architectural strategy possible.

In contrast, if the hydrological demands for the Fabrications
installation by Office dA are negligible, then the advancement of
folding as an instrumental device is demonstrated through the
development of the "stitched seam" (ills. p. 41). Researched and
developed with Milgo Bufkin, the stitched seam acknowledges
the thickness of metal sheathing by laser-scoring offset seams
with correspondent dimensions, ensuring structural stability
while also enabling the continuity of material. Notwithstanding
the sartorial metaphor, the stitch is the result of a material
extraction, not joinery; in turn, the precision of its CNC logic
offers minimal tolerances, mass customization, and a tectonic
logic that overcomes the strict conventional divisions between
structure and skin. The detail, in fact, is in service of a broader
conceptual aim that pushes to the extreme the phenomenal
motivations of tectonic thinking: to demonstrate the radical
schism between retinal and constructive thinking. The installation is conceived as an anamorphic projection, producing the
illusion of a flat rectangular panel, whose discrete units appear

Gramazio & Kohler, Gantenbein Winery facade
(Bearth & Deplazes, principal architects of
Gantenbein Winery), Fläsch, Switzerland,
2006, non-standardized brick facade,
fabrication.

perfectly plumb and level from a privileged vantage point –
a device that relates to conventional checks and balances on
the construction field. While the construction of steel panels
underscores the elemental and aggregative differences between
each panel and their requisite parts (the jig, fold, and reveal),
the anamorphosis helps to conceal the traces of its very construction in the flattening out of the perspective. From a broader
technical level, the installation is also built without bolts; steel
folds are wrapped around structural jigs adopting plug welds
to conceal the traces of construction, supporting the tension
between conceptual and technical agendas.

Within the context of contemporary culture, the Fabrications
installation speaks to a tendency that is well outlined in Greg
Lynn's foreword to the "Intricacy" exhibition.[2] In the essay,
Lynn offers a theoretical vantage point that helps to situate
much of current thinking within the terrain of tectonic thought.
Lynn identifies how computation and the digital platform
have produced the possibility of a new attitude towards the
detail, drawing emphasis away from the uniqueness of the
joint and instead supplanting it with the idea of the detail as
omni-present, as a distributed system, or as a field condition.
Implicit within the intricate is the bias towards continuity,
monolithic singularity, and self-similar organic relationships of
part to whole, overturning traditional hierarchies, types, and
collage-based assemblages. In turn, various pedagogies of the
past decade have given priority to material thinking and the
subsequent means of aggregation, to geometric speculations
and systemic permutations, and more recently, to scripted
procedures that have attempted to automate much of the
conceptual apparatuses that aim to re-center the work of
authorship around parameters.

Digital Research

Within the context of the exhibition, the Tongxian Art Project
illustrates Lynn's point by way of the "variable bonding,"
a masonry bond that abandons the traditional adherence
to the Common or Flemish bond in lieu of an organizational
configuration that enables multiple architectural possibilities
by using the detail to engage integrative strategies: structural

optimization, environmental calibration, programmatic
adaptation, and other architectural contingencies. This
proposition was maybe best illustrated in Casa La Roca, where
the experimentation was tested between bricks, blocks, and
tile, all of which displayed their own unique innate potentials
(ill. p. 53). Tongxian, though conceived on a parametric
conceptual platform, is in fact delivered in archaic terms, using
CAD files as its instrument. This thinking takes a radical leap
forward with the aid of R-O-B, an apparatus unavailable at the
time of Tongxian, but an instrumental protagonist in the work of
Gramazio & Kohler, who take the same conceptual platform to
a new technical level (ills. pp. 40, 56). Their work with masonry
essentially re-confirms the premises of the Tongxian project,
in part due to the aggregate nature of masonry blocks, which
define the configurability of joinery within the system. Instead,
their research with Foam and the Disintegrated Wall offers new
conceptual hurdles which escape material unitization, and a
scenario whereby the joint is divorced from its conventional
geographic alliances: thresholds, corners, junctions. Instead,
these experiments are either the result of pure geometric
speculation or a negotiation with material behavior. The Foam
research, akin to the work of Roxy Paine, takes advantage of
the viscosity of the material to gauge robotic instrumentality
and test the limits of mimesis, where organic matter confronts
systemic fabrication. In the case of the Disintegrated Wall,
excavation and geometric patterning operate with utter
independence of the panels that drive the experiment; the
panels dematerialize as the configurative logic of perforations,
by way of the Voronoi diagram – a special kind of decomposition
of space determined by distances to a specified discrete set
of objects in the space – takes front stage. In the perforated
wall, the eventual abandonment of the panel sets the stage for
the complete independence of aggregative logics, geometric
speculations, and their subsequent effects. In essence, freed
from the shackles of unitized construction, the architect invents
other alibis that can drive formal derivations – testing functional,
performative, and technological parameters through the digital
media to advance architectural malleability towards inventive
terrain, bringing a material agency to intricacy beyond the realm
of mere visualization. Still, the dominant results of their research
have resulted in surfaces, with lesser spatial consequences.

Other parallel researches engaged in the intricate by the likes of Ali Rahim have produced geometric propositions with greater formal and spatial range, even when they operate with complete irreverence, indifference, or innocence to typological questions. For this reason, Rahim's towers may either have missed the boom in Dubai or they simply could not work out the *pro formas* in time (ill. p. 169). Whatever the reason, what is lacking in the towers is a sense of indispensability – the idea that the form, in some way, contains a narrative that cannot be value-engineered. Others testing similar territory, such as Kengo Kuma, in his Granada Performing Arts Center, show more strategic alliances with typological and functional attributes, linking the hexagonal geometry with the vineyard seating, the rakes of staircases, and the structural logic of the proposal – all in all, constructing an alibi that organically binds the detail to the broader geometry.

The Acrobatics of the Cover-Up

If the intricate operates to spread the realm of the detail, to dematerialize, and to offer variability in the joint, its predisposition towards patterning helps to camouflage all those architectural mandates that come to crowd, compromise, and complicate conventional architectural strategies. For this reason, the techniques of the minimalists cannot be overlooked as part of this debate. If their tendency towards reduction, silence, and abstraction is well documented, the joinery that makes this architecture possible is also instrumental to its cause. For instance, the butt-glazed joints of the Glass Pavilion of the Toledo Museum of Art by SANAA help to dematerialize the glass walls, but they can only be paired up with the broader efforts of erasing all other evidence of architectural bureaucracy: the apparatus of mechanical engineering, structure, fire suppression systems, and the host of programmatic equipment that overwhelms conventional work (ills. pp. 42, 43). The stubborn and insistent battle for the primacy of affect over substance requires the understanding that the majority of joinery and detail is kept behind the scenes precisely so that the detail is not fetishized on the surface or in the foreground. For this reason, the Toledo Museum enjoys several hundred carefully located beam penetrations above the level of the ceiling so as to protect the sanctity of the extended flat roof slab. This enables SANAA

SANAA, Glass Pavilion, Toledo Museum of Art,
Toledo, Ohio, USA, 2006, interiors.

SANAA, Glass Pavilion, Toledo Museum of Art,
wall section detail.

to play with transparency, reflectivity, ambiguity, and a range of other effects produced by the layering of glass, in order to establish a significant relationship with the glass "content" of the building, unhindered by the brutal proliferation of architectural requirements. The strange absence of lines in the presentation drawings then, are to be taken literally, as if to evacuate her architecture of all detail; in turn, this is accompanied by a thick manual of working drawings that extensively locate each and every joint that is suppressed within the backstage of her buildings. If the Glass Pavilion extends the landscape of the museum into the surrounding park, the Lichtenstein Museum by Morger & Degelo and Christian Kerez indulges in a similar sensibility to different ends (ills.). Working with black polished concrete, amplified by dark glass and mullions, the building is designed to reflect the landscape around it. The polish of the surface dissolves the aggregates, as if refined terrazzo, concealing any and all expansion joints. Again, evacuated of all detail, what remains is a void, a reflection, and a desire for architecture to disappear – a desire which cannot approach fulfillment if betrayed by evidence of the detail.

Performance and Its Predicaments

Still, the majority of projects do not permit the luxuries of budget or the added leniency of code that is somehow bestowed on rarefied minimalist projects, and thus their rewards are few and far between for the greater mass of architects. Nonetheless, the idea that the emancipation from the detail – or the visible detail – can lead to a tectonics of ephemera, a perceptual phenomenon, or a dematerialized affect, is a seductive proposition, using material conceits to point to immaterial potentialities. In response to this, the work of Philippe Rahm brings up further challenges by dealing precisely with non-retinal techniques, using atmosphere, thermodynamics, and the environment not merely as alibis for the building's performance, but as rationale for form itself (ills. pp. 44, 183). If his rhetoric displays an innocent yearning for environmental determinism, it is made more complex by a self-conscious play between spatial and material projections that pit form against performance. Enhanced by a myriad of charts and thermal diagrams, projects like the Interior Gulf Stream and the Convective Museum lay

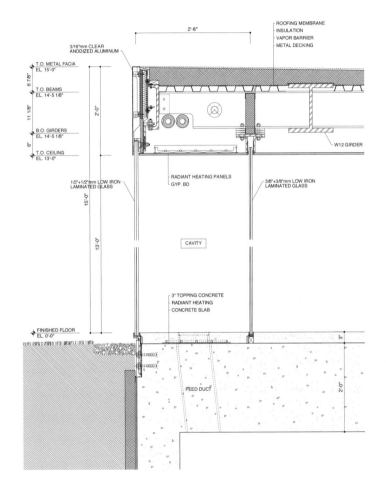

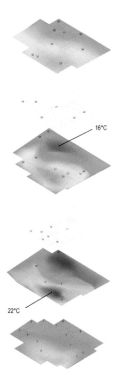

bare the materio-linguistic biases of an architecture in search of an alibi. Rahm finds himself in a classic predicament: that while form is always informed by some sort of performance, it is at the same time never determined by it independent of external cultural forces that engage language or the vocabulary of material influences. One is reminded that even if Boston Symphony Hall is regarded as having one of the world's best acoustics at the level of performance, that still does not explain its detailed syntactic differences from the Concertgebouw in Amsterdam; as such, architecture, it would seem, thrives precisely from a certain autonomy from performance, or at least it gains productively from this friction. Still, Rahm's position points out how we are in a historical moment where the rigors of environmental modeling can produce a credible link with form, if only to challenge conventional typologies, organizations, and material distributions. For the moment, his work remains in progress, and thus further elaborations of this argument will only be enhanced and compromised as he takes on building projects, a chapter that has yet to come.

Difficult Synthesis

Of the thinkers that have confronted contemporary culture and the construction industry with some measure of simultaneous directness and irreverence, Rem Koolhaas stands out. In the context of the various tendencies outlined here, his utter lack of care towards the detail can be construed as a polemical stance. In his earlier work, such as the Kunsthal, the prosaic use of industry details in brutal juxtapositions, intersections, and banal connections almost leads one to believe that it could be the result of carelessness, incompetence, or lack of sophistication. Yet as his work has developed, Koolhaas's emphatic refusal to get sucked down into the preciousness of details stands out for its consistency, and more importantly for the emphasis placed on conceptual strategies – almost as if the noise rendered by the detail could hinder the clarity of his arguments. More recently, his denial of the detail in the junction between the columns and the skin of the Seattle Library is one such example, where added I-beams unceremoniously thicken the zone of the diagrid skin without any sense of decorum (ill. p. 45). Instead, the superposition of I-beams can be said to underline the simultaneous figurative and configurative importance (cf. pp. 48-61, 62-65) of the diagonals within the building's structure and skin, making any emphasis of the junction a kind of diversion (ill.). Maybe most importantly, Koolhaas's contribution comes in the way in which his cultural preoccupations with hybrid programs and urbanism have led him to formal experiments that foreground difficult architectural reconciliations. In this sense, his work evades the classical possibilities of establishing an easy relationship between the part and the whole. The detail, in turn – even if not a precursor of his design process – is then implicated in his preoccupations and made to take on a cultural significance as it mediates between industry conventions and architectural mutations.

Given the complexities required by hybrid programs and typologies that characterize today's architectural patronage, one of the currents that challenge architects is the formal preoccupation with synthesis in general, as each tradition attempts to overcome classical organicism on the one hand, and collage techniques that tend to produce fragmentation, blunt juxtaposition, and simultaneity on the other. It is perhaps in this area of "difficult synthesis" where the detail is put to its ultimate test, where systems fall apart, where technologies overlap, where geometries intertwine, and where easy solutions no longer suffice. Not all architects are predisposed to taking on these types of problems, but those that do are not guaranteed an easy success either. Consider Steven Holl's Whitney Water Purification Plant, and his audacious attempt at fusing the main barrel vault with a tangent stair – miring him in the geometric predicament of reconciling the relationship between a single and a double curvature, the surfaces that contain the stair and the main vault of the building (ill. p. 46). Suffice it to say that if the act of drawing through the geometry could have shown the problem of conjoining these two volumes to be of sufficient difficulty, then the building process only confirms the crisis as the sheet metal shingles refuse to abide by the mandates of compound curvatures. If Holl does not succeed in organically reconciling the two volumes, he also erodes the volumes sufficiently such that their legibility as distinct entities is compromised; maybe most problematically, the resultant form serves to undermine the self-consciousness that is so much part of the critical culture of the architectural enterprise,

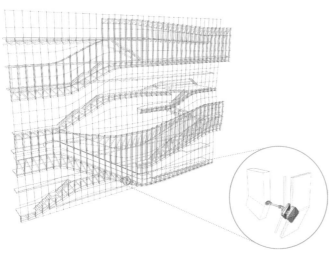

and tragically obscures the difference between willfulness and oversight. Preston Scott Cohen has taken on a similar problem in his torqued circulatory promenade in the Tel Aviv Museum of Art, named the Lightfall (ills. p. 47). His calibrated focus is on geometry as the building block of the atrium ensures him that the rigors of the ruled surfaces will embrace the adjoining ramps with deliberate resolution; in turn, his use of concrete – a liquid medium producing a monolithic *poché* – conceals the geometric gaps between the inner surface of the atrium and the edge of the ramps on the opposing sides, offering him, as it were, a tolerance for error that remains unperceived. Such a move also absolves him of further integration of the complexities that come with layered systems, hybrid construction techniques, and essentially the dependence on detail. Through this sleight of hand, he is able to achieve formal continuity and spatial singularity in a circulatory system that is, in fact, fragmented, parceled, and aggregated. In the same trajectory, SHoP addresses a similar formal problem in their slab for the Fashion Institute of Technology in New York (ill.). The staircases that ascend and bind the various vertical commons are pushed to the outer skin of the building, exposing the vertical promenade to the city. The staircases are displaced in accordance with adjoining rooms, views to the city, and lateral programs, creating distortions in the skin that register the impressions of its adjoining program. The skin takes on the burden, not only of indexing and accommodating programmatic necessities, but also the technical mandates of the building, including the structural, environmental, and weatherproofing logics. Most importantly, unable to hide any of these contingencies, the skin is forced to mediate between the performative aspects of its mandate and the building's larger responsibility towards the city and the identity of the institution, holding in suspension the relationship between its singularity of expression and the various fragments contained within. Equally important, it is precisely because of the exposure that the glazing system renders, that the larger thematic imperative of an architectural agenda is led to supersede any functional or performative dictates. Adopting material and tectonic devices as the medium of addressing complexity and contradiction, the strategy acknowledges a problematic that persists despite the ongoing evolution of forms, idioms, and spatial regimes in architecture.

Preston Scott Cohen, Lightfall,
Tel Aviv Museum of Art, Israel, 2010,
model and sections.

In the context of the agency of material detailing, the idea of the difficult synthesis exposes the necessities of discursive narratives and strategic choices within the broader panorama of architectural practices. The foregrounding of details and construction logics can be viewed as much to expand and innovate in expository ways as the selection of certain media that help to silence, undermine, and conceal the instrumentality of material use. Both strategies ultimately uphold the deep-seated bias of architecture's tacit allegiance to materio-linguistic practices. The acknowledgement of this condition can be seen as a source of liberation, but also poses significant challenges. On the one hand, it demands of the architect a re-acquaintance with the techniques of the medium – something that has been lost with the advent of specialization – on the other it requires a more nuanced level of critical faculties, ensuring that the architect can distinguish between the potentialities offered by material speculations and the redundancies of material fetishization. The denial of the material playing field, whether out of innocence or ideological stubbornness, is ultimately a self-defeating and tacit abdication of power and critique in those areas over which we have the greatest political dominion – foreclosing the possibility of the determination of specification, the seizure of architectural opportunities, and the innovation of practice by way of its tectonic underpinnings.

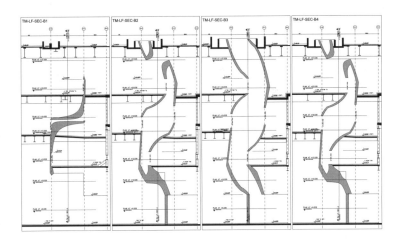

Notes

1. Of the many canonic arguments the Greek Temple has served to illustrate, the question of its joinery, connections, and details is, in many ways, the most salient. They tell a story about architecture that remains until today rich as a problematic and controversial in terms of principles: namely, the disjunctive relationship between the facts of material construction and their desired effects. Consider, if you will, the triglyphs and the idea that they somehow materialize the end grain of wooden beams as they rest on the architrave. If the fiction that wooden members somehow reappear in a different life in the form of stone is not conceptually fantastic enough, then imagine the crisis that is unleashed once the triglyphs migrate from the side of the temple to its front, under the pediment. What does it mean, operating within the paradigm of signification, when the ends of beams run perpendicular to the grain of the temple's structure? Is this a mistake, or is its adoption so systematic that it is absolved of such a characterization? Alternatively, are we allowed to interpret this as an act of irony in a historical moment when the temple is seen as sacred? Is it a conceit of ornamentation, or are all the triglyphs already enforcing the regime of ornament? Or consider this: had the triglyphs been flushed out with the face of the architrave – submerged into invisibility – would we have access to this vast repository of interpretations or the ethic that is associated with them? One may be prone to say "no," but then one would precisely be missing the rhetorical impetus behind much of modern architecture, minimalism, and a range of work whose motivations get richer with silence. Conversely, it would also miss the nuance that even the most technical of architectural requirements can rarely, if ever, determine a singular outcome, overcoming any possibility of structural, functional, or formal determinism.
2. "Intricacy," exhibition of the Institute of Contemporary Art, University of Pennsylvania, USA, September 3-November 7, 2003.

Aggregation

Nader Tehrani
Justin Fowler

Kruunenberg Van der Erve Architecten, Laminata House, Leerdam, The Netherlands, 2000, interior detail.

The necessity for aggregation, or the process whereby many parts are brought into a whole, would seem to be a fact that the discipline of architecture could take for granted. Whether built in wood, stone, steel, or concrete, one would be challenged to find a piece of architecture that is not the result of a painstaking assemblage of elements that attempts to form something larger than the sum of its parts. Even concrete, whose aggregate constitution is launched in a liquid state, is mediated by formwork, whose construction process is the result of fabricational intricacies related to aggregation, and whose imprint leaves an indelible mark on the concrete for its lifetime.

At the same time, there is good reason to reconsider the theme of aggregation, because it arguably points to one of the most irreducible aspects of the medium, something that is either quite often overlooked, or in many cases forgotten altogether as abstract processes come to overwhelm the conceptual basis of the architectural task. How could it be that the conceptual task of architecture could become so remote from problems of building, of putting things together, of making – in essence of aggregating? The answer to that may lie in an age-old and productive problematic that has come to bear on architecture as a discipline: architecture offers something in surplus of mere building, and one of the cornerstones of its theoretical underpinnings, tectonics, tends to dislodge the relationship between building as fact and building as effect.

The persistence of matter – or materials – and their requisite limitations of dimension, weight, and construction modules cast onto architectural practice a set of parameters that force a confrontation between abstraction and the real, perception and fact, the actual and its effects. The problematics of aggregation come to haunt those designers whose conceptual practices are devoid – or innocent – of its omnipresence, but also in the practices of the self-conscious, the presence of aggregation oozes through even where it is being most suppressed – in precise and tailored ways – making its absence an index of its very importance.

Tectonics

The persistence of tectonic thought within the discourse of architecture is a phenomenon whose longevity can be attributed to architecture's inability to escape the conceptual pairing of the facts of construction with the poetics of effect. This persistent presence, however, does not speak to the imperviousness of tectonic thought to the attacks launched by the various movements that have sought to dethrone it, as the study of tectonics has largely been marginalized by, among other things, the development of the spatial narratives of modernism, the paper architecture era, the emergence of the diagram, and the tactical social projects of the informal and the sustainable. Tectonic thought is now often deemed to be a nostalgic and outmoded relic of localized resistance to the supposed nuance of network culture. Vague notions of shape, performance, atmosphere, and ecology have come to dominate the disciplinary vocabulary. In their refusal to address the issue of the building as the primary site of contestation, such formulations of contemporary architecture have effectively managed to sidestep the crucial intellectual and practical concerns prompted by a rigorous study of the means and methods of construction and the way in which they have and continue to be deployed across a range of scales in the production of a vast array of effects. In the absence of tectonic considerations, architecture severs its capacity to generate effects specific to the discipline and risks diluting its social and political agency by ignoring the instrumentality of its medium. So while architecture's recent tendency to relegate debates regarding the act of building to technocrats, developers, and engineers may provide designers with the illusion of greater conceptual latitude, the same tendency also represents a surprising willingness on the part of architects to abdicate a significant amount of their power to influences beyond their control.

The Architectural Figure Configured: Part-to-Whole Relations

The practice of building can be represented by a productive tension between the figurative and the configurative. Figuration in the purest sense involves the utilization of tectonic means

in service of a legible form. The Eiffel Tower is perhaps an obvious example, but broader architectural typologies such as the Basilica or the Rotunda also serve to underline the idea that the discipline has evolved to the point where sophisticated assemblages of parts have come to amass to a larger entity we recognize as a figure. While the figure's component parts may be readily decipherable, the overarching form is neither dictated nor limited by its constituent parts. In turn, external factors such as setback regulations and site boundaries may also figure a building, without any acknowledgement of disciplinary decorum regarding type, language, or construction. Thus, figuration can occur both as an appeal to constructive expression in the vein of Frank Gehry (ills. pp. 63, 67, 71-74) or as an analytical breakdown of pre-existing codes as in the stereotomic operation of subtraction played out in Hugh Ferriss's monolithic renderings of Manhattan skyscrapers.

Configuration, on the other hand, involves the systemic deployment of parts, privileging the unit of construction, whether it be the brick, the beam, or the module of inhabitation. Such an operation of aggregation does not determine *a priori* a legible final figure, yet it precisely anticipates form by way of the materials, methods, and rules of assembly. Safdie's Habitat '67 (ill.) and Kurokawa's Nakagin capsule tower are the prototypical modern examples of such a configurative mode of design, where the aggregation of parts produces a rich and multi-faceted spatial complexity. Despite the predisposition towards informality, these operations are not absolved of a larger submission to organizational rigors, and thus, Safdie's Habitat must measure up to the performance of the "Italian hilltown" inasmuch as Kurokawa's tower needs to absorb and overcome the technical mandates of the skyscraper type.

Gottfried Semper was one of the first architects to recognize the intimate relation between construction and poetics. In his proposed four elements of architecture, he not only identified distinct components of building formation (hearth, wall, mound, and roof), but also tied each to a specific material characteristic (ceramics, textiles, stereotomy, carpentry), which acted toward the production of a unique set of effects. In his system, Semper separated the rigid load-bearing frame from the soft enclosure that defined interior space. Though originally based on Semper's observation of the hanging textile enclosures of Assyrian dwellings, such a formulation also has a certain linguistic ontology, as some languages, such as Spanish, differentiate between the interior corner (*rincón*) and its exterior equivalent (*esquina)*. The implications for this distinction have reverberated throughout the history of modern architecture, from Adolf Loos's distinction between the abstract public facade of his homes from their sumptuously clad interiors, to Koolhaas's separation of the Manhattan skyscraper envelope from its programmatic logic in his analysis of the Downtown Athletic Club, to the willful disconnect between Gehry's sculptural surfaces and the geometries of his interior spaces. To a greater or lesser extent, however, these examples fail to capture Semper's rigorous logic of reciprocity between the material quality of the component and its respective method of deployment within a larger system of construction and signification. And though one may reject the essentialism of Semper's choice of material associations and his preference for monumentality, what can be adopted from his line of thought is its focus on the systemic linkage of form and material as a generator of precise architectural effects that originate from within the discipline, yet exert an impact within the greater realm of cultural production and communication. If Eisenman pursued a conception of architecture based solely on the linguistic constituents of architectural form devoid of material considerations for purposes of disciplinary autonomy and cultural critique, then a reconsideration of Semper's mode of architectural thought should be seen as an alternative method of disciplinary specificity offering, perhaps, an even more incisive model of extra-disciplinary agency – essentially linking formal and linguistic operations to material agency and its requisite means of aggregation.

Patterning and the Problem of the Corner

A discussion on aggregation is invariably linked to certain techniques, modes of construction, and their loopholes. Aggregation is also linked to patterning, as all assemblies are somehow bound by systemic configurations that establish the rules and exceptions of a building practice. For instance, the aggregation patterns of brick construction speak directly to the innate relation of the tectonic unit – with the particular demands imposed by its material characteristics – to the effects produced through its systemic deployment. As with any traditional system of pattern-making, the problematic moment is the way in which the system addresses the corner or the edge. This moment of exception forces tectonic systems to either privilege the dominant field of the pattern – only to break it at the corner – or to recalibrate the system such that the exception is called on to generate the logic of the pattern itself. In brickwork, the common bond, with its staggered alternation of stretcher courses, must break its logic and incorporate headers once every six rows giving the wall lateral strength, and in turn address the exceptionality of the corners by cutting bricks. The Flemish bond, by contrast, incorporates the exceptional moment of the corner to produce a syncopated arrangement of headers and stretchers across the field of the pattern, giving a more integrated and distributed lateral strength to the wall. The distinct logics of these two modes of aggregation produce markedly divergent structural and aesthetic effects.

Although Semper was a proponent of the material expression of building tectonics, he took a position supporting the idea that ancient Greek temples had been adorned with polychrome paint. Such a notion was vigorously opposed at the time by Kantian scholars who held fast to the idea that material purity was a more profound and rational way to build and that, by extension, a society as enlightened as ancient Greece would no doubt build in such a manner. The tendency to speak of tectonics in ethical terms, thus assigning a moral imperative to a particular style of building, has been a key factor in the contemporary marginalization of tectonic thought. Kenneth Frampton has maintained a critical bias throughout his career that has tended to conflate the poetic production of effect with the appeal of an ethical imperative. Such an argument suggests that effects lose their moral validity when detached from a holistic sensibility of tectonic articulation and material expression, thus perhaps ruling out the possibility of certain complexities and contradictions that are part and parcel of every construction system.

An alternative to this stance would be an acknowledgement of the fundamental rhetorical status of the surface as a positive fact, acknowledging the superficial structure of a building as its tectonic imperative, and seeking reciprocity between deep and superficial aspects of the building not as inevitable facts, but rather as curated and imposed points of emphasis. To replace the legacy of Frampton's largely top-down approach to tectonic scholarship would require an almost grassroots re-conceptualization of tectonic practice as a mode of inquiry that investigates and exploits the specific potentials embedded within particular materials and their respective systems of aggregation. The ghosts of tectonic essentialism can only be exorcised by such an analysis of the limits of material potential, as a practice that both embraces and struggles against these limits will invariably be equipped to offer architectural solutions based on the negotiations of actual performance and expression, not one or the other.

Two- and Three-dimensional Patterns

For the most part, tectonic culture has looked at modules and units as the main protagonists of aggregation. Field patterns, for example, have historically fallen within the domain of two-dimensional thinking, consisting of processes of single-variable manipulation, focusing on the figure or the ground, but rarely both. Such limited thinking exists across a range of scales from wallpaper to urban plans where primacy is usually devoted to a consideration of the guiding module, or that produces a pattern. The herringbone is such an example, using the relationship of perpendicular units to characterize the overall directional field. Some notable exceptions have offered a different view, imagining not only the figure but the ground – the space of residue – as an equal partner in the formulation of patterning. Sigurd Lewerentz, for instance, used the space of the mortar, not the brick, as a malleable figure, enlarging it at will to create openings within the field of the brick wall. This simple observation has been the most central consideration of the expandable/contractable bonding that Office dA envisioned for the Casa La Roca (ill. p. 53), adopting the dimension of the mortar as a parametric vehicle to introduce the possibility of light and air in an otherwise impermeable wall. The notion of the variable tectonic pattern has also been extended to achieve spatial results; SHoP's Urban Beach project for PS1 established a systematic taxonomy of flattened sections that became spatial only upon the moment of their serial proliferation – a two-and-a-half-dimensional process that extrudes patterns with incremental shifts, as it were (ills. p. 172).

FOA's Yokohama ferry terminal project is also indebted to the lineage of modular thinking, even if its form does not betray the marks of such a lineage. Here the pattern emerged from a decidedly three-dimensional conception of construction. A certain feedback operation occurred whereby sections were extracted from a larger form, yet these components were structural necessities for the formation of the whole rather than mere orthographic slices through an abstract volume. The visual trope of modular inhabitation reached its seemingly premature climax with Moshe Safdie's Habitat '67, a work whose tectonic legibility set the standard for parallel explorations by the Metabolists and more recent projects organized around cellular inhabitation (ill. p. 50). In the case of LOT-EK's prefab shipping container camp, the module of the unit is kept intact in terms of its visual signification, yet the method of aggregation is not necessarily derived from the unit's inherent material characteristics.

Frames, scaffolding, and other mechanistic devices are often employed to produce the effect of aggregation. In the work of Lynn, Rahim, and others, the isolated module is often less discernible and becomes eroded within a more seamless whole that approximates the performance of an aggregational assembly without exhibiting the more overt visual traces of construction (ills. pp. 93, 98, 169). At the same time, however, even the most seamless design conceptions can only reach actualization through a rigorous negotiation with necessities of fabrication such as module dimensions, construction joints, and environmental dictates which all reveal the rhetorical status of continuity as one of many possible architectural alibis.

This conflict between the performance of tectonic aggregation and its image is a major point of contestation regarding the role of effect in tectonic thought, returning again to the tension between tectonic facts and the poetics of construction. Beyond

purely tactical explorations of material layering for purposes of technical investigation, practices that utilize such means must embed them within a larger spatial or effect-driven narrative. Ultimately, processes of aggregation are a means to an end rather than an end in themselves. Such techniques cannot be divorced from the way in which they are situated and integrated within the larger logic of any particular built project.

Along these lines, one can begin to formulate a range of configurative approaches and scenarios that vary in both their techniques of aggregation and their desired effects:

1. Literal Configurative Expression ("Honesty") for Figurative Spatial Abstraction

Constructed as a temporary structure for the Hanover 2000 Expo, Peter Zumthor's Swiss Pavilion utilizes timber beams in a relatively orthodox and undifferentiated fashion in the production of a series of abstract atmospheric spaces. To achieve the effect of a lumber yard, massive horizontal planks of ruddy pine separated by thin larch members with square profiles are stacked without the use of bolts or artificial adhesives, forming dense, yet porous walls held together by stainless steel rods in tension that run vertically across the stacked members, holding them in compression with the stressed steel springs attached to the rods. This spring-loaded construction system allows for the walls to gradually contract as the timber dries and accommodates any additional deformations in the wood. By avoiding the use of secondary joinery methods, the wood used in the pavilion could be sold as seasoned timber at the close of the Expo, demonstrating awareness that the lumberyard metaphor can be transformed into ecologically grounded performance without diluting the original design intent.

2. Literal Configurative Expression for Phenomenological Effect

Baumschlager Eberle's Rohner port building presents a deviously simplistic figure of a cantilevered rectilinear volume of reinforced concrete, balanced and anchored to the ground at a single core. The figure's perceptual defiance of gravity is but the first of its phenomenological manipulations. The interior, too, is almost banal in its spatial organization and its material

palette, but here, wood is deployed in a configurative manner
to amplify the effect of the narrow space. Larchwood planks of
uniform width are placed end-to-end upon each of the room's
longitudinal surfaces, directing the view outward through
the glazed room-sized aperture framed by the relentless
outward directionality of the room's seemingly continuous
wrapper. What is unique about this interior is the way in which
a technically unsophisticated unit and system of aggregation
are placed into tension with an atypical approach to interior
cladding that refuses to acknowledge the traditional distinction
between floor, ceiling, and wall. In this system, variance is
ignored altogether in favor of a literal directness of material
presentation that simultaneously heightens and dissolves the
appearance of the material. The directionality of the wood
is indispensible in the construction of its argument, and the
graining effect established through the consistent method of
material deployment conspires with the perspectival intentions,
expanding the perceived depth of the space and extending
the bounds of the volume into the landscape beyond. The
Rohner port project exemplifies a way of working that achieves
a complex effect through leveraging a minimal systemic logic
against typological conventions.

3. Literal, Yet Counterintuitive, Configurative Expression for Phenomenological Effect

Methods of material layering or aggregation are often deployed
in a manner that displays a certain literalness or deference to the
traditional properties of specific materials. If Zumthor's Swiss
Pavilion can be seen as an abstraction of log cabin construction
techniques that leverages the inherent structural potential of
stacking wood, then Kruunenberg Van der Erve Architecten's
Laminata House exhibits an equally abstract, yet counterintuitive
handling of their material of choice, glass (ills. pp. 49, 54). The
Laminata House, built as a celebration of the city of Leerdam,
Holland's glass capital, is constructed of 13,000 sheets of precut
laminated glass arrayed sectionally in a manner that parallels
SHoP's PS1 project. Using transparent glue, the layers of glass
are adhered together at their surfaces, producing striated walls
that vary in thickness from 10 to 170 cm. Though this variation
adjusts to define different spaces within the house, the glass
layering acts less as a programmatic register, as in the SHoP

project (ills. p. 172), but rather modulates the presence of light
throughout the house, producing a syncopated sequence
of phenomenological conditions ranging from complete
transparency in the wall apertures to the total opacity of a
masonry *poché* wall. Refraction effects, heightened by the
air bubbles present in the glue between glass layers, produce
ghosted images of inhabitants as they move through the main
corridor. The house does not offer a radical reinterpretation of
interior space, and in fact, its austerity betrays its position within
a lineage of stereotomic thought, where the rooms appear
carved from a solid. Nevertheless, this effect is achieved via an
additive layering process that performs in ways that masonry
construction cannot. The normative organizational layout of the
Laminata House may actually work to its advantage in the sense
that its phenomenological manipulations become more legible
when placed in tension against its clearly defined residential type.

4. Configuration That Erases Its Own Trace
for Figurative Motives

Steven Holl's body of work straddles the line between the
figurative and configurative, as his projects tend to reflect
his desire to "build the site" by addressing programmatic
considerations via a figural language. Among others, his Fukuoka
housing project in Japan is largely concerned with an indexical
registration of the interior program on the building facade. The
interlocking surfaces convey the volumetric interplay within.
Simmons Hall, by contrast, attempts to employ a neutral surface
grid of windows so as to heighten the contrasted effect provoked
by the carved voids that signify communal spaces within the
normative dormitory block (ills.). The programmatic legibility
that characterizes much of Holl's early work appears here in a
more perverse form that frustrates the perception of scale. To
achieve a regular gridded surface effect, Holl uses L-shaped
aluminum panels that aggregate across the surface to produce
a series of equally sized square apertures. Floor slabs occur at an
interval of every third window and no trace of the structure can
be read on the facade. Surface aggregation is thus employed in
a sleight-of-hand manner to dissolve the spatial aggregation of
the dormitory modules behind the facade, revealing two distinct
aggregation systems being deployed at cross-purposes to erase
the perception of the unit of construction.

5. Configuration as Structure and Image

Gramazio & Kohler's facade for the Gantenbein Winery in Fläsch, Switzerland, addresses issues of structure, light, and image with a single surface strategy (ills. pp. 56, 57). Utilizing parametric digital design processes to situate 20,000 bricks in a pattern meant to evoke oversized grapes bulging from the volume of the winery, designed by Bearth & Deplazes, the architects used a robotic arm to assemble the units into larger rectilinear surface modules that could be assembled on site within a grid of concrete bays. Here, the surface is simultaneously calibrated to produce a specific image, acting as a billboard for the building program, and to produce a variable range of openings to permit indirect light and air to penetrate the facility to aid in the grape fermentation process. The overt pictorial effect, coupled with the production of a seemingly plastic surface, is accomplished via a single unit of construction that both reinforces and erases its materiality. This material consistency, which is leveraged for a range of effects, stands in stark contrast to work by BIG and Herzog & de Meuron, which often goes to great lengths to achieve a similar pictorial and phenomenological complexity. Bjarke Ingel's Mountain apartment project presents a more virtuosic barrage of means to achieve a similar pictorial effect. The rich aggregational logic of the apartment units determined by programmatic requirements and the desire to provide ample light and terraces to each apartment produce a powerful image. The entire arrangement, however, is both symbolically reinforced and preemptively undercut by the screenprinted image of a mountain at the base of the complex. Its presence represents a certain one-liner provocation that emerges from the notion of the building as iconic metaphor rather than a coherent work where literal representation emerges from configurative logic. Semper's distinction amongst different tectonic elements paved the way for such an extreme separation of pictorial expression and structural logic, yet the Gantenbein Winery facade offers perhaps a more operative mode of practice that produces a variety of effects through the calibration of limited means without resorting to either a nostalgic notion of material honesty or a wanton deployment of dissonant techniques.

Office dA, Villa Moda Sports Club,
Kuwait, 1995-present, programs and
typologies.

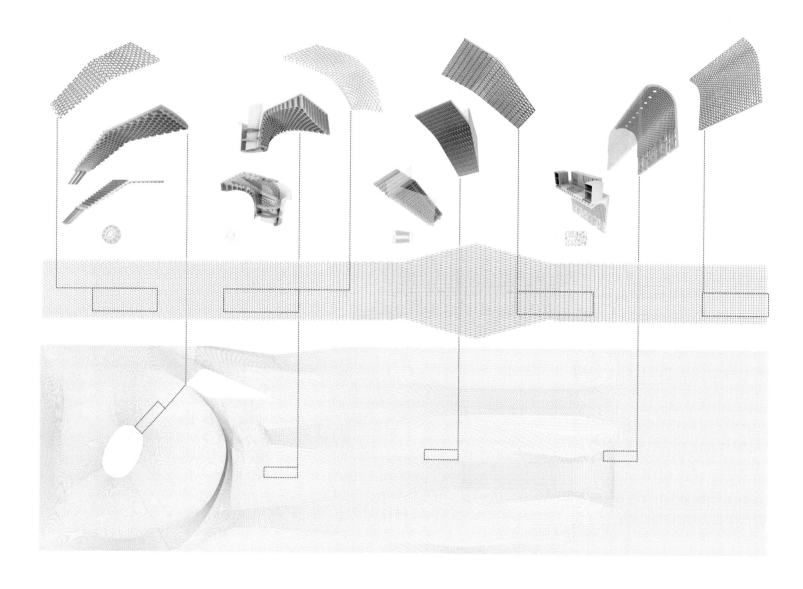

6. Configurative Variance for Spatial and Tectonic Performance

Office dA's Villa Moda Sports Club and Issam Fares Institute employ configurative tactics to achieve effects that go beyond the expression or erasure of its material means and attempt a direct negotiation between the local dictates of their respective sites (Kuwait City and Beirut) and a discipline-grounded experimentation with geometric and aggregational variability.

The basic organization of the Villa Moda proposal can be described by four decks of varied thickness and geometries (ill. p. 58). Beneath the ground level, there is a parking deck, which supports service deliveries, mechanical space, and technical support equipment for various programs. The ground level is characterized by an undulating public surface, supporting the main functions of the arena, convention hall, souk/mall, aqua center, and hotel lobby; the surface dips and rises in accordance with the programs (i.e. swimming areas and the arena), but also in relation to the extended public zones such as the commercial level. The public ground is covered with a singular and extended canopy: a coffered structure that accommodates blended programs, circulation itineraries, structural mandates, and vertical cores. The identity of the proposal is in great part the result of this invention – a large "carpet" or the canopy of a great banyan tree, giving shade to the public zones and protecting the ground from the sweltering Kuwaiti heat. Though undulating, this canopy is based on a conventional grid, drawing from a more repetitive layout of residential units that coffer as the fourth layer of this system. The housing forms a two-storey crust to the canopy, excavated to draw light and air into the courtyards, as well as allowing the passage of light into the public spaces beneath.

The project's aesthetic effect emerges from a more direct confrontation with the advent of geometry and patterning as displayed in Kuwaiti history, though implemented in abstract and allusive ways. Since each building type manifests a need for its own autonomous organization, form, and figure, there is no universal geometry to bring together the various fragments. To this end, the appropriate geometry was identified for each type, based on the figural biases they display: circle for the arena, triangle for the theater, and square for courtyards, among others. The way in which these geometries are brought together is unique: instead of typological aggregation or fragmentation, we assemble the dissonant geometries through the technique of metamorphosis, grafting together a wide range of irreconcilable types. As a technique, this is deployed by the transformation of geometric cells onto which we keep adding vertices. Thus, for instance, a square cell may be altered by the additions of two vertices to create a hexagon, and in turn negotiate the transition of a square courtyard type and a radial arena. The precise orchestration of plan typologies and a correspondent structural condition creates an opportunity to maintain the seamlessness of an organic geometric logic while permitting typological diversity and heterogeneity. This aesthetic effect is also augmented by the adoption of and reaction to local materials, climate, landscapes, and textures – again adopted as allusive signifiers of the regional flavor.

The structure in this typology is not independent of the architecture. The scale of the programming allows the structure to inform the specificity of the architectural shape. The structure is analogous to the sponge-like form and material-to-weight ratio of human bone: a trabecular structure in which material is concentrated efficiently in response to the applied, or anticipated, loading while minimizing weight as in Wolf's law for human anatomy. What appears random in bone, or as mass customization at the scale of building structures, is in fact an efficient use of materials, providing material for strength and stiffness where it is needed most and reducing the material quantity in areas where it is not needed. This effect can be provided as distinct, crisp changes in material cross-section or in a more sinuous nature as proposed here. In areas of high moments, shears, or in response to concerns of serviceability, the form of the slab system morphs from a typical, orthogonal, uniform depth rib system into a system of deeper ribs, wider ribs, and/or more closely spaced ribs. The changing shape responds to the intensity of the loading and the need to provide strength and stiffness to the system. This variability in coffering geometries is at once structural and aesthetic, signifying programmatic diversity through configurative dissonances.

Office dA, Issam Fares Institute,
Beirut, Lebanon, 2006, exterior renderings.

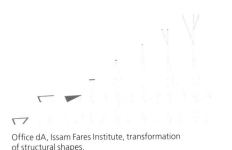

Office dA, Issam Fares Institute, transformation
of structural shapes.

In a similar way, Office dA's proposal for the Issam Fares Institute at the American University of Beirut offers a strategy that negotiates between the figurative and the configurative in reciprocal ways (ills. pp. 60, 61). Located in a bosk of trees, the project is as much the result of a negotiation with nature as architecture – the trees offering substantial challenges in planting new structural piles amongst the roots of the Ficus trees on the site. Working with a geometric unit – this time not two-dimensional, but three – the project identifies a key parametric potential within its logic: that the triangle, once truncated on three sides, becomes a hexagon, establishing the two figures as genetically linked. This simple observation offered the possibility of a variety of transformations for structural shapes that would be needed to negotiate both urbansitic and programmatic complexities. The geometries offered a way to incorporate columns, *pilotis*, transfer beams, and walls, among other structuro-spatial elements by way of a single organizational unit. The building then, deviously works to camouflage itself within the context of the trees, while adopting a configurative strategy that capitalizes on the structural, spatial, and programmatic possibilities of the organization to integrate commonly held contradictions into a cohesive architectural figure.

7. Entropic Configuration

Approaches to layering and aggregation are largely conducted as systemic endeavors embodying a replicable logic or employed for a specific spatial or figural effect within a defined context. The possibility nevertheless remains, however, that such configurative material techniques can be conducted in the absence of a discernible logic or intent. Massachusetts-based artist Tom Friedman has made strides toward this end with works such as Inside-Out, where objects cascade from their cardboard box container, spilling across the floor in a seemingly random assemblage of found objects. His work with polystyrene packing peanuts also follows in this vein, yet here, the unit is fixed but its aggregation is not limited by material constraints, as they adhere together upon any surface through static.

Ronan and Erwan Bouroullec have pushed this approach toward more spatial ends with their Algues, injection-molded tentacle-shaped polypropylene components that link at the ends. The modular elements have 19 eyelets and can attach together at any or several of these points using small plastic pegs. Although the pieces set certain limits on their configurative potential, these restraints are minimal and, in fact, can produce a variety of user-determined tectonic effects from semi-transparent interwoven screens to entire spaces.

Conclusion

Aggregation and tectonic configuration refer to strategies that attempt to go beyond the honesty to materials as an ethic. Instead, they establish a more critical, if devious relationship to the narrative intent of a project. Navigating between figuration as a goal and configuration as its path, aggregative practices attempt to bring an increased intelligence regarding material agency, means, and phenomenal effects to a building project. Methods of material aggregation and configuration become mere exercises when detached from larger effects-based strategies and logics of construction. Architecture always contains an excess, or a surplus which is unaccounted for by technique alone and in fact, architectural agency emerges at the precise moment when technique breaks down, requiring a direction and an intent to deftly negotiate the uneasy tension between tectonic facts and the poetics of effect.

Joints and Junctions

Thomas Schröpfer
Elizabeth Lovett

Frank Gehry, Guggenheim Museum, Bilbao, Spain, 1997, facade detail.

Architectural details bear witness to the limitations we face when using tools to enact change on a material's raw nature. The multi-axis rotations and translations of tools, once sufficiently encoded into the traditional know-how of a craftsman, are made available through architects only within their ability to communicate them definitively to an operational tool. An architect is not a craftsman, and therefore relies wholly on a system of communicative tools to enact change on materials. The sophistication of these communicative languages ultimately expresses itself in the joinery of a project. The architect's traditional methods of projective drawings have stripped their dictates to singular, planar operations lacking content concerning depth, sequence, and unambiguous geometric definitions. The complexity of the joints and junctions of a project corresponds to an ingenuity in the representation and documentation of design intent. Joints and junctions of an architectural project are also expressive of an ingrained building culture in tension with a design intent as well as the design intent's struggle to express itself through communicative and operational tools. These are the considerations that govern the relationship creators have with their materials, from the highly specific but intuitive nature of a craftsman to the abstract but universally defined relationship of the architect.

To understand a joint or a juncture in the context of a created object requires a depth of knowledge that extends well beyond the simple comprehension of a layering of parts. Material properties and constraints are often discussed as the central concern in the joinery of an architectural construction and while critical in the final resolution of the connection, the materials are only part of the deterministic equation. Joints and junctions in a composition of materials are never isolated incidences of material adjacencies. They impose and reflect a greater structural and expressive logic across the whole architectural form. Degrees of tolerance necessitated between materials are deterministic of sequences of assembly, hierarchies of information and sometimes effect change on the original formal desire. Joints and junctions in architecture are the resultant balance of a process, form, structure, and desire.

The Role of Detailing in the Act of Architecture

Discussions around architectural detailing often center on the rubric of part-to-whole relationships. Buildings are admired for consistency between their formal concepts and their material junctures. This articulates itself in several ways: The first is a moral prescriptive once described as "total design." Hailed by the early modernists and the arts-and-crafts architects, the idea of designing a building's expression from its form through the details seems naive today. Few architects could maintain a practice in which every project's material treatment is uniquely considered. It left little opportunity for long-term development of material processes across projects or within a building industry. While there was much invention in the realm of material joinery, the building culture as a whole saw few systematic changes in material attitudes. Development was limited to the internal workings of architects and firms. Emphasis on joinery in these terms focuses disproportionately on the uniqueness of the details of an architect or of a project. It prioritizes the figure and ignores the fabric while adding a layer of imposed morality toward a family of building techniques. While this lends a greater appreciation for the intricacies of individual projects, it also leads to an episodic disciplinary conversation. The omission of the mundane, inexpressive details denies the culture and constraints of the construction industry and its influence on a project. The detailing is reduced to a few signature operations and loses the tension between fabric and figure from which a project springs.

The part-to-whole understanding of architectural operations also takes the form of an argument between a bottom-up and a top-down approach to design. A project labeled as bottom-up supposedly begins with an architectural operation whose aggregation is deterministic of its final form. A top-down design begins in a determined form and subjugates the materials to it through the details of its construction. However, the existence of a project that lies wholly within either of these camps is doubtful. An experienced designer understands the non-linear nature of balancing the pressures of materiality with the ambitions of form. The false layering of a simplified narrative to the development of these architectural projects takes them

Michel de Klerk, Het Schip housing block,
Amsterdam, The Netherlands, 1921.

outside of their contexts and treats them as isolated acts. Again, the figure is emphasized and the fabric from which these material operations arise is ignored. While the intent of applying these categories to architectural projects may have been to find a common ground by which to compare them, it has the effect of polarizing them and placing them outside of the normal material operations of the building community. Discussions in these terms promotes little creative impetus and serves primarily to generate *more* discussion. A truer investigation into architectural details asks us to consider the specific operations to which our tools subject materials. The part and the whole are elements of the discussion, but the root of any argument of material detailing lies within the act itself. In this light, the signature details of a project are expressive with regard to their willful distinction from the typical; both the fabric and the figure are considered.

The actions themselves are the result of a long history of choreographed movements enacted by a tool on a material. Each material inspires a specific set of movements. For instance, the grain of wood requires directionality to be considered when sanding, carving, or cutting in a manner that stone or brick would not. However, the brittleness of many stones will determine the speed and force of operations when forming them into new shapes. Depending on the material, simply removing mass can involve as many factors as cutting angles, back rake angles, speed, sequence, chipping tolerances and jig constraints. Most of these considerations are handled at the level of the craftsman, bypassing the architect and often the contractor. However industrialized the fabrication process has become, most of these concerns are still handled by the vocation most connected with the material. They troubleshoot the process until it is streamlined to get the best results out of the most material. In spite of this, designers are forced to engage with these processes when they require an exceptional condition. Decisions favoring one specific condition over the typical standard begin to change the motions of tooling upon a material.

Fabric and Figure in Architectural Joinery

Architects always build in relation to localized building practices. Although propagated by their continued employment by architects, these practices were developed outside of the architectural profession by contractors, builders, local artisans and in response to available materials. Architects design either within these practices, in spite of them, or in conversation with them. A term often employed is "vernacular," however its connotation with primitive or undeveloped building methods prevents us from using it here. The fabric of architectural joinery is in constant development and can require a high level of technical skill. It is the result of pressures from the materials, an industry of procurement and delivery, and representational methods of designers and implementers. Moments of architectural ingenuity reveal themselves in relation to the established practice of building. When, in 1905, the City of Amsterdam established the first building code and appointed Johan van der Mey as Aesthetic Advisor, favored architects were given the opportunity to work directly within the building tradition in new and inventive ways. Based primarily in brick, a series of civic and workers housing projects pushed the traditional Dutch language of brick to new heights of expression. Michel de Klerk's Het Schip housing block is the most salient example, displaying not only a series of new architectural flourishes but also allowing the brick to aggregate over entirely new forms (ill. p. 64). Deviating from the rectilinear nature of both the Dutch tradition and the unit of the brick, the swelling and curving forms pushed bricklayers to test the limitations of older forms of aggregation, exploring a cantilevering unit similar to corbelling. However, the expressionistic detailing of the brickwork was not a series of wholly new inventions. Many of the elements of the traditional Dutch brick facade were kept, if in an altered state. Typical cornices and window frames were essentially old features made to adapt to new forms via creative re-designs in the details of their connections. A looseness in the position of the bricks within the mortar allowed for the curving brickwork without changes in the unit itself. Directionality of the brick was also challenged as layers of brickwork displayed different bond patterns, often for pure effect. The resulting hierarchy of horizontal striations contributed to the overall effect of these slicker forms.

Office dA was quick to acknowledge the gradient between the fabric and figure of architectural detailing. They write that "the first interpretation emerges from the idea that the detail becomes necessary when two things need to be joined – that is, when two materials need a joint, when two parts of a building require a connection, or when two irreconcilable architectural conditions require mediation."[1] Their Toledo House outside Bilbao, Spain, bears witness to the ingrained building culture faced with an onslaught of imported and updated construction techniques (ills.). Bilbao put integrated CAD/CAM techniques on display for the world during the building of Frank Gehry's Guggenheim Museum (ills. pp. 63, 67). Office dA's Toledo House however is a gentler grafting of modernization with localized traditions. Building off the local Basque construction practices, the house utilizes a timber frame and masonry infill composite system. However, new spatial effects are achieved because new techniques are integrated into the assembly. The design called for laser-cut marine-grade plywood, which defines the outlines of an irregular form. They serve structurally in the same manner the timber frame previously served. However, they also take on the role of guides, allowing for an amorphous wall. The form is limited by the two-dimensional cutting technique, which limits these guides to planar cuts within the elevation. The curvature between the guide planes is estimated by the builders. We see the tension between the older methods and the newer ones in the resolution of the facade. Digital design lends itself to the creation of smooth curves, however the masonry unit permits smoothness only when stacked to form a planar surface. Barring the condition in which the traditional construction unit is altered, the resolution of the exterior facade curvature is controlled by the size of this unit, the degree to which it can cantilever over the one below it, and the interval of plywood formwork placed within the construction process.[2] The play in facets and gaps along the residence are a result of a negotiation between intended form and existing construction unit, between new techniques and traditional operations. In engaging with the existing building culture in order to achieve an atypical building, the architects take an active part in determining the construction processes. Office dA's direct role in providing a building jig in the form of the wood frame required the office to be intimately aware of

Frank Gehry, Guggenheim Museum,
facade detail.

67

the details of assembly, as well as the exact definition of the design's curvature at varying horizontal planes of the building. In a manner similar to the traditional construction of a wooden boat hull, a master designer provided exact profiles of the form at planar intervals, allowing the craftsmen and the constraints of the material to approximate the position of the intermediate space. While this degree of communication of formal properties operates well in some materials, less forgiving materials require a new means of formal communication between architect, builder, and tool.

American and Japanese Joinery: Conditions of Complexity

The degree of complexity within the fabric of joinery is maintained by a close connection between the material, the craftsman, and the architect. There are positive and negative aspects to this degree of material control. The industrialization of American wood frame construction, for example, illustrates the speed and accessibility of a construction industry based on a strong division between vocations, the homogenization of material, and the codification of construction techniques. Construction became affordable, less skill was required for assembly, and a relatively simple means of communication was needed to convey the overall design through to the material details. Lightness, temporality, and efficiency became design parameters in the resulting framing systems. Early American balloon frames were known to travel across the plains via wagon and later by trains. Today the average American wood frame house can be assembled with as few as three to four workers. The trade-off comes in the uniqueness of each finished product, flexibility within the design process, and professional understandings between the building vocations. Tailoring conditions become a matter of piecing together parts prefabricated for other uses and are often the cause of a palpable tension between cost and design. The material itself is not expressed but is optimized and while its constraints are represented through repeating formal traits in the resulting architecture, its natural distinctions are suppressed. The actions upon the material are simplified in a manner that reflects the communication between the architect, contractor,

and ultimately the construction worker. A combination of orthographic drawings and written specifications have steered the procedures performed upon the raw materials toward planar operations that are performed sequentially.

The reverse example to American wood framing is that of the Japanese. Codified by families and guilds over the course of 1,500 years of construction, Japanese wood joinery exemplifies a deep-seated respect for the material and for the tools that work it. Carpenters go through a rigorous process of mentored work to master their craft. For example, 15 years of carpentry experience is considered necessary to perform the task of a temple carpenter and to become fluent in the tools of the trade.[3] It is not surprising that a tradition celebrated for its detailed joinery would put a great emphasis on the tools of their trade. The tools themselves are referred to as *dōgu*, translated "instruments of the Way [of Carpentry]." While the instruments themselves have evolved to include both traditional and electric tools, the pride taken in them remains strong. The tools connect the carpenters to the material, the overall design intent, and to the cultural tradition. Although there have been attempts to graphically describe many of the primary connections in Japanese joinery in the Western method of orthographic projections, they fall short of being able to convey the complexity of the sequence of operations required to perform these joints. This is in part because the joinery itself is not born from or did not respond to these representational techniques. The personal instruction given to carpenters during their training allows for the transfer of a body of three-dimensional and processional information that flattens out in the form of two-dimensional drawings. Len Brackett describes the difficulty of translating Japanese joinery into Western graphics in the foreword to his own joinery handbook saying, "the design of the joints is really quite simple and that, of all the things in the book, layout is considerably more difficult. Western geometry is the product … of an intellectual process, a process for which I have great respect. This Japanese layout, however, is experiential – it is "hands on" – and deals with a carpenter's ability to visualize on a three-dimensional scale."[4]

Constraints of Description: Utzon and Gehry

The frustration many architects feel in the struggle to communicate specific complex processes is not limited to Japanese joinery. Often a designer's intended form, at the scale of a building or of building detail, is not conducive to traditional architectural representation, and consequently defers from the established construction delivery processes. In these cases a designer must also create a feasible means by which to make and assemble the design within the tools and materials available to him or her. Although today there are an increasing number of tools and methods available to operate on materials, they are also becoming highly specific to singular uses as a means of adding efficiencies. Clarity becomes singularly important in the attempt to push a new material application through the design-build process. While traditional architectural methods of information transfer are still effective in some arenas, they are woefully inadequate when the building culture is unlikely to be able to fill in the gaps with experience.

When Jørn Utzon submitted his proposal for the Sydney Opera House, he had never even seen the site (ills. pp. 69, 70). The project was to be designed from his office in Denmark, with major consultants located around the globe, and a body of builders that were disengaged from the design. Such is now the norm in modern building. Because of the separations between the different building vocations, a more elaborate set of communicative tools was needed. Utzon's initial sketch was dynamic, inspiring, and very uninformative. This is meant in two ways: firstly, that it communicated little materiality, and secondly that the sketch itself was uninformed by any constraint of fabrication. However, the scale of the project would lead the design development team to adopt geometrical rigor and advanced communication techniques in order to find common ground between overall form and material detail.

While the challenges in achieving the ambitious design of the Sydney Opera House were numerous, the problem of joinery was paramount in every re-design, cost escalation, and eventual expressiveness of the overall form. The initial competition entry, soon satirized as a "magnificent doodle," took little account

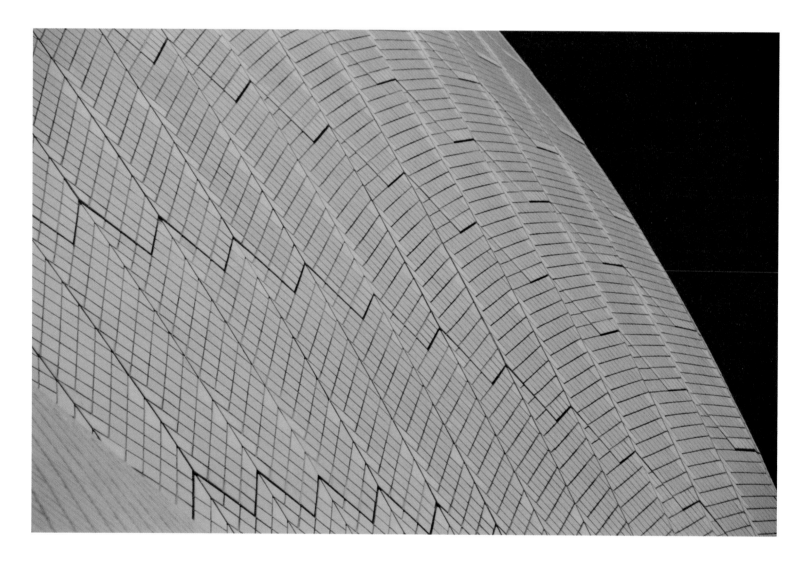

of the constraints of materiality. Originally conceived as thin concrete shells, Utzon intended for the interior surface to be smooth and rib-less, "like the inside of an egg".[5] The prominent engineers of the day immediately realized the unlikeliness of this structural solution. Both Pier Luigi Nervi and Felix Candela expressed concerns about the geometry of the shells, which was not inherently self-supporting. Utzon was encouraged to work with engineers Ove Arup and Partners. It was Arup who first described the difficulties with having all of the shells being shaped uniquely. The problems boiled down to the fact that the detailing of the original shells did not allow for repetition in any major elements. It would have been prohibitively costly in time and money to design hundreds of unique conditions. A standard set of elements could not have been defined, and the architectural language would have been the ad-hoc composite of constantly negotiated constraints. The geometrical rigor required by the constraints of joinery gave the overall form an integrity that otherwise would have gone unconsidered. The combination of the structural instability and geometric irregularity led Utzon and Arup to re-design the shell structures, as well as the entire fabrication delivery method. What was lacking in Utzon's design was a means to communicate the nature of his curved surfaces. Without a clear definition of form, the engineers could not calculate forces and the contractors could not plan for material components. Arup sought to find a form that expressed Utzon's design intent but that also had the qualities of mathematical definition and geometric consistency, thereby enabling analysis, placement, and repetition. Arup articulates this to his clients in 1958 saying, "By defining the surfaces geometrically, each point of the surfaces can be given spatial coordinates and a basis has been created for the calculation of the forces acting on the shells."[6] Eventually the shell structure was abandoned in favor of ribbed vaults. Utzon was convinced of the ribbed scheme because of its material integrity. A shell structure would have required a complex double skin of steel and concrete, with the concrete being of limited structural use. The ribbed scheme however highlighted the second initial problem of the geometry in that now the structure required a series of large non-repetitive ribs, all of which would have to be constructed on site. This led to the final proposal in which the shells were all constructed as fragments

of an identical sphere. The spheres provided both definition and repetition.[7] Having resolved the greater geometry, the constraints of fabricating the components became paramount. The new proposal allowed for a fabric of similar elements to come together in standardized joints. The ribs were divided into segments of 15 ft/4.75 m lengths, totaling 2,400 units. The geometry allowed these to be cast with only four molds, though ten were used to speed up construction. The construction crews became so adapt at casting the repetitive elements that the process was completed ahead of schedule and rib units had to be stored off-site. Construction of the ribs also employed one of the early uses of epoxy as an adhesive. Typical concrete seams would have slowed progress as it required a longer drying time and would have created a more visible joint.[8]

The Sydney Opera House's form finding calculations were one of the first large-scale applications of computers in architecture. The only computers available at the time belonged to university departments. Arup engineers traveled to Southampton in order to use the university's computers, which they were learning to operate as they progressed through the design. While they were initially used to determine complex load calculations on the shells, they went on to become necessary in many elements of the detailing of the building, most notably the tile work and the glass facade. Complex calculations for the tiles were needed to handle the placement and the combinations of standard and non-standard tiles.[9] The tiles themselves were designed by Utzon in combination with a Swedish firm, Hoganas, when no existing tile could be found to suit the qualities of reflection that Utzon desired. After numerous experiments in shapes, materials, and finishes, a combination of square white tiles with a transparent glaze and matt off-white tiles was chosen. The matt tiles would be used along the edges to soften the form, while the glazed tiles would softly reflect light patterns across the shells. The square tiles were laid diagonally in chevron shapes that corresponded to the localized geometry of the ribs. Originally Utzon imagined the tiles would be laid directly onto the shell structure. When the design changed, he suggested laying them directly onto the ribs before they were assembled. While this would have helped in determining placement, it would have been problematic during the erection of the ribs and no guarantee could be made about

Gehry Partners, Vila Olímpica,
Barcelona, Spain, 1992.

the waterproofing or the finish of the surface of assembled joints. Instead, a layered joinery was proposed in which groups of tiles were cast into ferro-cement "lids" of 25 different shapes, sized under 19.5 m² for easy transport to the site. These lids could be prefabricated off-site and attached to the ribs as construction progressed.[10] While the assembling of these chevron panels was relatively simple, the management and inventory of a total of 1,000,000 tiles required substantial computational modeling. Within each chevron, the internal tiles were identical squares. These squares were one of six standard sizes. The external tiles were then custom-designed and cut to accommodate their unique location on the shell and to absorb any differences between the idealized geometry and the as-built reality.

The high level of complexity of the tile design sprung from Utzon's determination to achieve a highly specific material effect. The nature of the material itself was lenient to small-scale differences between the designed and the built conditions. The mortar of the tile and the sheer number of the pieces melted discrepancies into the overall pattern of light reflections. Such leeway was not present in the glass enclosures. As a primary weatherproofing element, the glass facades to the shells required a highly exact assembly process. There was little tolerance in the connections between the glass and the steel and bronze mullion system. While the facade had been given geometric definition (the shapes defined by a cylinder intersecting two cones), the ideal geometry differed considerably from the reality of the shells' built conditions. While the exact dimensions of each cut of glass could be determined in an ideal world, on-site specificity was nearly impossible to achieve. It was this set of problems that led Arup to begin to build one of the earliest parametric computer models of a shell and facade system. The relationships between the material connections needed to be defined in geometrically relative terms, rather than dimensionally specific ones. As adjustments were made in the greater geometry of the shells to reflect differentiations from the idealized forms, the changes would trickle down into the dimensions of the smaller elements. However, as in most parametric systems, the manner in which smaller sub-elements changed to fit the new geometries had to be controlled through a specified hierarchy of parameters and

constants. These imposed their own feedback to the greater geometry, allowing and disallowing sets of alterations and given constraints. This is an important shift in the way in which the material components and joint conditions were considered. Rather than the fabric being comprised of dimensionally consistent identical pieces, the common condition becomes one defined in relational terms. Pieces with wildly different physical shapes are grouped in families. The figurative joint becomes one, which must be defined as unique in the context of greater geometrical language. In this manner, the part-to-whole relationship between form and detail is no longer limited to a few expressive details encapsulating the ideals of the project. Instead, the whole affects its embedded logic on the shapes, families, and material hierarchies of every single joint in the construction.[11] The Sydney Opera House pioneered by necessity new means of describing surface geometry across the building vocations. The relatively young technologies used by Arup to develop an informative model have since evolved tremendously. With these, a new set of mathematics has been revived in the discipline of architecture. Calculus and computational geometry, both centuries old, have been reintroduced as languages to describe architectural forms and allow for precise definitions of joints and junctions. Thanks to this enhancement of vocabulary, designers today are not restricted to simple geometries, such as catenaries and spheres.

No architect demonstrates the potential of these new tools better than Frank Gehry, who constantly materializes forms we have only experienced in natural settings. He has achieved these constructions within a highly codified building delivery process. He needed to invent a means to communicate his formal intentions to craftsmen. In today's stratified building culture, this language required an unprecedented depth and precision. Borrowing software from airplane manufacturers, Gehry and his architects began to reinvent architectural communication. While designing and fabricating the Vila Olímpica fish-shaped canopy for the 1992 Olympic Village, tight construction deadlines turned the design team toward remodeling the physical fish into a digital program (ills. pp. 72, 73). However, architectural software was built either for two-dimensional drafting or for three-dimensional visualization.

Gehry Partners, Vila Olímpica, canopy detail.

Gehry Partners, Weisman Art Museum,
Minneapolis, Minnesota, USA, 1993.

While the first digital model of the fish was highly accurate to the physical model, the digital surfaces lacked the embedded surface information that would allow for a precise placement of points in space. Because the surfaces were described as polygon approximations and not with polynomial equations of descriptive geometry, the information could not be translated to the numerically controlled tools needed to fabricate the pieces efficiently.[12] Essentially, the same problem existed for Utzon and Gehry: how would one communicate the exact size, shape, and placement of a component in a space that could not be fully described in two-dimensional drawings. Utzon resolved this by simplifying their intents to fit well-known and more easily calculable geometries such as catenaries, hyperboloids, and spheres. Gehry's team continued to evolve the modeling and representation tools to allow for the description of more complex curvatures. Adopting CATIA, the now well-known software by Dassault used by the aerospace industry, Gehry's office began to remodel the physical models by the same means one would attempt to use in a constructed drawing; via plumb lines, measurements, strings, and geometrical relationships. The success in quickly achieving the Olympic Pavilion's detailed connections led Gehry's office to integrate the new software into their larger projects. This was in large part due to the difficulty Gehry had in describing his designs to his contractors. The two-dimensional representations appeared more complicated than the shapes themselves. The inability to communicate effectively increased the time and cost of building the project and limited the types of geometry Gehry could use. Despite Gehry's office's proficiency and experience in descriptive geometry, without the new software, the architecture still had to be simplified in order to be communicable. The last project completed wholly by hand in the office was the Weisman Art Museum (ill. p. 74). All of its facade curvature was based on cut platonic solids.[13]

While much attention is given to Gehry's hand sketches, it is his office's discovery and adaption of new descriptive tools that have opened the doors to a more varied family of forms accessible to architects. The value of the descriptive software is not in its ability to generate form or design in lieu of the architect. It is its ability to describe the architect's intent in a manner that is precise and useful to the craftsmen who can handle the detail. In effect, it is comparable to the years of training and experience a Japanese carpenter undergoes, in that it has three-dimensional and temporal information ingrained within it. It provides models of assembly, sequence orders, and embedded material constraints. However, none of this information is generated by the software itself.

Countless professionals are required to build an intelligent working model. Parametric digital models now require the modeler to engage in the constraints of construction, from the tolerances end-materials allow, the constraints of tooling abilities, to the limitations in jigs, molds, and formwork. As consultants across the industry share this family of descriptive digital models, they can again begin to work in a collaborative way, reconnecting the architect and master planner with the vocation engaging in the joinery of materials. This bridging of the gap between the building professions that was created by a project delivery system communicated in two-dimensional drawings brings back older questions of authorship, collaboration, and professional roles. However, its increasing popularity is building a new fabric of joinery that integrates both local practices with individualized form. The fabric of details becomes that of topological similarity rather than dimensional similarity. An exceptional joinery condition is one that differs from the geometrically set language of the others, offering a unique condition. In this way, architecture again becomes relative to itself, giving a part-to-whole unity that is endemic to the nature of design, and reflective of a culture of building.

Notes

1. El Khoury, Rodolphe et al. *Office dA*. Minneapolis: Rockport Publishers, 1999. p. 6.
2. *Ibid*. p. 56.
3. Nakahara, Yasuo. *Japanese Joinery: A Handbook for Joiners and Carpenters*. Washington: Hartley & Marks Publishers, 1983. p. 7.
4. Brackett, Len and Landers Rao, Peggy. *Building the Japanese House Today*, New York: Harry N. Abrams, 2005. p. 9.
5. Murray, Peter. *The Saga of Sydney Opera House*. London: Spon Press, 2004. p. 13.
6. *Ibid*. p. 20.
7. *Ibid*. p. 34.
8. Smith, Vincent. *The Sydney Opera House*. Sydney: Paul Hamlyn, 1974. p. 15.
9. Murray, Peter. *The Saga* .... p. 30.
10. *Ibid*. p. 40.
11. Schodek, Daniel, et al. *Digital Design and Manufacturing*. Hoboken, NJ: John Wiley & Sons, 2005. pp. 29-33.
12. Lindsey, Bruce. *Digital Gehry*. Basel, Boston, Berlin: Birkhäuser, 2001. pp. 32-34.
13. *Ibid*. pp. 38-39.

Weaving
The Tectonics of Textiles

Toshiko Mori

Toshiko Mori Architect, stair for house in Casey Key, Florida, USA, built by Goetz Custom Boats, 2004.

In material research, there is a need to find a more holistic and comprehensive understanding of material culture. The study of materials draws on two principal understandings of the subject: an experiential and a technical understanding. On the experiential side, textiles provide differentiated and nuanced intangible qualities that are difficult to quantify and describe; yet their impact can be quite powerful. Texture, pattern, and tactility all embody enormous potentials to invoke emotional responses from humans. Textiles can carry in them memories and associations that appeal to the human sensibility offering softness, accessibility, and texture. As a second basis of understanding, the techniques of fabrication comprise how a material can be manipulated, processed, and eventually applied to a purpose, transforming its pure ingredients into a complete whole with a specific utilitarian role. By exploring the tectonics of textiles, one not only appreciates an impressive multiplicity of its methods and applications, but also recognizes the potential embedded in a seemingly primitive technique and its emergence as a major material technique of the 21st century.

The tectonics of textile production involves such methods as weaving, knitting, knotting, braiding, plaiting, layering, laminating, felting, seaming, quilting, sewing, embroidery, and stitching. They are techniques often associated with crafts, and in particular, those made by women who are thought to pass traditional skills and artistry from generation to generation. Textile production can be traced back to the ancient worlds of Egypt and Mesopotamia, and found universally throughout history. Each culture and civilization developed unique design, material, and color palettes informed by their geography, climate, and available materials. In ancient Peru, it is said that textiles were used as a communication and recording device to transmit messages and document stories. The pervasiveness of textile production across cultures and time can be attributed to its familiarity and accessibility. They are techniques that can be mastered by diverse segments of a population, from the young to the old, from men to women, and from weak to strong.

It is this ancient, primitive, vernacular technique that is leap-frogging into the most sophisticated and versatile fabrication methods. Today, the same methods used to produce traditional clothing and fishing nets are employed to fabricate high-performance products ranging from athletic gear for competitions to high-tech medical devices, and from military gear to outer space exploration tools. These innovative textile products and applications suggest a far-reaching potential for the future of textiles and textile tectonics across a diverse array of industries. They have taken new forms and processes, promoting continued development and innovation, which have great implications for their application in the architectural world. There are two paths of exploration for textile tectonics, both of which I hope to explore in this chapter. The first is the idea of new surfaces using textiles. The other is to extend the attributes and concept of textile tectonics to re-conceive architecture.

The Process of Weaving

The textile fabrication process is one of the few techniques that encompass three modes of production: hand-made, mechanical, and digital. The translation of the hand-made technique of weaving to mechanical production is intuitive and predictable. The jump to digital production, however, provides an interesting insight into the original structure of weaving, as it is surprisingly compatible with digital processes. Weaving is a binary process, similar to electronic circuits, where warp and weft comprise the technique's fundamental organization, just as the "on" and "off" do for circuitry. In fact, some of the early jacquard loom pattern cards were models for early FORTRAN computer programming cards. Computer programming processes are similar to pattern-making processes in weaving, both sharing a mathematical foundation. Traditional weavers have to understand the precise relationship between the planar pattern and the linear dimension of yarn. He or she has to constantly balance the warp and weft structurally to create a stable fabric. When this intuitive yet precise craft-based knowledge and wisdom converged with computational logic, the exponential growth of textile production quickly led to the development of high-performance materials. Thus, the similar languages of weaving and digital processes allowed for textile production to jump quickly from mechanical production to a digital one. In the new generation of textiles, the process is made more precise, the composition more calculated, and the range of scale vast.

"Josef and Anni Albers: Designs for Living," exhibition, Cooper-Hewitt National Design Museum, New York, New York, USA, 2005.

With these multiple production methods, textile fabrications offer a great flexibility in the quality and quantity of product. Woven fabrics can be produced individually or collectively; they can be custom-made, mass-produced, or even mass-customized. Each fiber and each thread of textile fabrication is in fact "data." The technique thus allows for a combination of complex sets of data found in the strands or layers to embed an enormous amount of "information" into the fabric. A playful example is Issey Miyake's A-POC project developed by Dai Fujiwara. The consumer cuts away at a piece of cloth to create clothing of one's choice. The A-POC rolls of fabric were embedded with information for the possible choices for many potential garments. The various ways in which the individual strands are combined yields a specific and unique product.

Physically, these individual threads of information are often made of lightweight and insubstantial materials. The lightness of yarn strands was what led textiles to be originally developed as garments and other portable equipment such as fishing nets, carpets, blankets, and scarves. Embedded in this technique is the knowledge for easy deployment, portability, collapsibility, and moldability. For example, the knotting technique employed in the making of fishing nets maximizes the surface area, uses very little material, and permits portability as it easily collapses into a compact volume. Acknowledging these inherent qualities of textiles, yet questioning their preconceived limitations, Anni Albers describes the relationship between textiles and architecture in her essay, "The Pliable Plane: Textiles in Architecture": "Both are ancient crafts, older even than pottery or metal work. In early stages they had in common the purpose of providing shelter, one for a settled life, the other for a life of wandering, a nomadic life. To this day they are characterized by the traits that made them suited to these two different tasks, obvious in the case of building, obscured, more or less, in that of textiles. Since the obvious hardly needs to be examined, let us turn to the less evident."[1]

At first glance, fabric appears to be a non-structural, flimsy, and floppy material that is incapable of supporting anything close to what steel or concrete could hold. Yet, with certain production methods, textiles can become tough, robust, and rigid. Textiles are durable; they survive continuous daily usage for many generations.

Their strength is based in their organizational composition. The rigidity in textiles is achieved through a dense weaving technique, layering of textiles, and the addition of seams in a geometric pattern that adds stiffness. There is native intelligence in using weak and negligible material mass, such as yarns, to create a considerable construct of impressive range. The accumulation of small units to make an ambitious larger whole is essentially a bottom-up process. It allows for the inclusion of dissimilar materials to free up a monolithic composition. In her numerous textile experimentations at the Bauhaus, Anni Albers worked with this idea by combining synthetic materials, such as metal foil or cellophane, with natural materials like cotton and linen. In doing so, she added to her projects the performative qualities of textiles such as sound absorption and light reflection (ill. p. 82).

While some textile production techniques allow for more rigid compositions, the fabrics' seemingly weak qualities of limpness and pliability actually prove to be the most advantageous attributes in its application to architecture. Textiles' flexibility allows the material to counter the conventional rigid and static manner of dealing with forces of nature. In fact, there has been a re-conceptualization of structural engineering that understands the unique characteristics of textiles as a potential model, thereby embracing a more efficient, lighter, stronger, and resilient new structural paradigm.

The threads act as both the distributional components and the binding components of fabric. When a fabric absorbs a local impact, the force is translated laterally throughout the surface, thereby requiring less depth of the material to resist. Textiles' floppy quality becomes an asset as it allows them to "yield" and "distribute" forces, absorbing the impact efficiently instead of resisting it with added mass and bulk. Bullet-proof panels made up of layers of fiberglass are a good example: when the impact of a bullet hits the surface of a bullet-proof panel, the woven fiber pattern on the top surface dissipates the applied force horizontally, transmitting the force and diminishing its impact as it travels toward the perimeter. Multiple layers of composite textiles continue to absorb residual forces, thus allowing less weight and bulk than a material with singular characteristics such as steel and concrete.

North Sails Mylar-laminated sail,
"Extreme Textiles: Designing for High
Performance," exhibition,
Cooper-Hewitt National Design Museum,
New York, New York, USA, 2005.

A New Conception of Surface

The key to applying textile tectonics to structural frameworks intelligently is the rethinking of structure as not just a matter of balancing compression against tension, but rather conceiving the surface as an area that transmits forces. The idea is to consider forces such as gravity and weight (vertical loads), and earthquakes and wind (lateral loads), as dynamic, so that their transmission can be calibrated precisely on the construction of the textiles' fiber alignment to create directionality. Creating a new framework for understanding forces of nature as dynamic will in itself contribute to a new way of thinking about architectural construction. Weaving patterns, conceived as an artistic expression, can be translated as a diagram of the transmission of forces, allowing the textile to assume a precisely calibrated geometry of a performative pattern. For example, North Sails' Mylar-laminated sail shows a force pattern by the careful placement of fibers such as carbon (black) and Kevlar (yellow) in critical points of force concentration (ill.). This allows for a minimal use of lighter and thinner materials while still achieving the same structural accomplishments of solid materials like steel and concrete. For example, carbon fiber can resist the same force as steel in just one sixth the weight of the steel, and in fact, has already replaced steel as the structural skeleton in boat building.

Textiles' inherent porous property, another seemingly weak structural material quality, actually proposes an interesting potential that may act against a conventional understanding of solid materials. Through the incorporation of negative spaces, holes, and air pockets, textile tectonics is one of the fabrication techniques that maximize the surface coverage while minimizing material use. This helps to vary the density and weight of the material through weaving patterns and processes, thus shifting the degree of stiffness.

This control over material density is also helpful in environmental control in a number of capacities. Advantages can be seen in increased air ventilation, and filtration of particulate matters. The air spaces found in porous textile tectonics are used to increase insulation values. This strategy can be found in "primitive" structures, yet the concept is highly intelligent and sophisticated. For example, some African huts use layers of woven bamboos to

promote ventilation. This technique also acts as a rainscreen and solar control device, as alternate porous patterns are applied in layers to prevent rain and sunlight to enter the hut. In essence, the textile tectonic serves to multitask. Textile techniques allow for otherwise contradictory performative goals to coexist. For example, geotextiles have weaving patterns that have the rigidity to prevent erosion, yet the porosity to allow water to pass through for irrigational purposes. They take advantage of the limited depth of the material and the differential in top and bottom of the textile patterns to allow a coexistence of seemingly opposing functions.

The ability of textiles to integrate multiple functions within very thin strata can be translated into future architectural applications and transform the role of intelligent facades that can respond to localized and generalized forces to create an effective and systematic approach, delivering performance on demand for changing environmental conditions. With a combination and assembly of diverse material palettes, textile facades can breathe, yielding against such impacts as bomb blasts, provide fireproofing and waterproofing, and corrosion-resistant skin that becomes a monocoque surface. Ultimately it combines performative and structural capacities, responding to climate, security, energy consumption, and light and air quality control.

Innovations and Applications in Engineered Textiles

Applications of engineered fabrics span a great range of industry products. They are as diverse in their fabrication processes as they are in their practical applications. In 2005, I helped advise and design the exhibition, "Extreme Textiles: Designing for High Performance," at the Cooper-Hewitt National Design Museum, curated by Matilda McQuaid. The exhibition displayed a number of industrially developed textiles that approximated direct architectural application (ills. pp. 80, 81, 85). Over 150 objects demonstrated the innovative techniques in textile fabrication, and their infiltration into a wide range of industries. The qualities found in these impressive textile objects have powerful implications for the future of textile tectonics in architecture.

Filtration devices are woven metal tubes, rings, and sponges that help to filter, trap, and block undesirable particles and

Moon landing equipment and gear.

High-performance gloves.

Felt gears (foreground left).

Glass fiber/Kevlar speed skiing helmet, carbon fiber recurve bow, carbon bicycle racing wheels.

chemicals. With the use of resistant materials and treatments, filtration technology works in both air and liquid. In felt, fibers are assembled instead of being woven. Made of wool, it is a soft but tough material that is absorbent and durable. Densified to increase rigidity, industrial gears made of felt absorb lubricant and silence the noise. Felt is adaptable to many fabrication processes, its carbon emission rate is low, and it can be recycled or composted. Collapsible booms work as structural components but are portable for outer space deployment. They are foldable and extendable, with a geometry of knotted joints that allow for both the flexibility for deployment and the rigidity at full extension. The use of textiles in medical devices advances a traditional technique, like embroidery, into a digital patterning field that develops free-form organically shaped patches to adapt to human organs and muscles. Fibers made of proteins eventually disintegrate and fuse into the human body. Some even combine a slow release of medicines to accelerate the healing process while monitoring health from inside the body.

As with any material or fabrication technique in a nascent stage of development, luxury and leisure markets start experimentation and trends in new materials and techniques. Competitive and extreme sports often have commercial sponsors to endorse product development to enhance athletic achievements. For example, a woven bicycle seat adds enough resilience to provide comfort for a long ride. It is responsive to the rider's weight distribution, making it more breathable and lighter than molded plastic seats. For that same reason, bicycles, bows, sports helmets, fishing rods, and skis are often made out of fibers and synthetic textiles; they resist impact, pliability can be controlled, they are lighter, and are resistant to various weather conditions, salt, and extreme temperatures. Climbing ropes are an interesting example of textiles' fusion of aesthetic and functional concerns. Ropes are coded with colors and different materials are combined in intricate braiding techniques to provide strength, dimensional stability, durability, flexibility, and lightness. They are able to hold surface friction for knotting and handling to be compactly coiled for easy portability.

In military and space exploration, protective gear is made out of multiple layers of textiles. The exterior layer forms the first line of defense against attacks and extreme weather conditions, while beneath the surface, layers function to insulate, provide bullet-proof protection, and offer temperature and humidity control. With the case of space suits, provision of water and oxygen is layered into the suit. There is a layer that consists of Mylar, Dacron, Nomex, Teflon, and others. Layered through conductive textiles, they create a micro-environment that also can process information, having electric conductivity and monitoring functions. It is a model for exploring cladding systems for buildings since many of the functions are similar in program to a building facade. Conceived this way, a textile facade system can be seasonally adaptable, becoming a first line of defense to assure security.

The landing airbag system designed for Mars Exploration Rovers uses a fabric construction made out of Vectran in a plain cloth weave, the most stable weaving pattern to assure stability. "Each bag has a double bladder and several abrasion-resistant layers made of tightly woven Vectran … Vectran provides equal strength at one-fifth the weight of steel. Weight is of premium importance for all materials used for space travel, and Warwick Mills, the weaver of the fabric for the bags, achieved a densely woven fabric at a mere 2.4 ounces per square yard, but with a strength of 350 pounds per inch."[2] The material is also able to perform at a severe temperature differential.

Gloves for various tasks also take advantage of layering different materials in response to specific functional requirements. The location of materials follows performative objectives such as protection from heat, abrasion, or incision, and the glove becomes an extension of manual manipulation of specific objects. Because of the flexibility and lightness required to allow hands to operate with fine dexterity, glove constructions are highly sensitive to human motor skill parameters. In essence, they adapt to become an extension of the human body. Textile tectonics in this instance allows localized intervention to improve and refine dexterity and manual skill. Within the construction of weaving, one can integrate electronic circuits, sensors, computer chips to create highly responsive textiles that can be worn in extreme environments, like those often found in space expeditions or military operations.

These innovations in highly engineered textile objects demonstrate the diversity of application of textile tectonics, and the potential for architectural design and construction. They clearly exhibit textile production's ability to serve multiple forms, scales, industries, and purposes. They are technologies that can be easily transferred across professions, inspiring diverse and rich collaborations among industries. This in turn promotes a translation of skills that inevitably leads to exciting experimentation and innovation.

Technology Transfer: Boat Hulls to Architecture

It may be surprising to know that, as an architect, I have been tracking the evolution of the boat-building practice for over 20 years. Specifically I have followed the career path of Eric Goetz of Goetz Custom Boats in Bristol, Rhode Island. Eric builds boat hulls for America's Cup Race boats and other competitions, as well as boats used for leisure (ill. p. 85). The boat-building business started with traditional hand-craft wood-boat construction. It required an intimate understanding of wood types, a close observation of wood grain, and a refined ability to assess the proportion and placement of lignin and cellulose of each species of wood. All of this translated into a highly skilled knowledge of wood geometry and joinery techniques. The boat builders not only had to know the types of wood but also the specific parts of the tree that best served particular boat details. Through practical knowledge they knew the variances of hardness and the weathering properties of one wood from the other. For example, hackmatack knees are known to be used to join the boat hull and seating elements because of their ability to handle severe weight and shear force. Boat builders had to carefully peruse wood inventories. They would store pieces in their boat shop that showed desirable characteristics for a specific future use, since they would not be able to order "ready-made" wood pieces. Since they were still dealing with a natural material, they also had to understand how it would respond once in the water, which can only be acquired through years of practice and operation. Not unlike weavers, boat builders had to study their material and have a thorough knowledge of techniques to allow them to achieve its optimal function and performance. The remarkable evolution of boat-building tech-

Various textile fibers and fiber-reinforced
plastics composites.

niques has become yet another example of the application of textile tectonics, and one that I was eventually able to incorporate into one of my architectural projects.

Composite building techniques started to enter the boat-building craft around the 1960s, when people began to focus on the role of cellulose in wood. Wood is made out of thousands of microfibers, with cellulose being the structural component of plants along which it transmits water and nutrients throughout. In wood, the patterns of cellulose are visible as the grain of the wood. In boat building, these patterns are aligned with the direction of external forces. As most economical textile fibers come from plants, it is natural to translate wood-building technology into a textile technology to achieve higher and more predictable levels of performative efficiency (ills.). Around the 1960s, glass-reinforced plastic, or fiber-reinforced plastic materials started to be used for more corrosion-resistant, maintenance-free, and structurally stronger boat building. The technique was also used to mass-produce fiberglass boats. Fiberglass textiles are draped over a wood-boat mold to be cured to form a shape. In order to produce fiberglass boats, a boat builder has to construct the wooden mold, which still requires the advanced techniques of wood-boat builders. The composite technology that used fiber materials such as fiberglass, Kevlar, and carbon fiber was a natural subsequent consequence for the next generation of highly competitive boat building (ills. pp. 79, 84, 85).

Specific fiber layout patterns can be designed through computerized design and simulation programs. In focusing on fiber patterns, one recognizes the forces applied to the material travel through and along the fibers. The fibers effectively transmit and translate those forces through the shaping of the boats. So the placement and directionality of fibers is critical to create a vessel with the least resistance. However, due to the structure of a woven textile, the overlapping fibers create undesirable micro-scaled knot. To avoid these knots in boat hulls and sails, the fibers are simply layered on top of each other. By combining fiber-weaving patterns, creating a layered pattern with one fiber on top of another, or reinforcing with stronger and more expensive carbon fibers at critical joints, one can translate the traditional wisdom of wood-boat building into a sophisticated

and intricate knowledge of digital-age synthetic production. Now, instead of collecting wood specimen, boat shops have rolls of composite textile materials that can be cut using scissors. According to Eric Goetz's mother, today Eric's workspace looks more like a tailor shop than a boat-building workshop.

Traditional wood-building practices also evolved into laminated wood techniques commonly known as the West System developed by the Gougeon brothers in the early 1970s. They focused on the use of epoxy resin as a structural adhesive for wood products. By laminating wood veneers with epoxy resin, they were able to make stiffer, stronger, and lighter vessels that sailed faster than traditional wood crafts. This technique is based on one of the two components found in wood: the lignin that binds cellulose in wood. This laminating technique utilizes the gluing methods to create more monolithic and smoother boats that face less resistance in water. Even in this more industrialized technique that uses chemicals, the skill of traditional wood-boat building is still essential in the layout of the wood and the principles are still closely aligned with early boat-building techniques.

The fundamental skill needed in composite materials is the same as in traditional boat building. The skill level cannot decline in either case. In fact the skill level becomes more demanding since the understanding for micro-alignments, and the detailed construction in digital fabrication methodology require a more sophisticated and comprehensive understanding in craftsmanship. Dai Fujiwara, who developed A-POC textiles for Issey Miyake through digital fabrication, also studied traditional boat-building techniques in Japan. He observed that northern Japanese wood-boat builders use the term "sewing" to explain the lap-joint technique of joining one wood plank to the other, evidence that boat-builder knowledge recognizes that the tectonics and structural integrity of wood resides in the alignment of its fibers. In the digitization of crafts, the distance between material knowledge and fabrication technique is reduced. It even accelerates in speed when applications combine multiples of material property analysis that lead directly into fabrication techniques. A broader approach is required, yet the fundamental principles are still embedded in the traditional wisdom of wood-boat building.

Goetz Custom Boats workshop in Bristol,
Rhode Island, USA.

Toshiko Mori Architect, fiberglass installation
for "Extreme Textiles" exhibition, fabricated by
Eric Goetz.

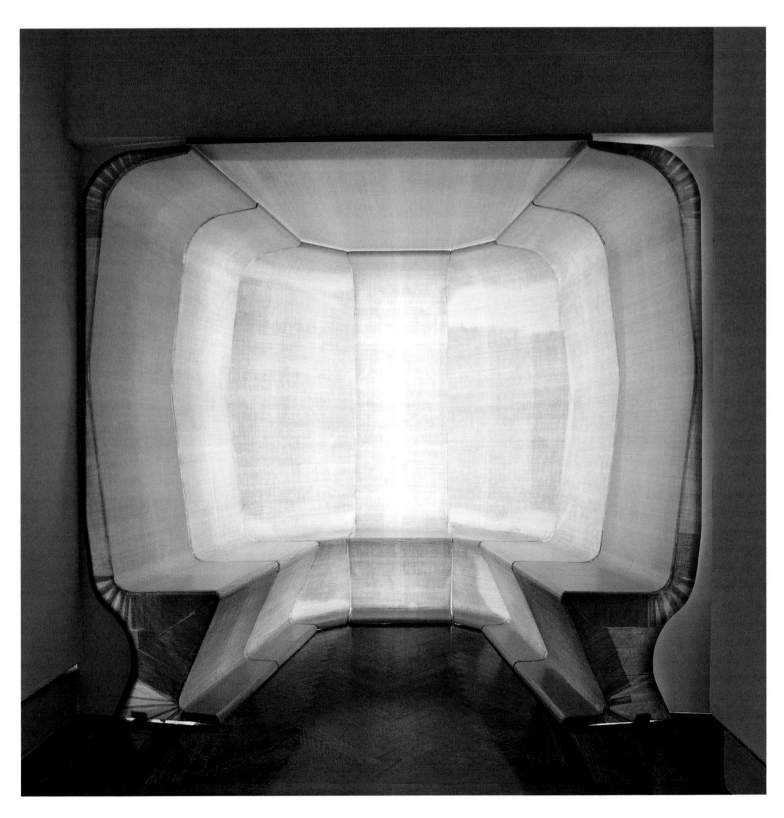

Toshiko Mori Architect, stair for house
in Casey Key, Florida, USA,
built by Goetz Custom Boats, 2004,
view and detail.

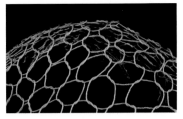

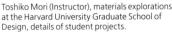

Toshiko Mori (Instructor), materials explorations
at the Harvard University Graduate School of
Design, details of student projects.

Working closely with Eric Goetz, I had the opportunity to apply the boat-making technologies of his workshop to one of my architectural projects. It exemplified the type of skill and technology transfer that is becoming more and more common. In this case, I designed an exterior stair for a house in Casey Key, Florida, that Eric fabricated out of fiberglass in his boat shop in Bristol, Rhode Island (ills. pp. 77, 86). Located in a hurricane zone, the house's remote site is prone to extreme winds, salt water, and solar exposure. The lightweight stair made out of fiberglass weighs less than 300 pounds, can be carried by two people and transported in one piece. The tread consists of seven layers: three on top and three at the bottom with a balsawood core in the center. The riser consists of nine layers: four on top and four at the bottom, also with a balsawood core in the center for stability and lightness. The stair hangs with ¼ in/63.5 mm fiberglass rods, constructed like fishing rods, supported by the roof.

The detail drawings of the stair are very different from architectural details that conventionally conceive stairs as combining and assembling parts. With this stair, there are no nails, screws, or additional material supports. It is a monolithic and monocoque construction made entirely of textiles. The difference in detailing a textile construction is the understanding of the continuity of materials. There are smoother transitions from one plane to the other, permitting the fibers to transmit directional shifts of forces, and some openings in the stair are folded cuts rather than punctures, in order to allow perimeter fibers to continue the force translation. The detailing of the stair takes cues from tailoring techniques such as draping, slitting, darting, pinching, folding, and rolling. As in a construction of a sleeve that requires continuity of material enclosure with the simultaneous existence of an opening, the armhole, the details transition from stair treads to handrails. The handrail itself is a rolled detail, often used in the bottom seam of a garment. Visually, it appears as if the textile is rolled down to meet the stair treads that then seamlessly fold out. Textile tectonics not only permits the stair to withstand its harsh climatic conditions, but also informs the design that, in the end, produced a clean and streamlined new aesthetic about continuous surface.

Textile tectonics requires the invention of a new detailing technique, by transferring tailoring methods and boat-building technologies. In the case of the stair, the construction is a rigid one, but it is completely plausible and desirable to conceive of building elements, especially facades, as more loose and flexible parts that become responsive components. The textile facade would breathe, filter, insulate, and protect, all at the same time. It would permit complex and compound functional properties to coexist. This ability to multitask is unique to this material, which can be highly heterogeneous in composition due to its unique fabrication processes. Its responsiveness and flexibility is a desirable attribute that can advance into architectural innovation.

Precisely because of its intelligent and ecological potential that allows knowledge flow, textile tectonics can be adaptable to diverse economies that are capable of survival in developing as well as highly developed countries. Their advantage, too, lies in their ability to appeal to a massive global population. Because of people's familiarity with the material, there is a great potential to deploy existing techniques, skills, and cultural resources to develop a 21st-century manufacturing model. An invention of a new material, and the prior experimentation that ultimately yields this, takes 20 to 30 years before it appears on the market for approved use. Textile tectonics takes advantage of existing manufacturing processes tested for performance. Existing factories can be easily reorganized without major change and existing products can find new opportunities. This is a particularly attractive quality for architectural advancements achieved through technology transfer, skill exchange, and knowledge flow. Since buildings are not consumer products, re-purposing existing technology is a very sustainable approach in material invention. There is also opportunity in that textile fabrication can exist both as a hierarchical top-down organized process, such as a multi-national manufacturing industry, and as a bottom-up process based in a local community. This presents an attractive possibility to develop hybrid manufacturing business models that can adapt to diverse economies, from emerging local rural economies to dense urban global societies.

Notes

1. Albers, Anni. "The Pliable Plane: Textiles in Architecture" in *Perspecta: The Yale Architectural Journal 4* (1957): pp. 36–41.
2. Brown, Susan (assistant curator at the Cooper-Hewitt National Design Museum). "Textiles: Fiber, Structure, and Function" in *Extreme Textiles: Designing for Higher Performance*. McQuaid, Matilda, ed. New York: Princeton Architectural Press, 2005. p. 38.

Modulation
Transformation by Shaping and Texturing

Thomas Schröpfer

Peter Zumthor, Brother Klaus Field Chapel, Mechernich, Germany, 2007, interior.

Synthesizing materials with cultural ideas is a fundamental architectural act, what Bruno Latour describes as a "nature-culture hybrid."[1] The shaping and texturing, or modulation, of material, which is part of the constructive act, may be found in any cultural context. Egyptian architecture exhibits reed pilasters that represent walls and columns carved from one stone, while stone columns were shaped to mimic papyrus bundles. The echinus between the column shaft and the abacus in the Doric order marks a modulated transition between the structure of the column and the load of the entablature. The volute uses a more organic, biomorphic form of transition between column and architrave. In Exeter Cathedral the thin stone ribbing of the tierceron vault gathers to meet in a colonette that has been carved to appear as if the stone ribs continue down the colonette; one piece of stone modulated to emphasize a structural continuity that does exist, but does not, structurally, need to be articulated. The continuous curvature of the entablature element above the lower set of columns in the facade of Borromini's San Carlo alle Quattro Fontane serves to unify the discrete sculptural elements, a mimetic gesture creating an amalgamation of components. In UN Studio's VilLA NM it is the total form of the building mass that is subject to modulation (ills. pp. 90, 91). Modulation, then, in the sense of shaping and texturing a formally undetermined material or volume, is a conceptual thread that approaches ubiquity. Methods of constructing and fabricating modulated forms of materials have undergone significant changes over time, but those developed over the last century remain, largely, relevant to contemporary explorations of modulation.

Contemporary modulation in architecture has not cohered as a concept: it is a polysemantic framework that defies the accord of unifying themes. A review of modulation must include divergent lines of thought that mostly apply to the same materials and methods and do not have distinct boundaries from each other: buildings rarely occupy only one conceptual domain. Modulation in architecture often contains a predominant line that is augmented and given depth by tangential lines of thought. In what follows, modulation is split into three categories: "Modulating Modulation" investigates latent geometries and properties found in continuous forms, "Modulating the Shaped" explores curving and carving, and "Modulating the Shapeless" deals with mimesis, encoding, amalgamation, and integration.

Modulating Modulation

Curvature

Mediating between concepts of modulation and their instantiation are the geometries and curvatures that translate concepts to materials. The curves may be generated by studied mimesis, as in the case of Michelangelo's carved stone, or by the flow of a line on paper, as in Zumthor's sketches for a field chapel, but in most recent work the governing geometry is generated by CAD software. There are different methods by which computers generate curvature (ills. pp. 92, 93). Programs such as Maya can simulate the effect of particle flows on soft bodies to generate form, or they can use coarser approximations of smooth form with subdivided surfaces. One of the most dominant curvature and surface generation techniques is the Non Uniform Rational Basis Spline or NURBS. Pierre Bézier, for Renault, and Paul de Casteljau, for Citroën, independently of each other developed the NURBS in the 1950s. Bézier and de Casteljau developed the curvature equations to accurately represent free-form surfaces of the type that make up car and ship bodies. Bézier's method of curve creation uses control points to form a curve that does not pass through these points, with the exception of the endpoints. The curve is parametric; when the generative points are moved, the curve changes shape. The Bézier curve (or the collection of Bézier curves to form a spline) is critical to modulated design because it is one of the most common curvatures used in CAD software. The Bézier spline, however, is only one among a great number of equations that can be used for representing splines, and it is not neutral. Rockwood and Chambers enumerate aspects of the Bézier curve that are important to its use in design:[2] The Bézier curve passes through its endpoints and is cotangent to its control polygon, meaning, especially, that the curve will be tangent to the lines that form the end segments. Scaling, rotating, or moving a Bézier curve's control points will predictably scale, rotate, or move the curve. The Bézier curve does not wiggle anymore than its control polygon, meaning that the direction of the curvature will not change back and forth unless the control polygon does. And the Bézier curve has

UN Studio, VilLA NM,
Bethel, New York, USA, 2007, interior.

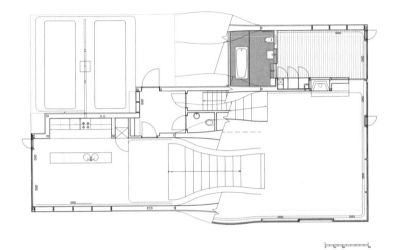

linear precision, meaning that if all the control points form a straight line, the curve becomes a straight line, which is not true of all spline equations. The predictability of the Bézier curve, both in the manipulation of individual control points and in operating on the curve as a whole, is crucial to its architectural use. As Greg Lynn describes the complexity of splines, "it is not necessary for architects to perform the differential equations that generate topological forms, as the equation for even the simplest spline is too complex for most architects to calculate. Instead, designers must understand the patterns of topology as they unfold dynamically with varying performance, rather than understanding them merely as shapes."[3] Of equal importance to the Bézier curve's predictability is the tangent behavior of the start- and endpoints. The longitudinal elevation of the VilLA NM, for example, uses splines and ruled surfaces to transition from one orthogonal box to another. This smooth transition and the tangent, orthogonal end conditions can all be expressed with a single curve; the shift in height can be brought into a single, continuous condition rather than two adjacent conditions. The Bézier curve shares a close relationship with the fillet (visually, if not mathematically); both rely on tangent relationships at their end conditions to resolve curves smoothly. Greg Lynn observes a critical difference between fillets, which have a fixed radius, and splines, which he describes as a flow between weighted control points.[4] In this sense the fillet is static, while the spline, derived with calculus, is dynamic. In terms of modulation concepts these differences are important, but in terms of shaping surfaces the fillet and the spline are cousins. The Bézier curve and the fillet are both exceptionally important devices in contemporary explorations of modulated transitions.

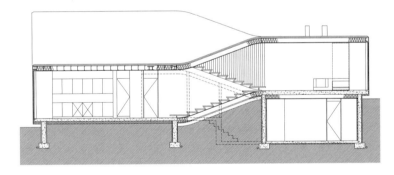

The projects shown in Ali Rahim's book, *Catalytic Formations*[5], and in particular his own project for a Reebok Flagship Store, represent a detailed exploration of the implications of splines and tangency with regard to modulation (ills. p. 93). Rahim uses particle densities, interpolated with splines, to explore topological form. Modulation here emerges from transitions between generating geometry and programmatically required forms in systems of tangential relationships. Stairs, for example, become texture on the floor, then twist up a wall to turn into structural fins for shelving. While Rahim's own writing is vague

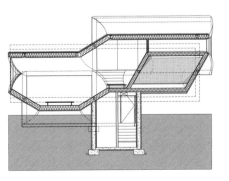

Bézier spline generated by four points, using control polygon endline tangency.

Interpolated NURBS curve using the same four generating points as the previous Bézier spline, no tangency exists at the end conditions.

Seven-point NURBS Bézier spline using endpoint tangency and showing resolution into straight line.

(Drawings by Eli Allen)

as to actual work processes in digital design, Greg Lynn's writings and his rigorous exploration of digital design provide a key to understanding Rahim's approach. The tapered stairs and shelves in the Reebok Flagship Store are instances of what Lynn terms "shreds," the latter in turn being a specific instance of what Lynn terms "isoparm apertures." Lynn has used the shred in several projects, among them the Predator installation. The specificity of Lynn's description of common technique is important because of his understanding of this method as a new generic technique. The descriptions of digital methods of rigorous modulation are, due to their clarity, worth noting at length. Here Lynn describes the shred:

"Topological surfaces are modeled as curve networks: curves that pass through or hang from control vertices, or points, in two directions. The U and V directions describe the bias of the curves. By duplicating two curves in the same position and then spreading the control vertices apart we were able to place shreds or slices that pull apart and then fuse back together on the surface. In this way the geometry of the apertures and openings is coincident with the geometry of the surface… The ubiquity and similarity of this technique in the mid-90s indicates that this technique has become the generic method for placing openings in a surface without violating the rigor of the surface itself."[6]

Rahim connotes how his analysis of particle flow can be understood in terms of Lynn's descriptions: "The system was actualized by connecting the particles with lines to generate curves and surfaces: the more particles or points regulating the curves, the more intense the transformations in the resulting surface."[7] The use of point-generated curves and surfaces in the Flagship Store project links it to Lynn's work, as well as to the Bézier curve. Rahim's design integrates multiple elements explicated by Lynn, like the stairs and shelving fins described above or the shelving system in the entry level of the store, an example of what Lynn has termed "teeth" and described as follows: "…the connection of disparate surfaces by co-planarity or blushing generates 'teething' across surfaces. The term 'teeth' describes any connection between surfaces where two curves are tangent or have coincident control vertices."[8] He explores teething in the Tadpoles project, a desk and shelving system

that uses teething to integrate multiple functional surfaces into a continuous, modulated form. Lynn's writings and research are important because of their clarity and their demystification of what Lynn terms "generic operations," while Rahim's virtuoso work achieves an integration of techniques into a relational whole: the Flagship Store combines shred, teeth, fillet, spline into a continuous whole, not just utilizing modulation techniques, but expressing modulation as a concept.

Rahim's and Lynn's projects also engage similar materiality, with Rahim projecting the use of vacuum-formed acrylic and molded fiberglass for the Flagship Store's interior skin and Lynn fabricating the Predator installation out of vacuum-formed plastic sheets. Each project involves the transformation of a planar material to form a modulated surface, a method discussed further in the section "Modulating the Shaped" below. Acrylic and fiberglass are both easily shaped over molds. In Predator, 250 CNC-milled foam panels are fabricated in order to serve as molds for the vacuum-formed plastic sheets.[9] Vacuum forming, a type of thermoforming, uses heat to permanently change the surface of a plastic sheet. Rahim postulates that this method and the ensuing materiality will "retain and even increase the formation's affects by giving rise to a range of climates and ambient conditions."[10] In referring to ambient conditions, Rahim alludes to the play of double curvature and light; he notes that "the vacuum-forming process changes the molecular structure of the panels, generating effects in the movement of light over the surface… patterns indented into the fiberglass ceiling also help to produce diverse qualities of light."[11] Describing the Tadpoles project in a similar vein, Lynn remarks on a mock-up, saying that the "lighting effects are produced by the cross-pollination of geometric excavations and material chemistry."[12] In relation to light, photographs of Predator and Tadpoles, as well as renderings of the Flagship Store, accentuate the reflection or refraction of light on or through the surfaces. The modulation of light in this manner must be seen as a result of the form-making. The use of double curvature, not for the purpose of form-making, but to modulate and to screen light, had been explored, some 50 years earlier, by Erwin Hauer.

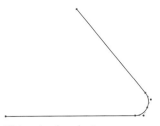

Fillet construction using tangency.

(Drawing by Eli Allen)

Ali Rahim and Hina Jamelle/Contemporary Architecture Practice, Reebok Flagship Store, Shanghai, China, 2005, facade and interior renderings.

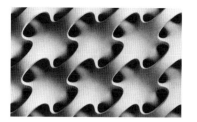 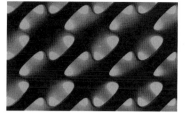

Erwin Hauer, Design I, 1950, details.

Light

In his experimental project Design I Erwin Hauer used continuous curvature as a way to explore light diffusion (ills.). Design I is cast as a single, repeating unit out of either Hydrostone (high-strength gypsum cement) or Portland cement.[13] The joints in the modular units are sealed so that the connection detail, and the unit itself, is entirely obscured; only the continuity of the surface curvature remains. Hauer's screens take on drastic change when front-lit or back-lit. In both cases, changes between light and dark are achieved through gradual modulation in light levels over the surface: the curvature creates gradients of light levels as opposed to sharp transitions. Hauer writes that "light that pours into the wall from the opposite side seems to adhere to the surface, to wrap around the sculpted forms and to illuminate even those parts of the surface that face away from the source of light."[14] Photographs of Design I bear out Hauer's description. Here light itself is modulated.

Modulating the Shaped

Curving

On an architectural scale, concrete is the only material available without inherent form, making it capable of taking on the modulations imposed upon it. While metals and plastics can be cast as well, this process is often too expensive to play out in architecture. Metals, glass, plastics, stone, and wood are all available as products with industrially produced form, in largely orthogonal geometries that makes products inexpensive to the building trade. These preformed orthogonal geometries can be manipulated to create modulated forms just as fluid in appearance as concrete.

Anish Kapoor's Cloud Gate makes use of precision CNC fabrication and rolling to curve metal panels over a structural skeleton (ills. pp. 25, 94). The coarse skeleton is completely concealed by the continuous curvature of the stainless steel surface. Here the modulation is achieved through the extreme precision of the cut-and-rolled panels, a high degree of engineering to ensure that the panels would not deflect,[15] and by continuous welds joining panels to each other and finally polished away.[16] Nader Tehrani has called the polished weld an erased detail; a technical necessity that is suppressed following a "perceptual imperative."[17] The transformation of the planar elements that form this surface is so complete that the finished sculpture ceases to read as an exercise in transforming planar elements and reads as a homogenous, modulated form. The polished metal of the double-curved surface greatly expands on the interaction of light that Hauer observed in his screen walls; rather than a play of light and shadow, Cloud Gate gathers the reflected light from the park and the city which surround it, drawing in their ever-changing conditions as permanent feature of the surface of the sculpture. Many of the techniques used to fabricate this form are fairly common; originally used in shipbuilding, they are increasingly applied to architectural works. Each panel's curvature was analyzed and the surface was divided to allow for acceptable deformations of the individual metal panels.[18] While the generic technique may be widely used, Cloud Gate is set apart by the extreme precision achieved and the erasure of the panel through continuous welding.

Zaha Hadid's use of double-curved glass panels for four Innsbruck railway stations is quite similar in structure to Cloud Gate: the panels are divided to minimize the degree of curvature in most of them, then mounted on an interior structure (ills. pp. 96, 97). The essential difference is the joint articulation that is erased in Cloud Gate and left as a thin joint line framing each individual panel in the railway stations. In Hadid's work the modulated continuity is read as an order that subjugates the joint, just as her work in concrete subjugates the marks of the formwork (which will be discussed in the section "Modulating the Shapeless").

Carving

Office dA's Lazlo Files at Harvard University's Graduate School of Design uses CNC milling to create an implied continuous surface, carved from a flat plywood sheet (ills.). As in Hadid's railway stations, joints are still needed (in this case the different panels are individual drawers), but the implied continuity of the fluid surfacing subjugates the drawers to the whole of the surface. Breaks in the fluid continuity across drawers allows for pulls to be integrated into the modulation system. The alternating grain of plywood lamination contours the depth of the carving.

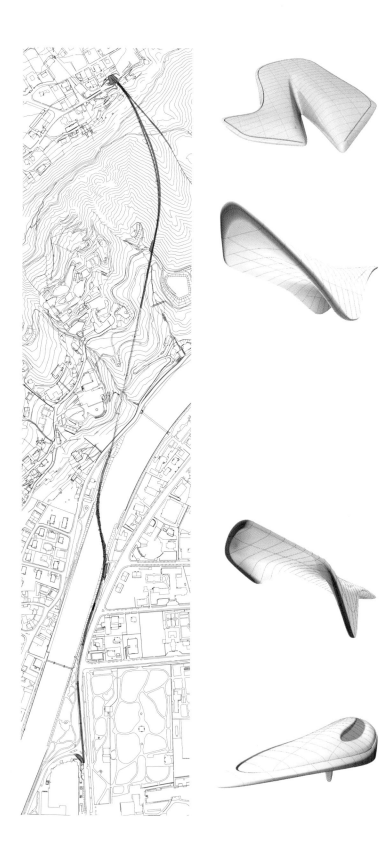

The exposed plywood layers set up an opposition between the planar, orthogonal material and the fluid form that has been carved to subjugate that planarity.

The sculptor Tony Cragg engaged similar methods. Cragg's works in carved stone, such as Messenger or Under Circumstances, utilize modulation as a method of forming distinct stone plates into a single image. The carefully polished continuity of the stone forms clearly a single, modulated whole, yet equally forcefully are the lines indicating the distinct components of this modulation. While, on an architectural scale, components are a necessity, on a small sculptural scale they need not be expressed: Cragg is exploring the relationship between the aggregation of parts and the modulated whole, a relationship completely suppressed in Kapoor's Cloud Gate. Germano Celant explains the tension seen in Cragg's work:

"Cragg's transition, following the work rooted in fragmentation and the assemblage of industrial scraps and waste, is towards compactness and unification, thanks to the choice of a single material, which is shaped and molded to create new forms and new images."[19]

In Cragg's modulated sculpture an essential tenet of modulation is revealed: an expression of continuity, of the ability to create whole forms. If a building is to represent a unified idea, it is appropriate to express it with a unified form. While Cragg explores carving as a technique, the ideas that give form to his sculptures are external to the process of carving, as opposed for instance to Office dA's plywood carving, which uses modulation as a technique to explore something inherent to the plywood, namely the layered lamination. Cragg's ideas touch on sensual, organic form and for that, they lead to another type of modulation, perhaps one of its oldest ones – that of mimesis.

Modulating the Shapeless

Mimesis

Mimetic modulation is an expressive approach. Mimesis encompasses both expressive form-making and biomimicry, both present in Classical architecture. Michelangelo's sculptural

Zaha Hadid Architects, Nordpark Cable Railway,
Congress Station and Hungerburg Station.

Ali Rahim and Hina Jamelle/Contemporary
Architecture Practice, Migrating Formations,
"Home Delivery: Fabricating the Modern
Dwelling," exhibition, Museum of Modern Art,
New York, USA, 2008, view and details.

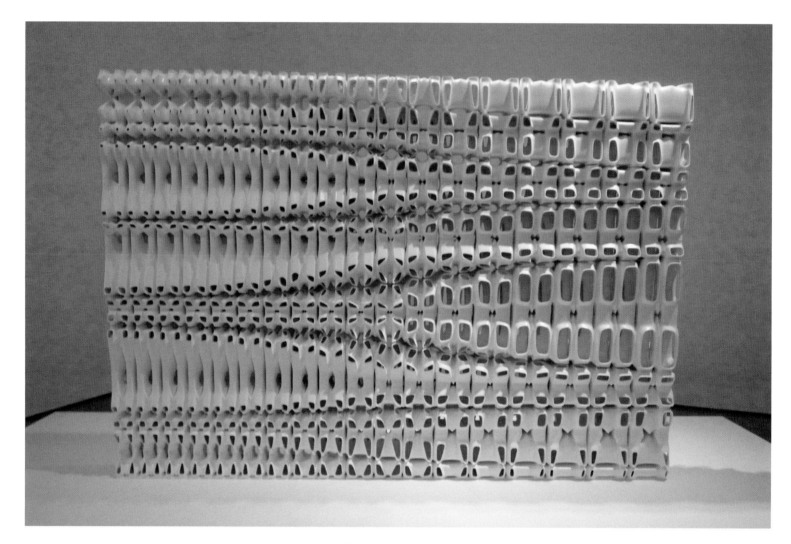

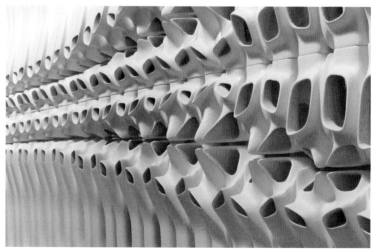

mimetic modulation is exemplified in the Pietà. The continuity of the marble surface aptly represents both cloth and skin. The highly refined polish possible with Carrara marble takes advantage of reflected light. The level of light reflections, similar over the different surfaces of the Pietà, accentuates the continuity of form, giving softness to the stone.

Erich Mendelsohn used mimetic modulation in his Einstein Tower in Potsdam. The tower was an attempt to give expression to Einstein's Theory of Relativity; the expression of the massing was an attempt to make visible the relationship of mass and light that the observatory's researchers were helping to develop. The expressive shaping of the tower was meant to resonate with the modulated forms that reinforced concrete would allow. At that time Mendelsohn was not able to achieve the tower entirely out of concrete, substituting plaster-covered brick for much of the structure. In his final section drawings of the tower, Mendelsohn distinguished which elements were to use concrete and which to use brick.[20] The sections are revealing: brick may account for some of the modulated surfaces in the tower, but it seems that many of the most dynamic elements (the sweeping entry, the lids of the windows, the thin balcony that tops the tower) were all achieved with the use of concrete. Concrete was used for its fluidity, its expressiveness, and its dynamism. The skin of plaster, stretched tightly and uniformly over the surfaces of the tower's exterior is a further unifying device, similar to the surfacing of Le Corbusier's chapel at Ronchamp (to be discussed below in the section on "Amalgamation").

Eero Saarinen's TWA Terminal offers the expression of dynamic flight. In an unfinished dictation, titled "General Statement," Saarinen said: " …one also learned that the structural and rational cannot always take precedent when another form proves more beautiful. This is dangerous but I believe true."[21] Saarinen had a tendency, played out in the TWA Terminal, to search for communicative, expressive form. Like Mendelsohn, Saarinen engaged in an attempt to express an abstract idea, in this case the idea of flight.[22] While mimetic modulation was the dominant thought in form-shaping, Saarinen expressed a desire to unite programmatic elements through mimesis (which would transform mimetic modulation into integrated modulation,

which will be discussed below): "As the passenger walked through the sequence of the building, we wanted him to be in a total environment where each part was the consequence of another and all belonged to the same world-form."[23] But unlike the VilLA NM the form here is not the consequence of the unification of different programs, but rather a totalizing enclosure of different programs: Mark Lamster points out that "Saarinen completed technical drawings only after the final form emerged following an extended modeling process."[24] Such a workflow suggests the predominance of formal modulation above programmatic modulation.

Encoding
In the process of forming materials there is an opportunity to layer information about the process itself. Such formwork markings can become the dominant logic of a modulated form. Carlo Scarpa's Brion tomb and memorial in Treviso emphasizes the discrete formwork elements by forming them into repetitive, linear patterns and allowing the rough linear formwork to texture broad planar surfaces. The textured concrete contains information that relates the concrete to other materials on the site through a shared geometric language. In Scarpa's Church of Nostra Signora del Cadore in Belluno the linear boards of the formwork are shifted in relation to each other to reveal the depth of the formwork elements rather than just the surface, creating a linear relief pattern in the wall. Earlier, this casting technique was explored by Frank Lloyd Wright in rather elaborate concrete masonry units: as exemplified in such houses as the Storer House, Wright cast specific geometric forms into concrete blocks and then used the blocks repeatedly to form a larger pattern.

Herzog & de Meuron's Eberswalde Technical School Library engages with the process of concrete's transition from liquid to solid with the use of cure-retardant. By printing photographs with cure-retardant rather than ink and allowing the surface of concrete panels to cure in contact with these photographs, the information from the photographs acts to encode the photograph in the concrete: where the concrete was in contact with the retardant, the concrete can be washed away to reveal the rough, dark interior in opposition to the smooth, light surface of the concrete, allowing the image to transfer.[25] As in the case of Wright's abstract concrete-patterned blocks, the image-imprinted concrete was used as a repeated unit. This is modulation on an extremely fine scale, allowing a single material to express multiple conditions, using the single material to unify an image even as the image differentiates the material.

Peter Zumthor's Brother Klaus Field Chapel (ill. p. 89) encodes the construction process, using a curvature formed by gathered tree trunks as an interior formwork and the tieback holes, plugged with glass, to allow points of light to penetrate the darkness of the chapel. The tree trunks were removed and the formed concrete was blackened with fire.[26] The fire echoes the process of concrete-shaping through formwork: it is a process applied to a material. The forming element itself (the formwork or the fire) is ephemeral in relation to the concrete, but the mark of the forming element will share the lifespan of the concrete.

Amalgamation

The amalgamation of discrete elements uses the continuity of one element to create a relationship and order to a set of elements that cohere through the modulated form that encompasses them. Le Corbusier's Notre-Dame-du-Haut exemplifies this manner of modulation (ill. p. 101). The roof serves as unifying element with great force in the chapel's interior. While the exterior is a fragmentary procession of curves, punctures, and small towers of whitewashed gunnite, the interior is dominated by the dark curvature of the concrete ceiling; all elements subordinate to the weight of the monolithic form. The wall construction functions, in technical terms, similarly to the roof: the smooth curvature of the walls hides a system of tapered columns connected with reinforcing struts; these separate structural elements are gathered together and made continuous through the smooth surface of the exterior walls.[27] This amalgamation of discrete elements resonates with the pour of the concrete roof and the gunnite spray of the walls: the concrete surrounds and hides the fragmentary rebar and the lath that give it tensile structure. This hiding of a coarse skeleton is almost identical in technique to the hiding of a structural skeleton below the smooth surface of Kapoor's Cloud Gate. The finite elements are contained, hidden, smoothed below continuous concrete surfaces.

More violent in its application of amalgamation is the Church of Sainte-Bernadette-du-Banlay in Nevers by Claude Parent and Paul Virilio. The small church consists, almost entirely, of site-cast concrete that is exposed both inside and out. The homogeneity of material was expressed just as clearly in the scale model, which was built of solid, polished blocks of wood. Rather than using curvature for explicit spatial integration, the curvature of the church forms an inward-facing, self-contained form. The material and spatial language used to express this defensive interiority is borrowed from the vocabulary of Second World War concrete bunkers. In an early article on "Bunker Archeology" Virilio wrote that the bunker had a physicality "allowing the habitat to be intimately joined with the hidden possibilities contained within the individual being,"[28] and Parent wrote that "the church has a menacing appearance: its opaque concrete carapace is defensive, even deliberately 'repulsive' in its relation to the surroundings, but at the same time it forms a protective interior."[29] This inclusive interior gathered the inhabitants forcefully, making them part of a unified condition. A separate concept from the bunker aesthetic, the church in Nevers is also an expression of Virilio's and Parent's interest in oblique movement and forms – the angling of surfaces that keep the body in continuous movement between states. Interior floors as well as the seating in the nave were placed on inclines to induce this continuity of movement. Virilio drew connections between oblique movement and a topological architecture.[30] The topological in mathematics is concerned with homeomorphism, a term that refers to the possibility to deform one geometric object into another. The topological transition is a way of looking at modulation; modulation, seen under this angle, is the continuous and smooth transition between two states. While much of the perceived modulation in Sainte-Bernadette derives from the filleting of walls and ceilings to form continuous surfaces, as well as the unrelenting homogeneity of material (concrete allowed Parent and Virilio to dispense with such details as flashing, which would have interrupted the continuity of the fillet from wall to roof), the conceptual territory breached in the church begins to lead to a different concept of modulation, no longer consolidating different elements, but integrating them into a new whole.

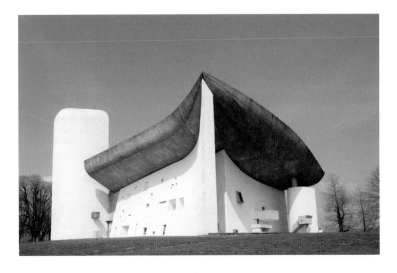

Integration

The integration of discrete elements uses geometric modulation
to encompass them and to bring them into a single system.
While amalgamation uses modulation to bring discrete
elements together, integration transforms discrete elements
so that they become one morphing system (this difference
might be likened to the difference between a mixture and a
solution: while the two might not be visually distinguishable,
in a mixture elements remain discrete while a solution is a
new, homogenous whole). Integration may be the purest form
of modulation; it is an attempt to merge the totality of the
building form and material with the concept. With integration,
modulation is seen in the massing and shaping of the overall
building, not only parts of it. Modulation, here, is not the
result of expressive desire or the mimicry of natural modulated
elements, but the result of an attempt to bring different
systems together in a totalizing, fluid synthesis. UN Studio has
developed a working method that relies heavily on modulation,
repeatedly citing its importance to their work and calling it the
"inclusive principle": "Achieving both an integral, relational
treatment of the elements of a building and a tightly woven,
efficient organization in which those elements exist is mutually
profitable, multi-use constellations are the overriding principle
behind our design models."[31] What is referred to as integral
and relational is achieved through modulation. The blob-to-box
model which, "at the scale of an individual building,… gives
the model for connecting disparate systems through sectional
transformation,"[32] is a clear visualization of the method of
modulation through integration. The VilLA NM demonstrates
such modulation using interstitial surface curvature in order to
integrate three boxes, each at a different elevation. The wall
curvature in the VilLA NM is fabricated in an analogous method
to the walls of Notre-Dame-du-Haut: prefabricated light-gauge
steel framing is covered with lath and plaster; the smooth result
unifies the discrete members used to structure the wall. The
deployment of this method, however, leads to a different result
than the one seen in Ronchamp; in the VilLA NM the finishing
of the wall leaves a single component: the orthogonal boxes are
brought, with the use of the connecting curvature, into a single,
continuous form.

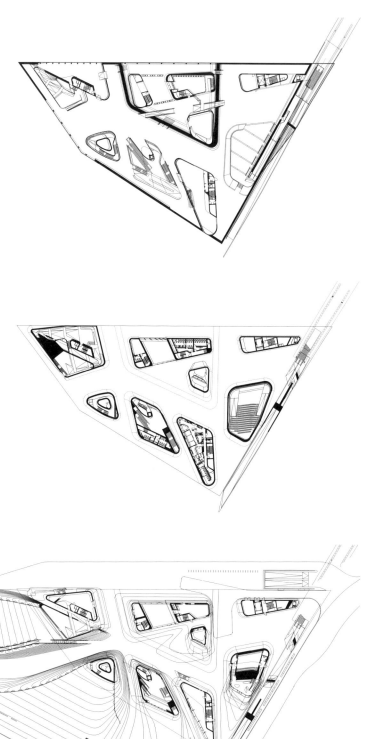

Zaha Hadid's Phaeno Science Center in Wolfsburg shows a similar systematic integration (ills. pp. 102, 103). The elevated exhibition box flows down to its shear wall supports through filleted concrete form. The fillet is again a curve segment with two end tangents and allows for a gradual transition between wall and floor. The tangential curvatures of the Phaeno Science Center allow the forms to flow into each other, the structure to integrate with space. In the fluid transitions and forms the structural concrete suppresses the marks of its formwork. The impression of the formwork is not erased through surface treatment but subjugated to the impression of the larger transitions. The discrete markings of the formwork are not the focus but rather used to reinforce the continuity of the larger form.

MVRDV's Villa VPRO in Hilversum uses poured concrete floor plates that have double curvature to make sectional transitions, integrating different floors of the building (ill. p. 104). Similarly, the building contains floors that use filleted transitions to turn to walls and then to ceilings. The integrated transition from floor to wall to ceiling is a ubiquitous, generic technique referred to as the single surface or continuous surface. It is also used, for example, in UN Studio's NMR Laboratory in Utrecht, Diller Scofidio + Renfro's Institute of Contemporary Art, and OMA's Educatorium.[33] The single surface forms a system that modulates between what are often distinct planes in a building. The double curvatures of the Villa VPRO's floor plates create sloping zones that are neither one floor nor another, but an integration of two floors; the curved surfaces are distinguished from ramps and stairs as a transition between floors, a transition not as a distinct element, but rather the deformation of two surfaces in order to connect one deformed surface to another. The ubiquity of single-surface projects exploring continuity demonstrates a current disciplinary interest, not limited to one architect or one style, in investigations of modulation through integration.

From Technique to Architecture

Integration is perhaps the most recent form of modulation, but it is certainly not the end result of all other methods of modulation, it is one exploration among many. Modulation draws together what is disparate or forms new elements as

Zaha Hadid Architects, Phaeno Science Center,
interior and exterior.

MVRDV, Villa VPRO, Hilversum,
The Netherlands, 1997, elevation, section,
and floor plans.

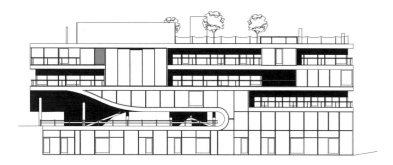

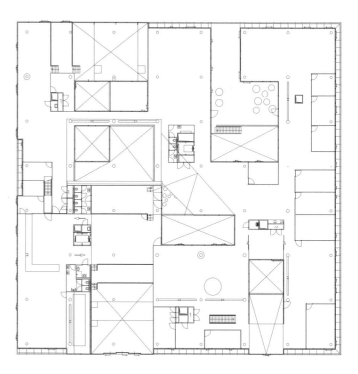

continuous divisions of single forms. The underlying concept of modulation is that many things can be achieved with one thing: walls become ceilings, stairs become shelves (or, perhaps, that many things can be made into one thing). A modulated form may synthesize many components or divide a single component; these operations are the connected inverse of each other. While modulation may be divisible into different approaches and methodologies, these are merely subdivisions of a single, textured and shaped concept.

Modulation is both material technique and architectural concept. The concept is explored through a material instantiation that is not itself architecture. As Jacques Herzog said: " …there is a paradox in this affirmation of the material aspect of architecture, because ultimately it is the moment when materiality transcends into immateriality that we are after."[34] The physical acts of modulation such as bending, casting, or carving are part of a family of techniques that are exploited for their connection to the concept of modulation. Engaging in techniques of modulation allows the architect to access the concept of modulation. Nader Tehrani puts this another way: " …a building is intensified through the elaboration of its own medium – a language of sticks and stones – to induce a state of architecture."[35] The wall of Ronchamp, then, with its gunnite skin concealing a system of distinct structural elements is both, the language and the perceived result – a taut unified surface – achieving the final architectural effect. It is through conceptual modulation, applied to or with material, that simple materiality or construction is transcended and an architectural act occurs.

Notes

1. Cited in Martin, Reinhold. "What is a Material?" in *Eero Saarinen: Shaping the Future*. Pelkonon, Eeva-Liisa, and Donald Albrecht, eds. New Haven: Yale University Press, 2006. p. 69.
2. Rockwood, Alyn, and Peter Chambers. *Interactive Curves and Surfaces*. San Francisco: Morgan Kaufmann, 1996. pp. 37-40.
3. Lynn, Greg. *Animate Form*. New York: Princeton Architectural Press, 1999. p. 25.
4. *Ibid*. p. 20.
5. Rahim, Ali. *Catalytic Formations: Architecture and Digital Design*. London: Taylor & Francis, 2006.
6. Greg Lynn FORM. Design Document 15: Greg Lynn: Form/Predator. Seoul: DAMDI, 2006. p. 92.
7. Rahm, Ali. *Catalytic Formations* … p. 53.
8. Lynn, Greg. *Architectural Laboratories / Greg Lynn and Hani Rashid*. Patteeuw, Véronique, ed. Rotterdam: NAi, 2002. p. 25.
9. Greg Lynn FORM. Design Document 15 … p. 134.
10. Rahim, Ali. *Catalytic Formations* … p. 53.
11. *Ibid*.
12. Lynn, Greg. *Architectural Laboratories* … p. 26.
13. Hauer, Erwin. *Continua: Architectural Screens and Walls*. New York: Princeton Architectural Press, 2004. p. 94.
14. *Ibid*. p. 10.
15. Hornzee-Jones, Christopher in *Anish Kapoor: Memory*. New York: Guggenheim Museum Publications, 2008. pp. 89-90.
16. Personal correspondence, Kate Bachman. Bachman's detailed description of the fabrication process for Cloud Gate also appeared under the title "Metal Fabricating in a New Millenium" on the website *The Fabricator*, published May 9th, 2006: www.thefabricator.com/ArtSculpture/ArtSculpture_Article.cfm?ID=1331.
17. Cadwell, Michael, and Nader Tehrani. *Strange Details*. Cambridge, MA: MIT Press, 2007. p. xi.
18. See footnote 15.
19. Germano Celant in Cragg, Tony. *A New Thing Breathing: Recent Work by Tony Cragg*. London: Tate Gallery Publishing, 2000. p. 52.
20. For the explication of the drawings see James, Kathleen. "Organic!" in *Erich Mendelsohn: Architect 1887-1953*. Regina Stephan, ed. New York: The Monacelli Press, 1999. p. 29 and 37.
21. Pelkonon, Eeva-Liisa, and Donald Albrecht, eds. *Eero Saarinen: Shaping the Future*. New Haven: Yale University Press, 2006. p. 344.
22. Stoller, Ezra. *The TWA Terminal*. New York: Princeton Architectural Press, 1999. p. 1.
23. *Ibid*. p. 3.
24. *Ibid*. p. 5.
25. Libermann, Valeria, and Gerhard Mack. *Herzog & de Meuron: Eberswalde Library*. Pamela Johnson, ed. London: The Architectural Association, 2000. p. 22.
26. Rossmann, Andreas. "Field Chapel Near Wachendorf." in *Detail*, 2008, v.48, n.1-2, pp. 12-14.
27. For a description of the wall construction and components see: Pauly, Danièle. *Le Corbusier: The Chapel at Ronchamp*. Basel, Boston, Berlin: Birkhäuser, 2008. p. 80.
28. Cited in Johnston, Pamela, ed. *The Function of the Oblique: The Architecture of Claude Parent and Paul Virilio 1963-1969*. London: The Architectural Association, 1996. p. 71 "Bunker Archeology" appeared in the March 1957 edition of *Architecture Principe*, a magazine published by Parent and Virilio. Virilio would later publish a book titled *Bunker Archéologie*, available from Princeton Architectural Press in an English edition under the title *Bunker Archeology*.
29. *Ibid*. p. 19.
30. *Ibid*. p. 11.
31. Van Berkel, Ben, and Caroline Bos. *UN Studio: Design Modules, Architecture, Urbanism, Infrastructure*. New York: Rizzoli, 2006. p. 26.
32. *Ibid*. p. 216.
33. It should be noted that Winy Maas of MVRDV explored this kind of surface transition as an intern at OMA. Costanzo, Michele. *MVRDV: Works and Projects 1991-2006*. Milan, Italy: Skira, 2006. p. 20.
34. *Immaterial/Ultramaterial: Architecture, Design and Materials*. Toshiko Mori, ed. New York: George Braziller, 2002. p. 81.
35. Cadwell, Michael, and Nader Tehrani. *Strange Details* … p. vii.

The author would like to thank Eli Allen, Master of Architecture Candidate at the Harvard University Graduate School of Design, for providing research assistance and drawings for this contribution.

Capturing
the Ephemeral

James Carpenter

James Carpenter Design Associates,
Refracted Light Field, Salt Lake Courthouse,
Salt Lake City, Utah, USA, 2003-2011.

The extruded glass tubes with a prismatic
internal profile gather, concentrate, and display
ambient light while refracting views and
reflections.

James Carpenter Design Associates,
Refracted Light Field.

The field of glass cylinders with an internal
prismatic profile concentrates light in its vertical
flutes and distributes it horizontally.

Opposite: James Carpenter Design Associates,
7 World Trade Center, New York, New York,
USA, 2006, podium screen and curtain wall.

Capturing the ephemeral may not at first appear to have any relationship to materials, but light phenomena, as any phenomena, exist only in the material world. We associate light phenomena with the careful observation of the material world. In a sense we consider materials to be inseparable from the light phenomena we associate with them – clouds, sky color, or rainbows. Light phenomena occur at every turn, but the distractions of our urban environment suppress our ability to observe them. Yet the built environment has the full potential to reveal the natural world, and the careful use of materials can lead to an environment enriched by our ability to experience the ephemeral more fully.

To achieve this we have formulated an approach that can effectively translate our observations of the ephemeral into the built environment. This approach has emerged from over 40 years of experience, beginning as an artist, working with glass, exploring film installations and light, and then working with scientists and manufacturers of glass and eventually with engineers and architects, now applying the full extent of our cross-disciplinary experience to the design of complete architectural projects. The artist's discipline is one of observation and this observation tells us about the world we live in.

Volumetric Light

The quality of light is explicitly related to the specificity of place. Light contains much of the information about our immediate environment. Every moment of ephemeral light informs our conscious and subconscious observations. As light interacts with the material world it reveals itself. Light and its interaction with any family of materials records and presents the information that defines the reading of our immediate context. We aim to synthesize these observations through the exploration of materials in general and glass in particular. By re-presenting this synthesis at a scale or context that is unfamiliar, light phenomena become an observable experience.

We approach architectural design through the architectonics of volumetric light. The architectonics of light considers the

material qualities of glass as having the most comprehensive ability to generate a volumetric quality of light. Light simultaneously occurs on multiple surfaces, thereby implying a depth to that field of light. This is a key concept that results in the building surfaces becoming sensitized to qualities of light through the use of materials; however, our approach to materials originates in our understanding of the extraordinary characteristics of glass.

The idea of the "responsive field" is fundamental to this approach – observation; synthesis of that observation; the testing of materials and ideas resulting in an understanding of how glass and other materials can embody the original observation. We think of materials beyond their typical place within a palette available to architects. We explore materials in order to find the qualities that are fleetingly observed in nature and that define a unique sense of place. Every material reacts to light, though some materials are more actively responsive. By taking advantage of those materials' characteristics, the surfaces can appear optically porous and dimensionally responsive.

The general understanding of glass is still quite limited. It is important to consider that many materials are glass, including metals, ceramics, and polymers. Most people look at a window and see that as the beginning and end of glass, when in fact glass is a state in which many materials can find themselves – a supercooled liquid whose jammed particles present localized discontinuous fields of structure and larger fields of dynamical heterogeneity within them. Its mutable characteristics offer an opening into a world of unfettered opportunities. Transparency is only one of countless capabilities and characteristics available to glass as a material. Photo-sensitive glasses, for example, can be described as having a latent memory: information can be recorded in the glass through exposure to certain wavelengths and reappears in response to temperature, while the glass remains transparent at other times. It is a very malleable material, but unfortunately in architecture, the manufacturer dictates the material and the designer has very little opportunity to manipulate the material beyond the manufacturer's determination. We have the opportunity to work closely with manufacturers to develop materials specific to our aims.

Hajime Tanaka, glass transition and jamming in a driven granular system.

Takeshi Kawasaki, Takeaki Araki, and Hajime Tanaka, glass transition in a polydispersed colloidal system.

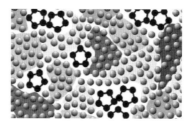

Hajime Tanaka, two-order parameter description of glass transition covering its strong to fragile limit.

This "first principles" approach to materials brings a new set of possibilities to architecture. What does it mean to work with a material that is generally defined as a supercooled liquid or a non-crystalline solid? What does it mean that a material is solid to the touch and manipulated like a solid when molecularly it is better described as a liquid? In the scientific community, the very definition of glass has long been and remains a matter of research. We understand that the glassy state exists across a huge field of materials from metals, ceramics, and plastics to colloidal solutions. The notion of jamming refers to very densely packed molecules, which as they become denser, slow down to the point where they are perceived as solids without the organized structure typically associated with solids. The field of granular physics practiced by Sidney Nagel, Heinrich Jaeger, or Hajime Tanaka among other scientists, has modeled these ideas so as to explore them in an observable manner (ills.).

Latency

Another unique quality of glass, and a conceptually powerful idea to be applied to materials in general, is latency. The term is used in the field of photo-responsive or photo-sensitive glass. Glass is essentially comprised of chemical elements, combined and put into solution. By adding certain metals such as silver halide, gold chloride, manganese oxide, or selenium oxide – all metals used historically in the production of photo-sensitive paper – and combining them with other chemicals such as fluorines, the manufactured glass maintains the appearance of a conventional piece of glass, but has the capacity to be manipulated using light. This manipulation can be as prosaic as developing a photo image in the glass, though it is interesting to note that the image exists in three dimensions since it occupies the whole depth of the glass. The particular choice of chemicals allows you to achieve intricate three-dimensional forms by selectively exposing parts of the glass to specific wavelengths of light.

The chemicals are melted together when the glass is manufactured in the furnace, then annealed. At room temperature the glass is then exposed to ultraviolet or infrared lasers or even by laying a photographic negative on the glass and exposing it to the sun. The glass at that point has the latent memory in it: it

is a clear piece of glass, but as soon as it is reheated close to the softening temperature, the image will appear. Within a non-crystalline field, there is now a matrix of jammed particles with photographically organized areas crystalline in structure. In other words, a solid field is suspended within a non-solid field. You can go further with this – under certain conditions the area that is unexposed (glassy) remains sensitive to acid, so you can take this sheet of glass and dip it into acid, thereby etching away the glassy area, leaving only the ceramic area – a systematic method of chemically machining the material. Latency and latent memory allow the organization of extremely complex three-dimensional structures used in many applications from communications to ceramic filtration systems.

Another application of the same process, developed during work on the photographic glass with Corning Glass, for Norman Foster's Hong Kong and Shanghai Bank, aimed at creating permanent louvers integrated into the body of the glass itself. This kind of louver glass was not further pursued, but this family of glass today includes solar-reactive glasses and glass filters. The initial research, which simultaneously explored glass as a photographic medium and a high-performance daylighting system, demonstrated the quality of glass as an ultimately malleable material: like a chameleon, it can take on almost any property, capacity, or role.

When I talk about light as information, I think of how light is invisible until it strikes something, be it water, dust particles, or any material surface, reflective or absorbent – that is when it manifests itself. Each substrate or subject that it strikes gives back the information about its presence in our world. It is also true to think of light as paradoxically revealing itself as it is interrupted by the material world. Something we never usually put together in our minds is that as light hits one object it is reflected away from us. Light is carrying the information from that reflective surface but it is also likely to strike many other surfaces, each surface being informed by the accumulated content of the light. Each photon is a record of its journey and interactions, and we aim to understand and reveal this cumulative body of information. It is a very complex thing. You can manipulate the transmitted and reflected light but consider also what is occurring within the reflective material, the glass

James Carpenter Design Associates,
7 World Trade Center.

Sectional diagram of curtain wall showing how
the linear lap and spandrel daylight reflector
interact with daylight.

Plan diagram of podium screen showing how
daylight is programmed by the outer screen's
prismatic wire orientation.

Plan diagram of podium screen showing how
LED lighting integrated within the wall interacts
with the screen's prismatic wire orientation.

Podium screen and curtain wall: LED light
is inserted between the two layers of the
prismatic wire screen.

The linear lap and spandrel daylight reflector
transform the full expanse of the curtain wall
into a responsive membrane.

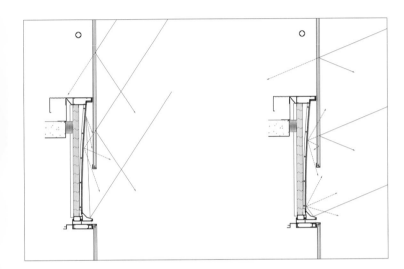

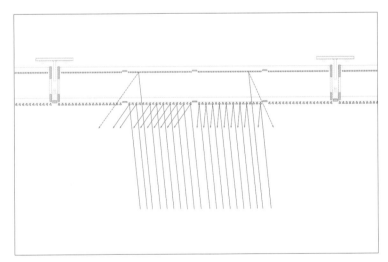

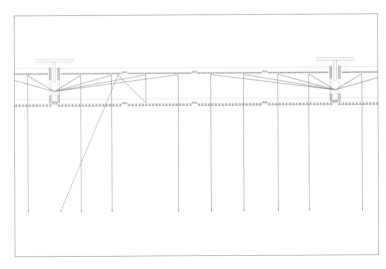

James Carpenter Design Associates,
Periscope Window, Minneapolis, Minnesota,
USA, 1997.

The window in this instance is a device that
constructs a new reality. It assembles diverse
sources of information existing in the exterior
environment and re-orders them through
superimposition to create a "new" perception
of that exterior.

The device during construction: it remains
visible from the outside while varying
conditions reveal more or less of the device's
parts on the inside.

The device is tuned to essentially synthesize and
deploy the everyday variety of light conditions.

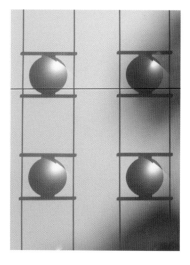

James Carpenter Design Associates,
Louver Screen, Israel Museum (architects:
Efrat-Kowalsky Architects, Lehman Architects
and Town Planners), Jerusalem, Israel, 2010.

100% scale paper model of Louver Screen.
The east and west exposures are protected
by the louvers' profile, which, despite
removing the view, does present detailed light
information from the outside onto the inside of
the louvers' screen-like plane.

James Carpenter Design Associates,
Louver Screen, Israel Museum.

Stills from computer animation study of light's
passage through Louver Screen.

itself. Glass is a remarkable material in that light passing through is slowed down by it at a molecular level and bent by its indices of refraction. The body and the surfaces of the glass add up to a tremendous amount of manipulation of visual information, but glass also reveals qualities that are inherent in the light itself.

We carry an incredible databank of experience that is significantly impacted by the memory of light, some of it consciously and much of it unconsciously. Our memories constitute one body of information while dreams and the unconscious mind are another body of information. Light reveals multiple layers of information in the course of its passage through glass. If light informs our unconscious memory, just as it informs our conscious mind, it seems possible that the process of revealing the usually unseen nature of light could also deepen a sense of nature that may be ignored but which has a powerful unacknowledged presence within us. By controlling light's transition across materials it is possible to transform the usually planar boundary into a volume of light. In extending the boundary between interior and exterior into a volume, the light's passage across space and its relationship to time can be better experienced. You might say that transparency is the least interesting characteristic of glass.

Expanding the Boundary Between Inside and Outside

In some respects this is metaphorical but with projects such as the podium screen and curtain wall for 7 World Trade Center (ills. pp. 107, 109), or the Periscope Window (ills. p. 110), both focusing on this notion of volumetric light, layers of materials have been set up optically to create or extend the perception of volume and the sense of light in nature. The aim is to extend the experience of the boundary between interior and exterior well beyond the physical depth of the building skin by understanding the optical and perceptual transition that occurs at that boundary. In 7 World Trade Center light from the deepest surface of the building is being broadcast back out into the public realm, as well as to the surface of the building. There are multiple sources of light from multiple depths, which are superimposed for the viewer to observe. The viewers may not understand exactly the physics of light and glass, but they

will acknowledge that they see something they have not seen before, something which connects them to the immediacy, familiarity, and topicality of nature.

The latency of glass can itself be a metaphor for the idea of the conscious and unconscious mind. In the case of the Periscope Window, the glass looks like a completely normal piece of clear glass although it actually contains information that is revealed only when subjected to significant optical operations. It is intentionally using several optical principles like reflected image, magnified image, and direct projection superimposed on one surface (ills. p. 110). When you look at that surface it is laden with multiple views of the world beyond the interior space, yet unlike a typical window, the Periscope Window is gathering information from points outside that would not be visible to the occupant. A window would normally give you a view outside, but in this case there is no view because of an immediately adjacent fence and neighboring building. The idea is to challenge our idea of what a view from a window should mean or look like. A window has the capacity to be more interpretative and informative of the broader context. The Periscope Window can collect pieces of the surrounding environment from a broad range of vantage points, providing a broader view of nature as opposed to the explicit view of nature from a conventional window.

These operations are not hidden – they are integral to the work. The flat plane of the interior etched glass intermittently conceals the working parts, yet at times, direct projections populate the Periscope Window revealing the lenses as objects in themselves. In this way information from the outside world, such as images of the trees projected on the glass or shadows cast, and the product itself, the optical parts of the window, exist and are revealed simultaneously. All the parts add up to present multiple phenomena simultaneously on the single plane of interior glass, thus powerfully suggesting the invisible accumulation of information seasonally and diurnally. Without this device you would not see what we have actually presented – a compilation of multiple experiences superimposed into one experience. By collating and overlapping all this diversely scaled information, you are presented with a vision of the outside world that might provide a more essential experience of place. The experience may be fleeting but the optical tuning of the device presents a constancy that helps manage the complexity of the output.

The Periscope Window takes all the characteristics of a simple piece of glass, expands them, and gives an explicit role to each of these characteristics – the front surface might be reflective, the back surface might be refractive, etc. By being manipulated in this way these characteristics bring to bear on the window another interpretation of what is going on outside. And this is why I talk about the volume of light or volume of information, because we are always trying to expand on this boundary condition separating interior and exterior, trying to understand how the boundary condition can be more readily manipulated to allow us a more complex view of the world.

Transparency, Reflection, and Refraction

Just as many people think of glass in an optically limited way, they similarly have never really understood the structural potential of glass. Structural glass is still an exception to the standardized approach to building with glass. Conceiving the structure as light and delicate as possible allows the glass to take on a more potent role in terms of defining your experience of the space. By minimizing the usually exuberant role of cables, stainless steel tubes, and all other components of the tensile structures, the latent information and phenomenology of light embodied in the glass can emerge clearly in its capacities for transparency, reflection, and refraction.

The Retracting Screen represents a particularly challenging yet pure example of structural glass (ills. p. 113). This glass wall in a private home emerges from the floor in order to screen a dining area from a gallery and retracts to open this space up at other times. Two layers of glass are located on either side of vertical rods that apply tension and compression to stiffen the glass assembly with a minimum of structure. In this way the glass can unfold its fullest potential to respond to the room's spatial characteristics and its relationship to the view through the clear glass boundary. The screen consists of an interior surface acting as a heightened plane of reflectivity and an exterior surface as a heightened plane of luminosity. To reveal the material in this way depends on the

glass itself being the primary structure so that its phenomenal impact on its environment is not obscured by extraneous structural elements.

The Structural Glass Prisms Window, well over 20 years old but remarkably timeless, responds to the wish for a clear window to observe the beautiful landscape surrounding a chapel (ills. p. 113). How to manage the material choices and structure of such a large window (9.75 m H x 3.05 m W x 61 cm D) and have it bring another level of spirituality, observation, or mystery into the chapel? The mullions of a metal framing structure would have stacked up and obscured the view from most points in the chapel. Instead, long vertical pieces of tempered glass span the width and depth of the opening, providing the primary structure while smaller horizontal pieces feature dichroic coating and at the same time stiffen the entire structure.

Similar to the Periscope Window's simplicity that belies the multiple levels of transmitted and reflected information, the Structural Glass Prisms Window is a device transposing the experience of interior space relative to exterior space. In each case, depending on the conditions, you may see a blank surface there, then fragments of the device may appear, disappear, or be very intense and there is the powerful cumulative effect of abstracted information experienced over the passage of time. The judicious use of materials has tremendous potential, yet time's influence over materials has to be understood. The diurnal and seasonal interaction of light within a particular site or space must be systematically calculated in order to strategically select materials that can embody the relationship of light and time.

Responsive Planes

Materials have the potential to act as responsive planes. They can be responsive to the environment, responsive to your vantage point, and responsive to qualities of light. In fact, the careful manipulation of materials results in optical devices that are highly responsive – these devices require that the depth of the device and its parts work precisely together. The operations that can be applied to glass – laminating, tempering, coating, polishing, etching, etc. – are informed by the pragmatic issues

James Carpenter Design Associates,
Retracting Screen for a private home,
Dallas, Texas, USA, 1993.

Two qualities of glass are layered to generate
the sense of simultaneity between reflection
and transmission.

Video still of glass testing.

The two layers of glass consist of an interior
surface acting as a heightened plane of
reflectivity and an exterior surface as a
heightened plane of luminosity.

The structural glass tension structure retracts
into the basement.

James Carpenter Design Associates,
Structural Glass Prisms Window for a chapel,
Indianapolis, Indiana, USA, 1987.

The window maintains the view out to the
landscape by using structural glass and
forgoing the need for mullions.

James Carpenter Design Associates, Reflection Threshold, New York, New York, 2007-.

Model showing the narrow alley with the screen layout and pavilion connecting the two buildings.

Mock-up view of the Sheldon H. Solow Library and Study Center windows as they would be seen from south of the alley at night. The screen is 66cm from the window assembly.

Mock-up of stainless steel tri-wire and textured, perforated stainless steel paneling. The tri-wire faces the alley, while the textured and perforated sheet faces the Solow Library's acid-etched glass windows.

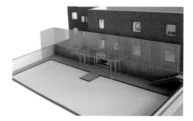

James Carpenter Design Associates, Reflection Threshold. Model with The Duke House to the west removed to show the screen's layout as it runs along the Solow Library's windows.

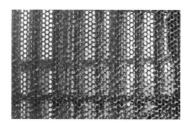

of thermal energy, daylighting, glare, and other performance requirements that deal with occupant comfort and functionality for the space. Then there are the contextual questions of the program, culture, traditions, and history and finally we mine the glass's potential to respond to these issues and generate the experiential qualities of light that bring a presence to the structure and a momentary pause to those that encounter it. Every project is a pragmatic process, but by the refined selection of responses to code, daylighting, and other issues of function and performance we allow those perceived limitations to become opportunities.

Small-scale models may be used for testing ideas surrounding these observations, a process that may result in material mock-ups for performance analysis (ill. p. 113). An example is the Reflection Threshold, which explores a location that has virtually no daylight, an alleyway which runs north-south between two buildings now owned by the New York University Institute of Fine Arts – the Sheldon H. Solow Library and Study Center to the east, recently donated to NYU, and The Duke House to the west, near Central Park in Manhattan (ills.). As a result, the narrow alley would become the connection between each eight-storey building. A pavilion was envisaged as connecting the buildings, but the minimal amount of light that filters down from above was considered a hindrance. The project is about enabling your eye to be sensitized to the modest level of ambient light and to capture and redirect light into this restricted environment. Specific surfaces can be deployed to allow the eye to observe in a more focused way while specific optics can be applied to render the light that is present. The pedestrians passing by on the street, looking down what they know to be a dark alley, are being presented with light from Central Park, captured by a metal tri-wire combined with textured and perforated metal paneling which extends the length of the alley on its east side.

From within The Duke House, which is on the west side of the alley, you will experience the vertical tri-wire wall with brighter horizontal tri-wire sections that align with The Duke House's windows. The wires of the horizontal tri-wire sections are oriented to capture the brightness of the sky directly overhead, and also you will always see an implied reflection of the window

James Carpenter Design Associates,
Dichroic Light Field, New York, New York, USA,
1995.

Polishing the ends of the glass blades generates
the glass's ability to register this one light
condition on the site.

James Carpenter Design Associates,
Moiré Stair Tower, Deutsche Post
(architects: Murphy/Jahn), Bonn, Germany,
2002.

View from the outside.

James Carpenter Design Associates,
Moiré Stair Tower.

Viewing platform at the stair tower's apex.

Details of the complex play of reflected and
transmitted images captured by the stair tower.

Metropolitan Life Building in New York: the phenomenon of light captured and diffused by water vapor.

James Carpenter Design Associates, Luminous Threshold, Sydney, Australia, 2000.

James Carpenter Design Associates, Luminous Threshold.

that you are looking out of, expressed as a brighter surface on the screen wall across the alley. The Sheldon H. Solow Library and Study Center on the east side of the alley contains many rare books and while it is appropriate that these be protected from direct light, users need not be deprived of a vivid level of light information. A light box provides the occupant with the sense of an extending luminous volume, simply by increasing the depth of the window's interior and exterior sills with reflective material – a device based on the idea of brick sills in England being painted white to create a brighter aperture than the window itself when you look through it. Thus an expansive sense of space is created. The design for this alley extends across every surface of the basement and ground level; there are different types of glass, stainless steel screens, and paving materials; the whole vocabulary of materials will turn the dark alleyway into an environment exquisitely responsive to light.

It is often the details that complete a device's ability to encompass a phenomenal experience of light. The Dichroic Light Field's dichroic glass fins feature polished ends which refract bars of light onto the screen under particular conditions (ill. p. 115). The Retracting Screen (as seen on p. 113) features beautifully polished edges which bring light into the glass, brightening the plane itself. Often a frosted edge makes the plane go flat. Even when we do acid etching we are very careful to retain the glass's optical brilliance. This comes down to a careful calibration of the glass's properties. We could describe the taxonomy of glass as being distilled to reflection, transmission, diffusion, absorption, refraction, and diffraction.

A mirror, being a completely reflective surface, presents itself either as the complete presence or absence of light. A mirror reflecting toward you is the presence of light and image, but the same mirrored surface reflecting away from you presents a void. There is a presence/absence quality to mirrors that I find remarkable. In the Dichroic Light Field, from one viewing angle all the light coming from behind you is being reflected away from you, so the field appears to be totally black and you just see the light reflecting back toward you from the fins against that void, while someone looking at it from the other direction sees the presence of light. The same mirror has two totally different readings.

Prismatic effects, pixelation, and fracturing can be described as subsets of reflection. The Moiré Stair Tower in the base building of the Deutsche Post in Bonn, Germany, contains selective areas of reflectivity, diffusion, and light re-projection in the glass, but more obviously it is about pixelating (ills. p. 116). Looking at the stair tower from the outside of the building this field of mirrored elements presents the landscape and sky behind you. When approaching you see more of the sky plane and also notice the blue squares facing the inside of the tower, which then merge with the blue of the sky. The mirror/blue elements were screenprinted onto the glass to heighten the levels of reflectivity and reflection. The project is essentially a mirror, but being presented as a field of rectangular dots, it begins to challenge your interpretative ability to read what you are seeing. It challenges your perception. The glass surface itself is reflecting the same information as the mirror dots, but by layering the reflective and transparent planes, the information is being reduced to the experience of ephemeral light.

Reconnecting to Natural Events

Materials are critical to deepen our experience of light, to reveal what is unique to a site through the experience of light, as light's interaction with the material world largely defines one's interpretation of place. A phenomenon as simple as clouds becomes much more complex under scrutiny. We take for granted the phenomenon of light captured and diffused by water vapor, and yet there is great beauty to be found in such observations. Luminous Threshold, a project announcing the entrance to Sydney's Olympic Park with a phenomenal experience which speaks to the industrial site's reclamation and transformation, investigates a synthesis of the natural phenomenon caused by water vapor interfering with the passage of light (ills.).

As we occupy a progressively more urban environment, we can become disconnected from the natural forces that prevail. Our approach to materials always begins with the questions: how do you reconnect people to the phenomenology of natural events in their day-to-day experience? How does the public realize that there is the potential within the built environment for something to take on a presence that is ephemeral, beautiful, informative, and enriching?

Responsive Materials

Sheila Kennedy

Mette Ramsgard Thomsen and Karin Bech,
Slow Furl, Brighton, UK, 2008, detail.

The ability to engage active materials to anticipate and provide for ranges of future use defines the design of distributed responsive materials and building systems. Two important ideas emerge from the root meaning of "responsive." To respond is to *answer,* and this presumes the posing of a prior question, which we identify as the necessary reconnection of material and disciplinary inquiry. But the word also contains a key nuance: it implies a question, but it is also a *promise in return*, there is a dimension of *responsibility* inherent in the idea of responsive materials. In addition to the posing of a disciplinary question, design with active materials suggests a further consideration, that it be *answerable to others*, for something larger than the design project itself. It is the potential agency of the architect in the making of this promise that interests us as it defines a state change in practice – the shift to proactive models of practice that explore the instantiation of thought and action in design.

New Materials, New Models of Practice

The increasing need to engage active, energy-exchanging materials in design and integrate decentralized forms of energy generation and distribution in building projects demands the creation of new *vertically integrated* models of professional practice. To address these concerns, the architect must organize – and often create – the products, technologies, and services that are required to synthesize technical, ecological, spatial, and social considerations of architecture. Further, the architect must find ways to situate and advance the discussion of active materials within the disciplinary discourse of architecture and in relation to the general public. The problems of *vertical integration*, which emphasize innovation and the rapid synthesis of new knowledge, are not well suited to the mainstream modern *horizontal practice model.* External consultants and designers in a horizontal practice model share a common understanding of existing building products and processes, which can be specified and deployed based on the successful repetition of known models based on known standards. With new materials and technologies, regulatory practices are not yet in place to systematically support this effort. Yet, at the same time,

the discipline of architecture offers enormous potentials for synthesis of information, incisive problem definition, and the ability to imagine and implement new realities.

To accelerate the implementation of active materials and technologies in architecture, new models of practice must be developed that simultaneously consider "doing" and "thinking." In these models, research, design, manufacturing, and construction are considered as part of an integrative platform that offers the potential to blend emergent and established knowledge bases.

Hybrid Materials

Active materials offer the greatest architectural potential, and pose the most interesting paradoxes, when they combine seemingly opposing or unrelated properties. This is seen in phase-changing materials (or PCMs) which are light in weight yet exhibit "dense" thermal mass behavior, or in solar luminescent materials that combine light reflection with absorption. Energy-gathering and -storing materials exhibit both "asymmetrical" and "symmetrical" behaviors over time, as stored energy (electricity) can be transferred to power applications with seemingly autonomous use cycles that are nonetheless related by their duration or capacity to daily natural cycles. Integrated in building materials, active materials create hybrid material composites that blur the modern distinction of high and low technologies, and offer ways to both make use of and transform standard building industry products.[1]

Design in the Fourth Dimension

One of the most significant developments in material culture is the shift from static material *properties* to dynamic material *behaviors.* The static nature of traditional material properties allows the architect to locate surfaces to achieve variations of opacity, translucency, and texture triggered by external forces such as the changing of light conditions, the shift of seasons, or the weathering of materials over time. The range of these external variations can be extended by CNC tooling operations, which selectively remove material to sculpt or

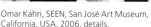

Omar Kahn, SEEN, San José Art Museum,
California, USA, 2006, details.

perforate traditional material surfaces, producing what has been called "digital materiality."[2] Active materials present an entirely different paradigm that engages design in the fourth dimension: time. Active materials change state *internally* in relation to energy exchanges, which may be triggered by external conditions of light, heat, or electricity. The question for architecture thus becomes not what is a material but *when* is a material; *when* does it change from one state to another, and how may its dynamic behavior be designed and experienced in the space of architecture? Active materials are not simply expressive; they hold the potential to become communicative, as their properties can be digitally controlled, and their output codified to signal external circumstances of the social collective (body gestures or activities), the building (sensors and monitoring), the city (networked resources), or the environment (weather and other atmospheric events).

The engagement of time carries aesthetic implications. The insistence of modernism on heroic structural expression is countered by the more subtle and perhaps more transgressive aesthetics of phenomena that reside hidden within materials until needed or activated. The modern tension between ornament and structure, form and performance, between thin surface and material depth, between inside and outside, front and back, servant and served are all put into question by active materials. Active materials may become *intelligent* when their aesthetics and performance are transformed by the agency of the designer. Without strategic design intent to explore and stage their architectural potentials, the physical behavior of active materials remains automatic. Design with new, disruptive materials and technologies is particularly interesting and challenging. While the public might assume that new materials are "high-tech" and high-performance, this is rarely the case. Disruptive materials and technologies such as solid state batteries, high-flux LEDs, solar nanomaterials, and even conventional polycrystalline solar materials, are often *underperforming* with respect to mainstream, established technologies. The design task is to understand the limitations of these materials, as well as their potentials, and to imagine for them an implementation vision that best suits their properties, leveraging their capacity to question mainstream practices.

The Power of the Many

Active materials and responsive building systems offer the potential to radically transform the concentration of building services within the architectural envelope. Distributed energy generation and the imperative to challenge existing architectural norms to find uses for efficient and disruptive technologies (solid state lighting, day lighting, micro-refrigeration, and localized heating) are driving the multiplication, distribution, and integration of building services into a distributed set of material surfaces that generate energy, distribute low voltage power, define space, and provide light. In distinction to the singular centralized infrastructure of modernism, it is possible to imagine a multitude of responsive material surfaces, a spatialized ecology of services in a dynamic, distributed architecture that carries the potential to be sensual, somatic, and tactile. In their engagement of time, the polyfunctionality of responsive surfaces in architecture challenges the modern credo of form following function. The plurality of functions will either call for spatial neutrality or for the design of materials and spaces that can physically adapt to different uses over time. This latter potential shifts the emphasis from the open plan to the re-configurable plan, which supports the coexistence of different activities in the same space over time. Re-configuration, or adaptive configuration, places increased importance on the architectural provision of adaptability, which engages the user in the co-creation of space. A material's responsive capacity in architecture is thus doubled, as the material responds both to internal energy exchanges and to an external range of formal configurations and daily functions, enabled by its material properties and the needs of its inhabitants.

Responsive Systems:
Potentials for New Environmental Practices

In responsive systems that are passive, material selection is based on an understanding of a material's properties, behavior, location, and proximity to activating sources. Once an active material is in place, the material's properties "automatically" create a response, usually an energy exchange, from one state to another. Thus, the design of active responsive material *systems*

Julius Popp, bit.fall, 2001-2006, shown at the
"Design and the Elastic Mind" exhibition,
Museum of Modern Art, New York, New York,
USA, 2008.

encompasses not only the understanding, selection, and siting of the material, but the design of a processing system which converts one set of information or phenomena into another set of information or phenomena, an output.

Closed-loop systems are historically associated with mechanical and structural engineering in architecture. Causality is foregrounded in a closed loop, and this can shift architecture's intentions and qualities away from the sphere of the reflective – of generating ideas about its situation – emphasizing instead design as a set of predictable outcomes, increasing architecture's likeness to a modern machine, and emphasizing predictable performance metrics. Open-loop systems receive information and continuously adjust to produce varied outputs. Open-loop system design can be randomized, or can vary within given design parameters. Open-loop output information or phenomena have the advantage of being more naturally diverse in their effects, engaging conditionality, variation, contingencies, and sometimes surprising outcomes.

Pushing the Envelope

Can the design of emergent responsive materials and systems be coupled with the disciplinary project of addressing environmental challenges? The "passive house" has recently come under scrutiny because the architectural materials required at the building envelope – triple-glazed glass, fiberglass insulation, etc. – contain a great deal of embodied energy, and their industrial production and transport are carbon-intensive. Environmentally sound architectural strategies are possible with responsive materials that hybridize passive and active elements.

These strategies are rooted in manipulating the physical envelope itself or in rethinking its boundaries as a set of distinct, lighter surfaces and spaces that are brought together in a climate concept within a responsive system. The efficacy of a responsive design can be defined in modern terms of system efficiency (i.e. the optimization of low expenditures of energy in the functioning of the system itself). This essay argues for an expanded notion of efficacy beyond performance – that engages the degree of *differential affective transformation*

that can be achieved by active processing – and the rhetorical capacity the design creates to provoke reflection. The discipline of architecture needs a set of critical terms to describe design intentionality in relation to responsive material systems – how and why one set of phenomena are processed into another set of phenomena and how design choices are made. An elegance principle of design intention is required where the *maximum affect* is produced by the system with the minimum material and energy expenditures.

Interactive Environmental Media: Emerging Design Strategies

Three pairs of architecture, industrial design and installation projects can be juxtaposed to demonstrate the coexistence of different working strategies that engage responsive systems to re-examine environmental questions of movement, energy generation, and air quality. These strategies outline a trajectory of thought for responsive systems that push the envelope by re-considering how the modern wall is conceived and what it does. At one end of this trajectory is the project of transforming the wall through movement, on the other is the disciplinary project of "unpacking" the wall and challenging the modern hegemony of the architectural envelope as a definitive and singular boundary condition.

The project pairs in this essay outline provisional strategies that are currently being tested at the scale of installation, research, and mobility design. Applications for responsive systems at the scale and longer duration of architecture and urbanism are still in their infancy. Each working strategy represents a different approach to motility, fabrication, and building industry; some foreground the visual or the tactile while others engage dynamic material components, material properties, or ambient environmental media. Yet until formal and programmatic strategies are de-antagonized and treated synthetically as integral aspects of responsive design, underlying questions of intentionality, prioritization, and problematization with respect to the discipline remain. What are the strategic conceptual design considerations regarding the audience and impact of responsive architecture and the types of problems that it takes

Mark Goulthorpe dECOi Architects, Aegis Hyposurface, Dynamically Reconfigurable Interactive Architectural Surface, Birmingham, UK, 2000.

on? How can these strategies be understood and positioned within the spectrum of singularity/reproducibility, modes of fabrication/ implementation in the building industry, and methods of resistance to or inscription within existing cultures of use? If responsiveness in architecture does contain a dimension of *responsibility*, then to whom is the work answerable and how does the designer position her or his work both as research and with respect to larger concerns beyond the boundaries of the design project itself? Can responsive architecture advance fundamental disciplinary issues – form, program, space, materiality – and achieve an impact at scale in order to respond to increasingly complex social, political, and cultural dimensions of environmental concerns?

Aegis Hyposurface – Adaptive Fritting Surface

Mark Goulthorpe's Aegis Hyposurface project – which received widespread public recognition at the "Non-Standard" exhibition in the Centre Pompidou – demonstrates a remarkable integrated system of interactive motility at the scale of an architectural surface (ills. pp. 122, 123). The Aegis Hyposurface prototype was constructed with ten framed support modules, each with triangulated metal plates driven by pneumatic pistons that react in real time to electronic stimuli from the environment, such as movement, sound, or light. Through a series of algorithms created for the project, individual triangulated surface "pixels" can be programmed and physically manipulated to shift shape and to change from form to form in a dynamic flow of movement. The Aegis Hyposurface effectively links information systems with physical form to produce a cladding surface that is dynamically variable. Aegis Hyposurface is perhaps the world's first dynamic three-dimensional screen: a 3D form organ.

At the conceptual level, this extraordinary piece of interdisciplinary engineering necessitates the reconsideration of modern attitudes of compositional logics, figure, ornament, and structure. Yet to achieve the surface in its fabrication, there is a clear front and back in the tradition of theatrical mechanics. The dimensional parameters of the support module's depth in section and the degree of each surface "pixel's" range of movement are the limiting constraints on the system's free play of motion, and reinscribe the system in a modern paradigm of

Mark Goulthorpe dECOi Architects,
Aegis Hyposurface, section, elevation,
perspective, plan.

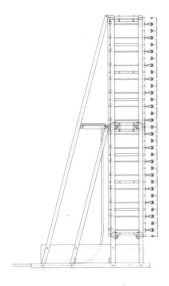

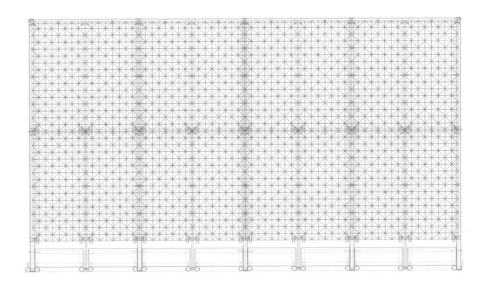

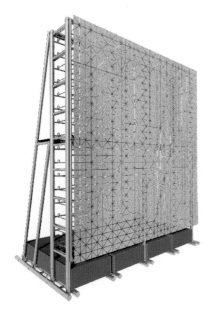

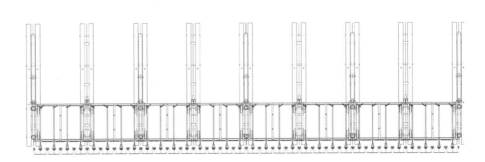

Hoberman Associates, Adaptive Fritting
Surface, „Ecological Urbanism" exhibition,
Harvard Universtiy Graduate School of Design,
Cambridge, Massachusetts, USA, 2009, details.

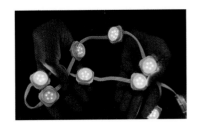

KVA MATx, Project for the HMS Laboratory at the University of Pennsylvania, Philadelphia, USA, 2009, detail, LEDs, renderings.

structure and skin, with the visual primacy given to the "front" of the surface. Even though careful design attention is given to normalize the installation process of the Aegis Hyposurface – the entire system can fit within the volume of an 18-wheeler truck; it is designed to be installed in a day by an ordinary worker with a forklift; detailed instructions are given on how to secure the pneumatic frames in order to resist the dynamic forces – the interactive formal qualities of the surface come with a trade-off of weight, human effort, and cost. These factors prevent the project from being as close as it might wish to the lightweight and more normative structure of a billboard or cladding system of a building. The project is an extraordinary aesthetic and technical accomplishment – it is no easy feat to make the surface dance in architecture – but it also raises strategic questions of what the vehicle and scale of responsive motility in architecture might be. What is its scale of use, its degree of singularity, its reproducibility, its fabrication strategy, and its degree of impact within the discipline of architecture and the larger context of the building industry?

Chuck Hoberman's recent Adaptive Building Initiative with Buro Happold engages the design and engineering of large-scale building components that move to respond to specific environmental conditions. Unlike the digital range of freedom created by the Aegis Hyposurface algorithms, Hoberman's projects are based upon mechanical translations of moving component parts from one clearly defined state to another. This strategy presents the practical advantages of highly efficient mechanical principles of motion: point pivots, rotational translations, and use of synchronized tension elements. Hoberman's Adaptive Fritting Surface uses a system of rotation driven by small electric motors, to move four layered Plexiglas panels in a 24 x 4 ft / 732 x 122 cm window, housed within a curved wall (ills. p. 124). This category of solution offers advantages in that it holds the potential for a more mass-reproducible "packaging" of a responsive window system that can be constructed of common building materials, interfaces, and motors. The use of rotation simplifies the range of action required by the mechanical servos and reduces the energy required to support the motion. Movement is concentrated at the corners, freeing the planes to move in relation to one

another, at times creating an unexpectedly rich range of intermediate "mis-alignments" before the system returns to its origin and the patterns repeat. Hoberman differentiates the responsive system by its ability to move, stating in a project exhibition text: "While conventional fritting relies on a fixed pattern, adaptive fritting provides a surface controllable transparency that can modulate between opaque and transparent states. This performance is achieved by shifting a series of fritted glass layers such that the graphic pattern alternately aligns and diverges."[3] The design is inspired by the adaptive natural processes of skin pigmentation. This approach to integration of responsive motility in architecture demonstrates the difficulties of scale and of fit to purpose attendant in the translation of biological processes to the hard, heavy planar materials of architecture, and the use of Newtonian mechanics, to put architectural materials into motion. Can fabrication innovations be developed for the manufacture of responsive systems in the building industry, or do they remain one kind of installations located within building projects? Can this category of solution compete effectively with imperatives for insulated glazing or operable windows that allow for ventilation, with all their normative requirements of cleaning/ maintenance? Or are solutions more purely demonstrative as an emergent dynamic aesthetic aligned with kinetic sculptures of Miró or Tinguely or the balance mobiles of Calder?

Slow Furl – SOFT HOUSE
The work of Mette Ramsgard Thomsen, and her collaborator Karin Bech, demonstrates the use of more radical strategies of integration at the level of flexible materials with inherently dynamic and responsive capacities. Thomsen's research team utilizes lightweight materials – often textiles – as these present the strategic combination of unprecedented material flexibility for architecture and minimal surface weight for motion. The use of textiles allows Ramsgard Thomsen to shed material weight and gain a greater range of possible motion, with less expenditure of effort and energy, while maintaining a high degree of material presence. The interactive installation Slow Furl was designed as a three-dimensional set for dancers that is both an object and an enclosure (ill. p. 119). Slow Furl explores the emergent concept of robotic membranes constructed of

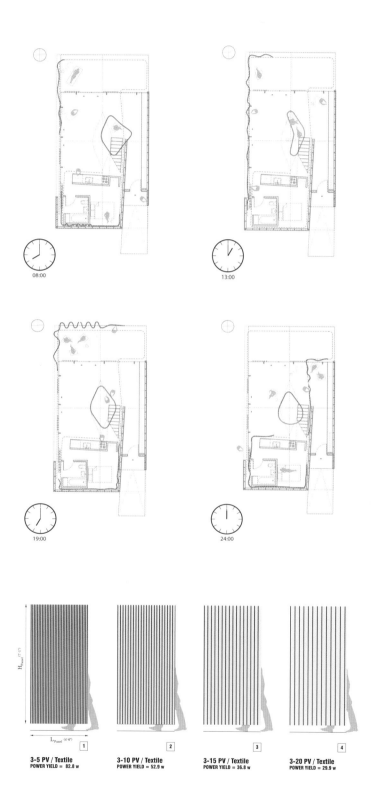

08:00

13:00

19:00

24:00

3-5 PV / Textile
POWER YIELD = 82.8 w

3-10 PV / Textile
POWER YIELD = 52.9 w

3-15 PV / Textile
POWER YIELD = 36.8 w

3-20 PV / Textile
POWER YIELD = 29.9 w

1   2   3   4

diaphanous cloth surfaces that are independently controlled by a sensing system – run by counterweight-assisted servos – that takes into consideration the resistance and weight of the fabric. Robotic membranes employ textiles as a technology as well as a material surface that provides the possibility of structural strength and movement. The material composition of the textile becomes a matrix for computation, integrating material capabilities of sensing and actuation. "Steel thread or carbon fiber allows electricity or data to pass through the material, making the textile the wiring that enables independent microprocessors to communicate. In this way, the membrane becomes an intelligent tissue 'aware' of its state and capable of sensing its larger setting and the space or activity it encloses."[4] Since these robotic membranes employ a distributed computational system, the aggregates of individual fabric cells can act or react independently to changes in their environment, generating complexity through overlay. While these explorations are currently limited to interior installations, Slow Furl opens the question of intelligent responsiveness over time and pairs this both with the idea of clothing – *habiles* – and with conventions or "habits" – how a built artifact may gain "habits" over time? The potential is for a new degree of material autonomy, and for a system of responsive motility that resides within the very properties of the material that moves.

A different strategy can be found in the augmentation and transformation of familiar "standard" elements and materials, as hosts and distribution mechanisms for responsive and/or dynamically active architectures. The SOFT HOUSE by KVA MATx transforms the household curtain into a set of energy-harvesting textiles that move to accommodate the changing spatial needs of living and working at home (ills. pp. 126, 127). Two curtain systems are explored. A central curtain under a skylight can be lowered to create an instant work room or raised to form a suspended soft chandelier that defines space in the open living area with solid state lighting. Perimeter curtains move horizontally along the southern building envelope on a standard track. Since track and curtain are always linked, the track is a strategic choice for a DC "ring" which distributes the DC renewable electrical power harvested by the curtain. The principles of the SOFT HOUSE energy network are

simplicity, adaptability, and intelligent cooperation among individual contributing elements. Mechanics are simple; it is not hard to move a curtain, the thin-film solar materials and textile host are flexible and lightweight.

The interest of the SOFT HOUSE project resides in the embedding of an augmented responsive energy-generating functionality within a familiar domestic textile curtain and its existing movement system – the track. As the textile surface engages space and household activities, it also reflects heat, shades sunlight, and provides the house with an additional layer of insulation along the window surface. The curtain is transformed while still retaining its traditional formal and material qualities of furling, flow, translucency, and movement – qualities which then become associated with the responsive technology. The deliberate acceptance of the curtain as type tends to de-antagonize the perceived differences between "smart" and "dumb" materials, high and low technologies, hand- and computer-driven craft. In the SOFT HOUSE project, the design of responsive technology expands to include a strategy for relocating the domestic practice of harvesting energy so that it can be integrated into an existing building industry and cultural patterns of use.

SOFT CITIES, the urban exploration of the SOFT HOUSE concept, is bound by both the limitations and advantages of pliable organic photovoltaic materials (OPVs). This class of photovoltaic materials presents a paradoxical paradigm that pairs inefficient energy conversion (in relation to conventional solar panels) with abundance in high throughput manufacturing processes and a very low carbon production footprint. Where conventional solar materials are evaluated by the standard industry metric of "peak efficiency," OPVs have a broad solar aperture and make energy – inefficiently – all day long, so a new metric of "total energy accrued per day" must be introduced into design considerations. The SOFT CITIES project in Portugal proposes to minimize the liabilities of OPVs and leverage their formal potentials at the urban scale as ambient energy-harvesting surfaces that can be flexible, cheap, inefficient, and everywhere.

To take advantage of the materials' flexibility, the design altered the ratio of voltage to current in the printable OPV structure, creating long, thin, pliable solar strands to maximize material flexibility and minimize connecting electric busways. Using computer-driven textile manufacturing equipment, the solar strands are integrated into a textile surface – creating a hybrid, which is part architecture, part mobile furnishing, and part infrastructure. Reproducibility of the retractable rooftop canopy design was prioritized. This helped to move the limitless resource model of centralized electrical infrastructure to a discrete (but mass-manufactured) product form for solar energy that would provide renewable light and be ready to use upon purchase.

However, there is a tension between the ubiquitous, generic nature of the global product and the degree to which such products can be successfully adapted to local material cultures. In Portugal, the rooftop canopies of the SOFT CITIES project evoked associations with the material culture of Portuguese lace and the tradition of rooftop laundry lines and grapevines. Certain materials, such as textiles, may enjoy a wider spectrum of associative properties that operate across cultures as a material common denominator. If so, then the stealthy overlap or deliberate mis-fit of their traditional associative values with those of their augmented performance in responsive architectures is a fruitful area for design. If responsive energy-harvesting materials are to have broader impacts, their associations, material properties, and degrees of autonomy or adaptability need to be studied and understood within the evolving history of material culture in architecture.

Copenhagen Wheel – Open Columns Project
The Copenhagen Wheel, a project of the sense*able* city lab at MIT, extends the idea of a hybrid product that serves both a familiar traditional purpose and a dynamic responsive role with respect to environmental ecology (ills. p. 129). A deliberate lifestyle product approach to representation and design is taken, where an existing lifestyle practice – the well-established Danish tradition of cycling in Copenhagen – is augmented (and in the Copenhagen Wheel literally boosted) by the addition of new mobility functionalities. The Copenhagen Wheel captures and stores generated energy, which assists the cyclist physically and

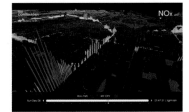

senseable city lab at MIT, Copenhagen Wheel,
2009.

senseable city lab at MIT, Copenhagen Wheel,
2009, information visualization.

monitors CO_2 levels, traffic congestion, and car exhaust along
the bicyclist's route. Carlo Ratti describes the Copenhagen Wheel
as "biking 2.0".[5] The compact, autonomous form of the design in
a detachable rear wheel "package" is explicitly intended to serve
as an instant 'upgrade' to any existing bicycle. The augmented
technology contained in the wheel hub works in synergy with
other "autonomous" lifestyle products. The system does not
need a dashboard screen, since the rider's iPhone can provide
one. Routes and information on CO_2 levels and traffic patterns
can be stored remotely through the connectivity of the urban
wireless network and viewed from any laptop. Here, mobile
technology both augments the familiar urban activity of cycling,
and also holds the potential to subvert it, or at least to re-purpose
the daily cycle by aggregating the commutes of thousands of
citizens as crowd-sourced information that may provide cities
with a low-cost method of urban air quality monitoring.

Projects like SOFT HOUSE and the Copenhagen Wheel share the
strategic intent to be mass-reproducible as hybridic new forms
of product/infrastructure. Although questions should be raised
about whether or not responsive mainstream designs produced
within the constraints of market forces can effectively carry
forward an alternative cultural or ecological agenda, this approach
demonstrates the potentials of engaging connective responsive
networks to bridge between independently manufactured
products and seemingly diverse and unrelated activities.

The ubiquity of many global products in the "first world"
building industry and the redundancy of consumer electronic
components, such as wireless ports, keypads, batteries, and
display screens, suggests that responsive architecture need
not be designed as a self-contained system, but may instead
be a conceptual organization that aggregates disparate
existing activities and industrial, consumer, and architectural
components. Within this emerging network paradigm,
responsive design innovation could include discovery of
parts and pieces like the bicycle or the curtain that can be
appropriated in an atomized strategy for distributed building
services or co-opted for augmented ecological practices.
The distributed "architecture" of these responsive projects
provides a reminder that sensing and energy generation systems

Omar Kahn, Open Columns Project,
University of Buffalo, New York, USA, 2007.

Laura Garofalo and Omar Khan

Omar Kahn, Open Columns Project.

gain momentum through the establishment of new forms and forums for collectivity, and the aggregation of information from multiple independent sources.

Omar Khan's Open Columns Project, an interactive installation at the University of Buffalo, explores the idea of emergent homeostatic systems that monitor the ambient health and quality of the environment while engaging the public to reflect upon the monitoring process itself, and the need for its presence (ills. pp. 130, 131). Open Columns is literally a conversation piece where the gathering of people in conversation creates a higher concentration of CO_2 in the air of the room. Sensors measure the air expelled by the onlookers, allowing the columns to deform and droop down, which in turn attracts people's attention and provokes discussion. The materiality and fabrication of the interactive columns draws upon what Khan has referred to as relational geometries, ways that self-similar assemblies or organisms propagate. The columns are made from very simple, self-similar rubber parts fabricated from a single re-configurable mold using two different Shore durometers. This fabrication strategy, often used in industrial design, here produces controlled spatial effects that can be designed and anticipated. Yet the system's materiality exceeds the reproducibility of complete control, and each deformation from the same atmospheric stimuli can produce a slightly different deformation in the rubber forms, according to the play of gravity and the inherent elasticity of the molded part. The variable and predictable elastic parameters of rubber and the strategy of *flexible* mold-making expands conventional industrial design manufacturing and suggests a new range of parametric materiality for interactive architecture.

Open Columns aligns itself with a modern avant-garde position of work that points to a condition or problem, in this case an invisible air quality, and raises awareness of potentially adverse environmental conditions as it monitors levels of CO_2 in the air. This approach provides much needed respite within the discipline of architecture, from the reductive terms of efficiency that have dominated the discourse of projects that address the environment. The uncanny material elasticity of Open Columns and its rhetorical capacity to elicit conversation and provoke

thought is clear, and it is intriguing to speculate on how or if such a position could be expanded to include more than monitoring and warning. Could such installations also contribute to the resolution of the very problem they point to? The potential for public dialogue, cultural reflection, and disciplinary inquiry is the larger, still open, promise of responsive architecture.

Notes

1. Kennedy, S. "Electricity, the Fairy and the Hollow Wall" in *PRAXIS 6 New Technologies://New Architectures*. Boston, 2004.
2. Gramazio, Fabio, and Matthias Kohler. *Digital Materiality in Architecture*. Baden: Lars Müller Publishers, 2008.
3. Hoberman, Chuck. "Adaptivity in Architecture" in *Ecological Urbanism*. Baden: Lars Müller Publishers, 2010.
4. Ramsgard Thomsen, Mette. "Textile Logics in a Moving Architecture" in CHI 2009: Digital Life New World.
5. http://web.mit.edu/press/2009/copenhagen-wheel.html

Materializations of Nanotechnology in Architecture

Peter Yeadon

Day after day, millions of Americans become engaged in a relentless battle against nanomachines, but they are not alone. Globally, hundreds of millions of people, perhaps even billions, rise to resist the interminable advance of these pests at least once a day, and wonder whether or not the problem is just being exacerbated by their actions. As one learns early on, it is very difficult to stop these troublesome foes. One strategy that is commonly employed involves some basic skills at brandishing crude, bladed implements; however a variety of fairly advanced lasers have also been shown to be very effective weapons for those that can afford them. The enemy I refer to, of course, is the human hair.

A single hair in the beard of a man will grow at a rate of approximately eight nanometers (nm) per second. That is to say, with each passing second, a hair will add roughly eight billionths of a meter to its length. In just 13 seconds, the hair will have gathered enough resources (i.e. carbon, oxygen, nitrogen, hydrogen, and sulfur) to amass another 104 nm of solid structure. This is a pretty small amount of construction and, admittedly, there's not that much to show even after a full day's work. What is remarkable, however, is that this self-assembling structure, in those 13 seconds, will have already become more massive than the largest creations of nanotechnology.

Nanotechnology is the study and fabrication of petite molecular structures that measure between 1 and 100 nm, in at least one dimension. Its fundamental objective is to gain complete control of matter, all the way down to the level of atoms, but it is not easily defined as a discipline in and of itself. Because nanotechnology involves the observation and manipulation of matter at the scale of atoms and molecules, it is an integral part of numerous disciplines. It includes researchers from material science, engineering, biology, computer science, chemistry, physics, medicine, and many other areas of expertise. The term really represents a range of technologies, not a singular technology; if you were to ask an assortment of scientists and engineers from a variety of disciplines what nanotechnology is, you would likely receive a rather broad range of definitions.

There is some debate, for example, as to whether or not nanotechnology refers to just single-molecule structures, or if it also includes structures that are made up of more than one molecule.[1] Compounding this problem of uncertainty are the seemingly arbitrary dimensional limits of nanotechnology. Some molecular structures, including single-molecule structures, are larger than 100 nm. So what could possibly be so significant about confining the dimensional limits of nanotechnology to 1 to 100 nm? Why not 1 to 999 nm or 1 to 100 molecules? Imagine describing architecture as the study and fabrication of all things that are between 1 and 100 meters, or decameters, in at least one dimension. Imagine the number of disciplines that could lay claim to being involved in architecture. Imagine, too, the numerous opportunities for collaboration.

Four Approaches to Nanotechnology in Design Innovation

As nanotechnology advances toward a new level of control over the behavior of matter, it will utterly transform the means of designers while manipulating our relationship to the physical world that surrounds us. There are four emerging methods, or means of invention, that illustrate how architects are thinking about design innovation through nanotechnology. That's right; so far, there are just four. But they are a beginning, however awkward and humble, and they do signify a certain resistance toward merely "rethinking" and "reinventing" existing architectural paradigms. These four approaches are: by mimesis, by application, by experimentation, and by speculation. Interestingly, these same four might also characterize the diverse modes of inquiry through which nanotechnology is being advanced.

By Mimesis

The first strategy is to copy what nature does already. With real-time imaging now approaching a spatial resolution of 0.5 Å, just 0.05 nm, microscopy has increasingly enabled scientists to observe biological and mineral specimens, characterize their composition, and synthesize materials that emulate their novel properties.[2] The recent improvements in biomimetic nanostructured materials, in particular, have benefitted from

Carbon Nanotube Arrays with Strong Shear Binding-On and Easy Normal Lifting-Off. Liangti Qu, Liming Dai, Morley Stone, Zhenhai Xia, and Zhong Lin Wang. From *Science* 322:238 (2008). Figure S14c. Reprinted with permission from AAAS. This SEM image shows a disordered array of vertically aligned carbon nanotubes (VA-CNTs) that have been mounted on a thin-film substrate of polystyrene. The nanotubes are similar to gecko spatulae, but this VA-CNT biomimetic adhesive has almost ten times the adhesion force of geckoes and can still release and reattach easily. A 4 x 4 mm film of VA-CNTs will support a 1480 g weight suspended from a glass surface.

Fabrication of sub-wavelength anti-reflective nanostructures using a bio-template. Guoyong Xie, Guoming Zhang, Feng Lin, Jin Zhang, Zhongfan Liu, and Shichen Mu. From *Nanotechnology* 19 095605 (5pp), figures 1a, 2 and 3a. Reprinted with permission from IOP.

Top: These SEM images of a cicada wing show a surface of 400 nm high nano-nipples. The nipples are responsible for the anti-reflective property of the wing. Each nipple tapers from approximately 150 nm at the base to 65 nm at the top, and mostly consists of chitin, a crystalline polymer.

Middle: This thin gold (Au) layer was deposited on the cicada wing, and was then removed to become a mold for casting polymethyl methacrylate (PMMA) films. The anti-reflective property of the cicada wing is inherited by the PMMA films, which reduce surface reflectivity considerably for wavelengths between 250 and 800 nm.

Bottom: This SEM image shows replicated nano-nipples, produced using the Au mold, as freestanding pillars on PMMA film. The researchers chose PMMA films because they are flexible, provide high resolution, and are transparent. These properties are highly advantageous for many applications that require anti-reflectivity.

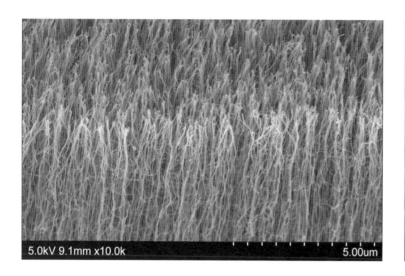

5.0kV 9.1mm x10.0k   5.00um

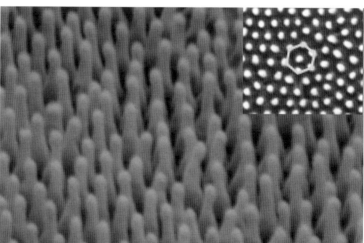

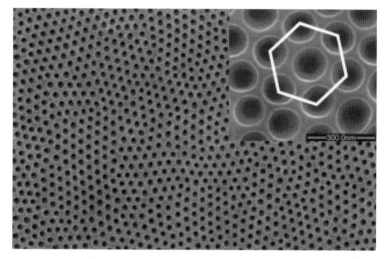

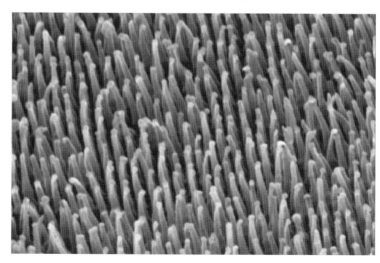

Clustered Sc-Zn Quasicrystals. Courtesy of U.S. Department of Energy's Ames Laboratory. Quasicrystals have been referenced as an important model for emulation in the architecture of Benjamin Aranda, Daniel Bosia, and Chris Lasch. Quasicrystals have an unusual symmetry, wherein their structure is both ordered and aperiodic. This cluster of rhombic triacontahedral quasicrystal grains was grown in solution. Each grain is roughly 1 mm in diameter.

Aranda\Lasch, Grotto Pavilion, PS1 Proposal, New York, New York, USA, 2004, detail model. Courtesy of Aranda\Lasch. Like quasicrystals, the Grotto Pavilion by Aranda and Lasch consists of a pattern of repeating elements that are not exactly identical.

researchers being able to observe and characterize organisms that have evolved during the past couple of billion years. By examining how the hourglass shape of aquaporins enables water to be efficiently transported through the walls of cells, for example, researchers have created polymer filtration membranes that mimic their shape to harvest pure substances. The high selectivity and permeability of the material permits target molecules to be separated faster, and with less energy. For desalination, water molecules pass through the pores, but the shape of the pores rejects the ions found in salt.

It is well known that nanotech researchers have studied the surface structure of lotus leaves and cicada wings to create biomimetic materials that repel water and dirt. To improve photovoltaics, researchers have also created synthetic molecules that mimic chlorophyll to convert light energy into electrical energy, and they have copied the eyes of moths and flies to produce anti-reflective surfaces that feature fine protuberances for capturing photons. They have created coiled nanopropellers that are just 27 nm thick and mimic the flagella of bacteria, for autonomous robots in fluids, and they have designed a molecule that changes shape in response to light, by studying the way in which plants move to protect themselves from too much sunlight. In recent years, researchers have not only focused on acquiring new knowledge, but they have also asked how we might make use of that knowledge, how it might be applied through nanoengineering. A single purpose runs through all of these examples: to use what we can learn from nature to improve our current capabilities.

Perhaps nature is not the proper term here as, at the nanoscale, when we get down to the scale of individual atomic elements, distinctions between natural and artificial become ambiguous. But we are beginning to see how the imaging of nanostructures is informing architectural design decisions. Benjamin Aranda, Daniel Bosia, and Chris Lasch, for example, have written about how "zooming in to the nanoscale, crystallography and its neighboring disciplines provide ample models of modularity through molecular frameworks that can be emulated at the building scale." [3] In conceiving their Grotto Pavilion, the collaborators found quasicrystals to be interesting because they have an unusual symmetry, wherein their structure is both ordered and aperiodic, meaning they do not have a pattern that consists of repeating elements that are exactly the same (ill. p. 135):

"The current research into the aperiodic structures of quasicrystals demonstrates that some materials can contain a perfect, long-range order without any three-dimensional periodicity, a quality that translates well into the world of architecture: modularity without a conventional sense of repetition. It is a search for the wild and yet perfectly stable order. The bridge between these disciplines, from the very small to the very large is geometry, the root of our investigation. What power do these rules that govern the very small have to organize material on the scale of the very large?"[4]

While "zooming in" and "zooming out," the architects found that it is a set of geometries, expressed through algorithms, which could be imitated. And all of that zooming in and out implies that it is important for us to witness, to see, to confirm how *this* can become *that*. But there has been a significant difference emerging between mimesis in nanotechnology (as demonstrated by biomimetic materials) and architectural approaches to mimesis, and it has a lot to do with the ability to zoom in and out. In the nanotech community, imaging is a means for researchers to understand things at the atomic level and make nanostructures that emulate those things. In the architecture community, however, the image itself has largely become the principal source of inspiration. It is the representation of the thing, not the thing itself, which often serves as the model for emulation.

This is difficult to circumvent; the imagery produced by microscopy is so exotic and compelling that its power in lending vision to the invisible is bound to excite all of us involved in the creation of architecture. At the same time, we need to be skeptical of the images we are receiving, and be aware of the fact that the tools that capture images can also influence and change that which is being recorded at the nanoscale. In thinking critically about using design analogies to nanotechology, architects will need to increasingly scrutinize the value and relevance of the metaphors that creep into mimetic practice, and we will need to be particularly wary of metaphors borrowed from other disciplines, such as grey goo. Perhaps then, our work will advance from that which is evocative toward that which is provocative. Nanostructures are so small that they exist in that strange territory between classical mechanics and quantum mechanics. Their properties are very different from those exhibited in bulk materials at the macroscale. This is not that; a building structure is not akin to a nanostructure. Indeed, a critical question to ask might be: why should these rules that govern the very small have any relevance to the design of the very large?

By Application

Because they are of a size where quantum effects influence their behavior, nanostructured materials have unique electrical, optical, and magnetic properties. They are significantly different from materials to which architects have become accustomed. But their creation does involve a set of constraints and opportunities that are very familiar to architects. They are the products of design. They require careful study, and there are important distinctions between that which is possible and that which is achievable, given our current means and resources. Nanotech advancements are also heavily influenced by investment, from public and private sources, which has shifted materials innovation toward health and safety, energy, transportation, security and defense, and environmental issues. And, the ability to design and engineer materials, atom-by-atom, molecule-by-molecule, has researchers considering the same questions a contemporary architect might ask. What should it be? How should it perform, or behave?

If we ignore molecular machines, for a moment, there are two broad classes of materials that are the products of nanotech-nology: nanomaterials and nanocomposites. Nanomaterials are nanostructured materials wherein the structural elements are smaller than 100 nm, in at least one dimension. A very large sheet of graphene is a nanomaterial, regardless of its width and length, because it is only one carbon atom thick. Nanotubes are nanomaterials, even if they are very long, when their diameters are less than 100 nm. However, nanoparticles are considered nanomaterials only if they are less than 100 nm in all spatial directions.

Many nanomaterials have a countable number of atoms, are smaller than 50 nm, and only become useful when added to other materials. When nanomaterials are integrated into the bulk matrices of other materials, we can produce nanocomposites for products, with enhanced properties that would not exist without the inclusion of these tiny nanostructures. Nanocomposites, in other words, have nanomaterials in them, and the products that are made of nanocomposites are rapidly emerging. In 2006, the Woodrow Wilson International Center for Scholars introduced an online, searchable inventory of 212 nanotech-based consumer products. About 15% of those products were cosmetics. The database has now grown to over 1000 items, with roughly three to four nanotech products hitting the market every week. Still, their emergence has been fairly inconspicuous, and the Center has found that public awareness of nanotechnology remains disappointingly low.[5]

For some time, industrial designers and apparel designers have been using nanocomposites in a wide assortment of applications, such as high-performance clothing and sports equipment. Swiss bike maker BMC offers light, strong bicycle frames that are nanocomposites made of carbon fibers, resin, and carbon nanotubes. The technology was developed by Easton, an American company specializing in advanced materials for sports, and their proprietary process involves evenly distributing carbon nanotubes into the resin that is used to bind carbon fibers together. Traditional carbon fiber frames have been found to be weakest in the areas between the fibers, where the resin is located. With the inclusion of carbon nanotubes, the strength-to-density ratio of the resin/fiber matrix increases significantly, resulting in lighter components and/or improved strength.

Even though the construction sector has been rather slow to adopt and develop nanotech innovations, especially when compared with the design fields that are allied with architecture, nanocomposites are steadily infiltrating the built environment on two fronts: by optimizing and enhancing the performance of existing building technologies, and by offering new material

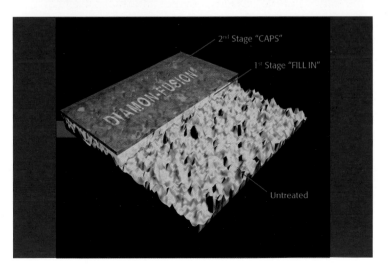

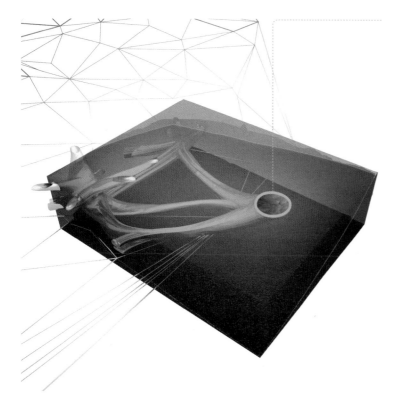

products that were not possible before. Even seasoned
practitioners are beginning to see the advantages of using
nanocomposites in their projects. Richard Meier's self-cleaning
Dives in Misericordia church in Rome uses titanium dioxide
nanoparticles in its cement to break down air pollutants, simply
by reacting to the divine intervention of sunlight (ill. p. 137).
At 40 Bond Street in New York, a residential building by Herzog
& de Meuron, the glass was manufactured with a hydrophobic
treatment developed by Diamon-Fusion International (ill. p. 137).
The two-stage process first smoothes the coarse surface of the
glass, and then adds a hydrophobic layer to repel dirt and water,
effectively reducing water consumption, energy, and costs
associated with cleaning and maintaining the facade.

Both the Jubilee Church and 40 Bond Street demonstrate how
nanotechnology is being applied to architecture: it is through
manufactured building products that are imbued with unique
performance characteristics; and, despite all of the hullabaloo
surrounding nanotech as a disruptive technology, its entry has
been surprisingly mute. Perhaps this is due to the nature of the
nano-enabled building products that have been created for,
and specified by, architects. Nanocomposites are exceedingly
discreet technologies. The vast majority of them are additives,
thin-film coatings, or gels. They are just there, working away.
Or they lie dormant, but ready, and do not exhibit their novel
properties until they are provoked to perform.

In this sense, nanocomposites are not unlike conventional
building technologies. Structural elements are constantly
working, even if it is just to support themselves, and smart
materials and sprinkler heads need to be stimulated in order
to react favorably. So it is not surprising to find architects
approaching the integration of nanocomposites in the same
way that they would any other building product. Architects
will consider the value of nanoproducts (e.g. cost, lifecycle,
performance, environmental impact, etc.) before specifying their
application. But, so far, nanotechnology has not seemed integral
to their work. Sure there are some coatings and insulants that
have been integrated by practitioners here and there; however
it is very difficult to demonstrate how nanotech is vital to their
work and has informed critical design decisions. Innovation

through nanomaterials and nanocomposites is not yet a priority. With respect to exemplary applications that exploit the potential of nanotech, no industrial sector is farther behind than the construction industry. This adds new urgency to a familiar question for architects: are we going to continue to make use of the products we are given, like consumers, or are we going to participate in the research and development of those products, like invested innovators?

By Experimentation

There are several recent advancements that would benefit from the participation of architects in their development and application. Some of these materials could have a highly visible impact on architecture, such as: transparent aluminum, luminescent quantum dots, third-generation photovoltaics, and liquid crystal elastomers that change shape in response to varying levels of light or temperature. Other materials will remain discrete. We will not be able to see EMF coatings that block wireless transmissions any better than we will be able to spot nanocomposites that automatically sense and repair cracks in structures. For most of these novel materials, however, we will perceive their behavior when they are provoked. We will just have to mechanically stress piezoelectric ZnO nanowires to witness the electricity they can produce, and silica particles will immediately disclose their presence when a bullet bounces off of a thin membrane coated with shear thickening fluid. Similarly, the controlled dampening capabilities of shake gels and magneto-rheological fluids will only become apparent in large structures during seismic activity.

Carbon nanotubes are another nanomaterial that should interest architects (ill. p. 140). They have improved the corrosion resistance of alloys, have helped remove perchlorate toxins from contaminated water, have been combined with nanoclays to improve the fire retardancy of plastics, and have formed controllable surfaces that can switch back and forth between super-hydrophobic (repels water) and hydrophilic (attracts water). It is well known that they offer exceptional specific strength, with the highest strength-to-weight ratio of any known material, and are currently being used to strengthen

polymers, golf clubs, surfboards, boats, and many other materials and products. A 1 cm diameter area of dangling carbon nanotubes, suspended 5 μm apart so that they remain invisible, is all that is needed to support a person so that they appear to levitate.[6]

Beyond stronger nanocomposites, carbon nanotubes offer a number of other novel properties that can be transferred to a very broad range of applications. Depending on their structure, nanotubes can be metallic or semiconducting. They are photovoltaic and are good electrical conductors, so researchers have used them to create lightweight, flexible conductive thin films and electronics, such as sensors, displays, antennae, speakers, solar cells, batteries, and supercapacitors. When a current is sent through a network of nanotubes embedded in a coating that surrounds a substrate, they can serve as a nervous system to identify stresses, defects, and cracks in a structure. Once located, a short electrical charge can be sent to heat the nanotubes that are at the location of a fissure, locally melting a healing agent that will fill the crack and mend the structure.

Due to its tubular architecture, a carbon nanotube can be used to shuttle whole molecules from one place to another, like an intestinal molecular conveyor, or disassemble matter atom-by-atom and reassemble it in another location. They can be used to trap and store molecules, such as hydrogen for our future fuel economy, and pushing water molecules through the tubes creates tiny hydroelectric generators that produce electricity.

When Lisa Iwamoto and Craig Scott created Hydro-Net, an urban vision for San Francisco, they fully embraced the strength and storage capabilities of carbon nanotubes (ill. p. 138). The proposal features a subterranean network of carbon nanotube tunnels, for hydrogen-fueled hover-cars to zip around in. The nanotubes store hydrogen and also permit its distribution for refueling vehicles throughout San Francisco. Carbon nanotubes are astonishingly strong in tension, which is why they have been considered for applications like the conveyance tether of the space elevator, however they are not very strong in compression and tend to buckle due to their tubular form. But that might not matter so much here. Whether intended

Multi-walled carbon nanotube. Courtesy of Dr. Robert Hurt. This TEM image of a multi-wall carbon nanotube (MWNT) shows how it is made up of many concentric tubes. The outside diameter of the MWNT is approximately 15 nm. Metal impurities inside the MWNT are discernible.

Decker Yeadon, thin-film carbon nanotube electrodes. Courtesy of Decker Yeadon. Thin films of multi-wall carbon nanotubes (MWNT) have been deposited on a flexible substrate at Decker Yeadon, and are being tested for electrical conductivity. The nanotubes were first dispersed in solution and then printed with varying densities using an ink jet printer. The firm is investigating ways to use MWNTs as flexible electrodes for electro-active polymer muscles, which will activate a facade system they are developing.

Decker Yeadon, nanotube-enabled EAP artificial muscles. Courtesy of Decker Yeadon. Schematic diagram of a nanotube-enabled artificial muscle. Changes in voltage induce movement in the composite material. The nanotube/polymer muscles (black) are bonded to both faces of a foam/gel sheet substrate (green). As voltage is applied to a face muscle, it expands, causing the entire composite assembly to bend.

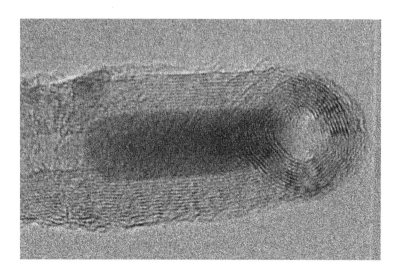

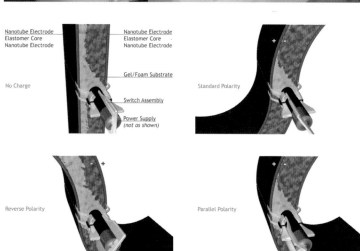

or not, Hydro-Net offers at least one situation where the form of the assembly might compensate for the limitations of nanomaterials; it may very well be that carbon nanotubes will perform well if fashioned into a series of uniformly-loaded compression rings.

Despite their extraordinary promise, architects have been reluctant to experiment directly with nanotubes, and nanomaterials in general. Perhaps this is due to their expense. The carbon nanotubes we experiment with, in our office, are more than 95% pure, have an outside diameter of about 15 nm, and have a surface area of approximately 220 m² per gram. At 110 USD per gram, they can become pretty expensive for a small firm to experiment with, but the price has come down over the past few years and will continue to fall as new techniques for making them emerge. Perhaps, instead, the reluctance to experiment with nanomaterials is symptomatic of the rapidity with which nanotech advancements appear. It is undoubtedly difficult to work with material technologies that are quickly evolving. This is one of the main challenges for architects that are interested in experimenting with nanomaterials, and writing about nanotechnology.

Experimentation in architecture and experimentation in nanotechnology are actually not that far apart. Both require research to produce new knowledge; which, if applied, can lead to new capabilities. Both require testing; which acknowledges that materials and form are only a physical manifestation of an ideal model that is based on principles (i.e. that which is made can only approximate modeled projections). Both are eager to make predictions, but are stuck in the present where impurities abound. As the problems and promises of nanotechnology in architecture become increasingly apparent, through experimentation and application, the chief advantage architecture will have over science and engineering is the humanities. It will enable us to maintain a fine balance between conviction and doubt, and, hopefully, construct compelling, convincing arguments that demonstrate leadership on the issue of the day.

Decker Yeadon, Kinetic Facade System enabled by nanotubes. Courtesy of Decker Yeadon. This proposal for an active facade system features a *brise-soleil* that is comprised of continuous ribbons of artificial muscles, shown left. The ribbons would be made of electro-active polymer actuators with carbon-nanotube electrode coatings. The ribbons can change position in response to the sun, becoming less/more dense and open/close to control solar heat gain. By configuring the controllable surface in this way, Decker Yeadon is also looking to significantly increase the surface area of a third-generation photovoltaic coating that might be added.

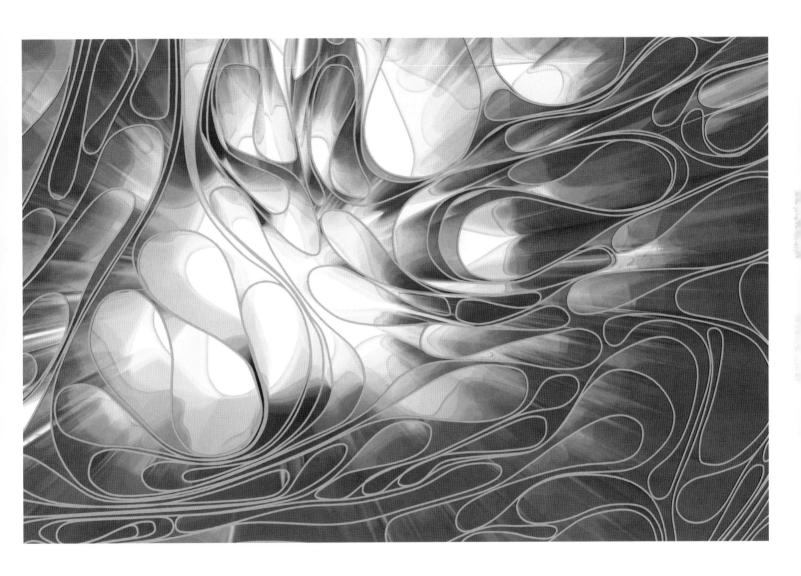

Daniel Pelosi, You've Gotta Have Faith, rendering. Courtesy of Daniel Pelosi.
Pelosi envisions a future where technological advancements will accelerate environmental degradation, and will be our salvation if we retreat inside. His project relies on a nanofiltration membrane to protect us from UV rays, and remove contaminants from rainwater and the air.

Nanocoil. Reprinted with permission from "Piezoresistive InGaAs/GaAs Nanosprings With Metal Connectors." Gilgueng Hwang, Hideki Hashimoto, Dominik J. Bell, Lixin Dong, Bradley J. Nelson, and Silke Schön. *Nano Letters* 2009 9 (2), 554-561. © 2009 American Chemical Society.
A 27 nm thick nanocoil with two metal connectors. The three-dimensional structure self-formed out of a planar InGaAs/GaAs bi-layer sheet. Researchers have demonstrated that nanocoils can be applied as artificial bacterial flagella, for tiny robotic devices, and are useful for converting linear motion to rotary motion.

Rack-and-pinion device at the molecular scale. Franco Chiaravalloti, Leo Gross, Karl-Heinz Rieder, Sladjana M. Stojkovic, André Gourdon, Christian Joachim, and Francesca Moresco. From *Nature Materials* 6, 30 – 33 (2007). Figure 1. Reprinted by permission from Macmillan Publishers Ltd.
Many molecular components for nano-machines appear to be similar to their large industrial counterparts, such as this rack-and-pinion mechanism (a). Researchers recently designed and fabricated a single-molecule pinion that is 1.8 nm in diameter. The molecule functions as a six-toothed wheel interlocked at the edge of a self-assembled molecular island that acts as a rack. Scientists monitor the rotation of the pinion molecule, tooth-by-tooth along the rack, by a chemical tag attached to one of its cogs. The chemical structure of the molecule (b) is two nitrogen atoms, carbon atoms (light blue), and hydrogen atoms (white).

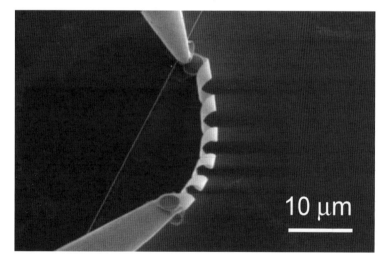

10 μm

(a)

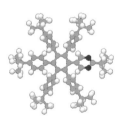

(b)

By Speculation

If we ignore the poor translations that emerge as research news passes through popular journals and into architectural projects – these are scientific hypotheses on what "might" be achieved, that become press announcements on what "can" be achieved, before becoming architectural pronouncements on what "is" being achieved – there are an increasing number of provocative architectural propositions that advance the debate on nanotechnology in architecture and society.

Encouraged by our fine tradition of visionary architecture, most of these propositions assume that advancements in nanotechnology will be good, and they help us envision why nanotech developments are important and worthy of our consideration and pursuit. To do so, visionary works often identify new technologies and show how they can help us address problems. In doing so, however, they are really obliged to demonstrate why nanotechnology is vital to a work. What problems can it address, and why should this merit our concern? Why is it necessary? Does it significantly enhance our current capabilities or provide us with an elegant, new economy of means that was not possible before? Hydro-Net, for example, demonstrates convincing critical inquiry, and the technology might be achievable, but are carbon nanotubes really vital to the work?

By far, the fewest and most successful propositions that consider nanotechnology in architecture venture into irony. These speculative proposals go beyond describing what nano-technology would do in a project, to offer arguments that contribute to a difficult debate. The projects show the promise of nanotechnology, while acknowledging the consequences of nanotechnology.

Daniel Pelosi's You've Gotta Have Faith project is an ominous proposition that examines the reciprocity between the problems and promises of nanotechnology, in the context of the year 2050 (ill.). The proposal involves significant alterations to the Prada flagship store in Manhattan, a piece of early 21st century technology. Prada is long gone, and so is our ability to find fresh air, clean water, and uncontaminated soil. The avarice of man

Molecular model of nanocar components.
Courtesy of Tour Lab/Rice University.
The nanocars fabricated at Rice University,
Houston, Texas, are only a few nanometers long.
The cars can move, at room temperature, at a
velocity of 4.1 nm per second. There is a light-
activated paddlewheel engine that sits atop
of each car's carbon framework. The wheels
were originally buckyballs, but were changed
to carboranes (carbon and boron) because the
buckyballs trapped the light energy.

Decker Yeadon, Carbon Nanotube Gripper
Fingers. Courtesy of Decker Yeadon.
Nanostructures are designed and tested using
advanced molecular modeling software.
Decker Yeadon uses NanoEngineer, a software
developed by Nanorex Inc., to examine and
develop various molecular components for
projects. The original version of their nBots
project features tiny fingers that enable the
nanorobotic devices to grab onto each other
and self-assemble into objects. This cross-
section shows three carbon nanotube fingers
that can rotate on a molecular bearing wrist.

Decker Yeadon, Rotaxane molecular motor.
Courtesy of Decker Yeadon.
Rotaxanes are light-driven motors which
have a ring molecule (shown near the center)
that moves back and forth along the shaft
of another molecule. The two bulbous ends
prevent the ring from moving off the shaft. The
most recent version of Decker Yeadon's nBots
project uses modified rotaxanes as molecular
muscles, to enable the tiny robots to move and
flex. Two rotaxanes are bonded, end-to-end,
and have two rings that use tethers to attach to
flexible molecular beams.

has led to extensive environmental degradation, to the point where we have to retreat to the interior of architecture to find salvation. It is neither love nor the bomb, but the environment that will bring us together.

Like a large HAZMAT suit, Pelosi's building relies on a multi-layer nanofiltration membrane to protect us from harmful UV rays and filter contaminants out of the polluted air and rainwater. Spatially inverting our relationship to our environment, he locates a pure, "natural" environment inside the envelope, while keeping our man-made environment outside. Ironically, the environmental devastation is the product of the same technological advancements that we have come to rely on. Here, technological pursuits are both the problem and the solution, and the project satirizes the folly of man, wherein we have convinced ourselves that we are capable of environmental stewardship, despite overwhelming evidence to the contrary.

Both Pelosi and IwamotoScott parlay their knowledge of current nanomaterials research into useful propositions that help us envision some of the future implications of nanotechnology. Their work signals a shift from the mores of reinvention to a culture of invention, and, in many respects, is made no less difficult by scientists' predisposition toward cautious predictions. That is not to say, however, that nanotechnology has not cultivated its own visionaries in the scientific community. The rise of novel materials with atomic precision has been complemented by many concurrent developments in nanoscale machines, which has generated some adventurous predictions for the future. From nanorobotic environments, to bitstreams in the bloodstream, to desktop nanofactories, the potential of molecular machines seems vast, unimaginable, and full of strange magic. Many of the propositions may seem inconceivable, but it is not unusual for technological prophecies to be considered unattainable for some time before they are shown to be possible, and then realized. It was not that long ago that flying at supersonic speeds would have been considered impossible.

When K. Eric Drexler's *Engines of Creation* popularized nanotechnology more than 20 years ago, it also laid down the visionary roots for molecular machines. The book spawned

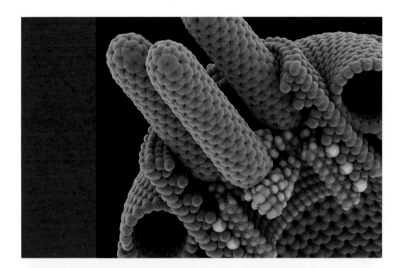

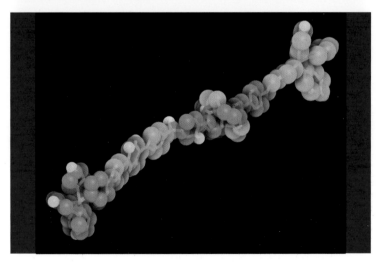

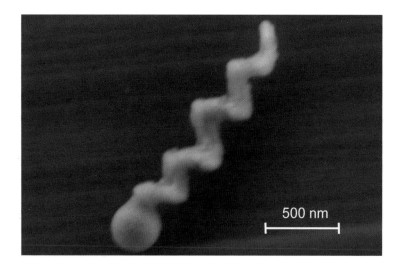

500 nm

the idea that nanotechnology would eventually enable us to make self-replicating nanoscale devices, and that a factory of nanobots could manufacture products from the bottom up, atom-by-atom, molecule-by-molecule, from a reservoir of stock chemical elements. Many researchers have been working on advancing these ideas, even while their detractors have claimed that it would be impossible to make such tiny machines with such precision.[7] But there is an abundance of evidence for molecular manufacturing around us, and perhaps precision is not as important as redundancy. Given the right conditions, a potato will make a potato. It is not an exact copy, but it is basically the same. We can replicate too, of course, and eventually perform activities that can be somewhat useful. Molecular machines are constantly replacing the cells in our bodies.

Globally, hundreds of molecular machines and devices are currently being designed and developed, many with a particular task in mind. Researchers have built single-molecule gears, switches, axles, wheels, brakes, rotors, locks, and rack-and-pinion systems (ills. pp. 142-146). They have made many different types of molecular motors, for single-molecule nanocars and other machines, that produce no waste, can rotate objects 10,000 times their size, and are approaching the speed of biological machines. Molecular machines have been taught to twist, bend, flex, lift, swim, swarm, steer, walk, and even pick up other molecules and transport them to a different location, like tiny molecular couriers.

Although some of these molecular machines might appear to be similar to their large industrial counterparts, they are quite unlike anything we have engineered before and can perform in ways that are utterly unprecedented. Our firm is interested in how clusters of roxatanes, for example, can be used as powerful actuator assemblies that flex like muscles, but produce no waste. These molecular machines consist of two interlocking molecules. One molecule has a dumbbell configuration, with a slender shaft of atoms and two bulbous stoppers at each end. The second molecule is a ring that entirely surrounds the shaft, but is not chemically bonded to the shaft and cannot slip off it due to the stoppers. By stimulating rotaxanes with controlled light, or electricity, the ring follows an excited electron as it jumps back

Decker Yeadon, nBots assembling into structures. Courtesy of Decker Yeadon. These movie stills show an array of rotaxanes/beams positioned directly below a sheet of graphene, which serves as the skin of each nBot. The graphene is bonded to the flexible beams and wrinkles like skin as the rotaxane muscles deform the beams and cause the whole assembly to contract. The nBots are soft, sticky, and wet. To stick to each other, they take advantage of van der Waals molecular forces provided by carbon nanotubes, which are similar to the setae and spatulae found on the toe of a gecko (ill. p.133). The nanotube hairs are strategically located so that each nBot can curl its arms to (re)attach to its neighbor, quickly building up mass, objects, and environments that can change in their appearance and bulk properties.

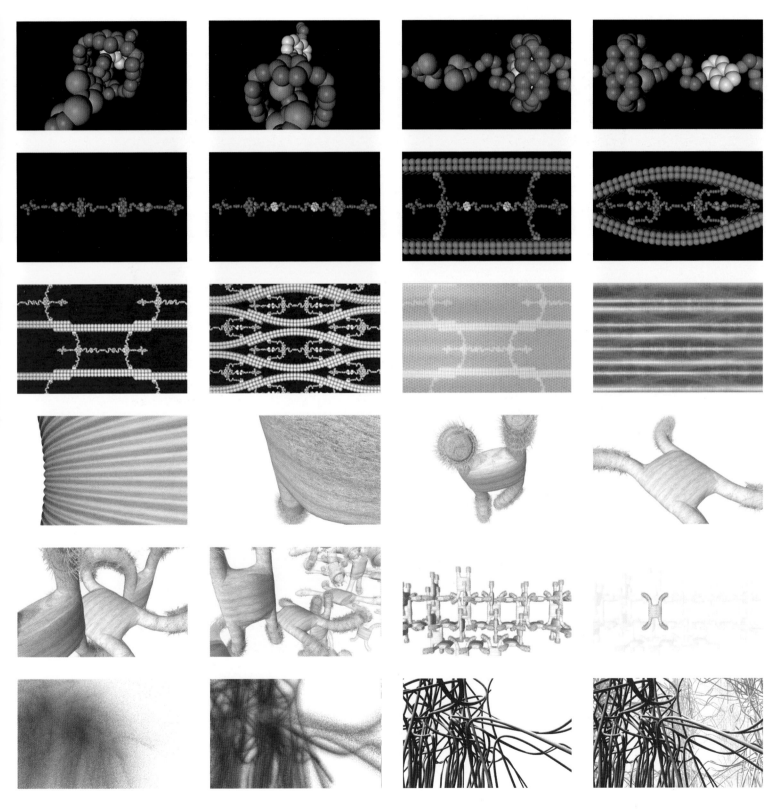

Folding DNA into twisted and curved nanoscale shapes. Hendrik Dietz, Shawn M. Douglas, and William M. Shih. From *Science* 325:725 (2009). Figure S5. Reprinted with permission from AAAS.

The programmability of DNA has led to numerous recent developments in nanotechnology. Here we see gears with twelve teeth that have been constructed by DNA. The DNA makes complex shapes by twisting and bending the molecules so that they self-assemble into useful forms.

and forth, from one location to another along the shaft. Here, a simple functionalized material is transformed into a complex device, wherein it is its own sensor, processor, and actuator.

Rotaxanes form the musculature of some tiny robotic devices that we are currently designing, called nBots, wherein they are positioned as an array directly beneath a skin of graphene (ills. p. 145). Our nBots would self-assemble into objects and environments, like the hard-bodied Foglets proposed by Dr. J. Storrs Hall, however the nBots would use carbon nanotube setae on their bodies to stick to each other, rather than mechanical grippers. Quite unlike Foglets, the nBots are soft, sticky, and wet, and they represent some recent thinking on the future of nanomachines. In particular, the first advanced nanobots will likely be wet, and will likely be made of biological components.

Researchers have already made enzyme-powered engines for nanomachines, which produce oxygen to cause nanotubes to move. They have created enzyme locks that open and close in response to visible and UV light, and they have engineered kinesin molecular motors that can pick up, transport, and deliver cargo. But, by far, the greatest interest and excitement is in DNA-based nanomachines, because DNA is programmable. Researchers can program DNA to bend and twist into complex shapes to make nanoscale components, and they have engineered a number of DNA nanomachines that can walk on surfaces. A DNA molecular motor has been realized, which changes shape in response to wavelengths of light, and DNA robotic arms are becoming increasingly capable of performing many tasks, including fabrication.

In fact, DNA-based nanotechnology has been used to fabricate materials and devices since 2006. Robotic arms can capture and maneuver other molecules and nanoparticles, and DNA nanofabricators have successfully manufactured other DNA machines that can walk. "The use of DNA to assemble nanomaterials is one of the first steps toward using biological molecules as a manufacturing tool," said Adam Lazareck, a researcher at Brown University, back in 2006. "If you want to make something, turn to Mother Nature. From skin to sea shells, remarkable structures are engineered using DNA."[8]

All of this is to speculate that, within this century, a designer might be able to use a desktop nanofactory to design and fabricate materials and devices, atom-by-atom, molecule-by-molecule. The domestication of atoms will certainly provide new opportunities for invention, but it will also have tremendous implications for architecture and society. What is the value of something, for example, if you can use molecular manufacturing to make an exact copy with such precision? By comparison, our current techniques for making architecture are still very crude; even our most advanced methods can be thought of as incremental improvements on cutting, shaping, casting, and placing bulk materials. In a way, that self-assembling beard is vastly more advanced. We will have no precedents to "reinvent" in the age of molecular manufacturing, but we will have a new opportunity to invent, and we can take some pride in knowing that we have also made that unwanted hair.

Notes

1. Professor Norio Taniguchi, at Tokyo Science University, first defined "nanotechnology" as consisting mainly of "the processing of separation, consolidation, and deformation of materials by one atom or by one molecule," in his paper titled "On the Basic Concept of 'Nano-Technology,'" in *Proceedings of the International Conference on Production Engineering, Part II.* Tokyo: Japan Society of Precision Engineering, 1974. pp. 18-23.
2. The stated resolution is based on the TEAM 0.5 transmission electron aberration-corrected microscope at Lawrence Berkeley National Lab's National Center for Electron Microscopy.
3. This quote was taken from "Nanostructures to Buildings: Generating an Architecture of Crystal Geometries," an abstract prepared by: Benjamin Aranda, Daniel Bosia, and Chris Lasch for: *NLSO (Non-Linear Systems Organization)*, University of Pennsylvania School of Design, October 10, 2005. http://www.design.upenn.edu/new/arch/nlso/NSO%20sponsored%20research.pdf [Accessed August 20, 2009].
4. *Ibid.*
5. Low public awareness of nanotechnology was reported in the Woodrow Wilson International Center for Scholars *News Release* no. 84-07, "Poll Reveals Public Awareness of Nanotech Stuck at Low Level," September 25, 2007. With a growing database of over 2000 postings, Nanoarchitecture.net has been the leading resource of information for architects and designers.
6. Pugno, Nicola M. "Macroscopic Invisible Cables" in *Microsyst Technol* 15 (2009). pp. 175-180; DOI: 10.1007/s00542-008-0653-9.
7. Chang, Kenneth. "Yes, They Can! No, They Can't: Charges Fly in Nanobot Debate" in *The New York Times*, December 9, 2003.
8. "Brown Engineers Use DNA to Direct Nanowire Assembly and Growth" in *Brown University Media Relations Press Release*, July 10, 2006. http://www.brown.edu/Administration/News_Bureau/2006-07/06-003.html [Accessed July 24, 2006].

Encoding
Digital & Analogue Taxonavigation

Liat Margolis

Lee-Su Huang and Gregory Thomas Spaw, Osnap!, installation at the Harvard University Graduate School of Design, Cambridge, Massachusetts, USA, 2009, vacuformed PETG plastic laminated with laser-etched dichroic film (3M's Radiant Light Film), detail.

Immersed in a surge of hyper-materialism, we find ourselves vacillating between our commitments to ultra-performance and environmental responsibility, and our fascinations with irreverent material mutations, outrageous morphologies, and sensorial maximalism of luxury and effect. Whichever fixation prevails, new materials – from self-cleaning glass, electroluminescent films, photocatalytic, ductile, self-repairing, and porous cements, to ultra-insulating foamed aluminum, and super-absorbent polymers that can rapidly soak up toxic spills – have launched us into a vortex of "hyperchoice" [1] and infinite material dialogues.

Inventions on the molecular level of material composition on one hand, and the influx of technologies that allow new aesthetic and performance possibilities on the other, have positioned contemporary materials in a perpetual future tense. This gluttony of material options and cravings for novelty have given rise to the contemporary models of material collections and classification systems. And while these new mechanisms of material research are largely contingent on technological prowess, they are also profoundly invested in the procedure of technological knowledge transfer – a cross-disciplinary exchange of often unrelated fields. Both those tenets are the basis for the content of material collections; and insist on new delineations and new ways of interrelating data in order to further dissolve the limitations created by conventional disciplinary boundaries.

The profusion of materials today and their frequent adaptation from one industry to another exhibit a certain resistance to architectural classification systems, such as the Construction Specification Institute (CSI), whose underlying code is dominated by predetermined architectural applications. If design innovation is reliant in part on hyperchoice and technology transfer, then material classification necessitates a flexible indexing structure that would link their intrinsic properties to a diversity of applications and hence transcend the "classificatory pigeonholes" [2] of architectural conventions. How do we organize a unified physical archive of contemporary material specimens that may originate in fashion, civil engineering, automotive and biomedical design? How do we inter-relate taxonomy distinct

to metallurgy, polymer science, and botany, such that it can generate cross-pollination among disciplines? And what is the relevance of material classification to the process of design as well as pedagogy?

Newness

An illustrated lexicon of current praxis, *The Metapolis Dictionary of Advanced Architecture* (2003), poses that in the context of information technology, which requires and facilitates new approaches to the conception of architecture and cities, architects cannot rely solely on the professional standardized conventions, but rather on innovation in design and the application of new techniques and materials. [3] The authors call for a relational and non-linear format for their dictionary in order to interlink distinct conceptual frameworks – "a matrix of terms, a mesh of codes" that is open to cross-referencing and allows for a shift in architectural culture. [4] They state: "If, in fact, the emergence of the new is almost invariably a cause of uncertainty (precisely because we do not know how to label it, and thus the difficulty of isolating the signs that are its expression and identifying the relationships of those signs with the existing ones) this necessary conceptual reactivation (and redefinition) of language is indispensable for a prospective action that does not stop at establishing a collection of fixed (and all encompassing) labels." [5] For instance, the *Metapolis Dictionary* permanently encodes our contemporary association between the term "blur" and the Diller and Scofidio Blur Building at the 2002 Swiss Expo in Yverdon.

Taxonavigation in design and architecture, much like the contemporary preoccupation with tagging, labeling, blogging, and wikiing has become integral to praxis and pedagogy. More recently, founders of Paris-based material library matériO, Daniel Kula and Élodie Ternaux, continue to acknowledge the pervasive interest in a synthetic and relational data structure, and more specifically expose a primary quandary (as well as the primary motivation to their own work) concerning the polysemy, or lexical ambiguity of material nomenclature. In their book *Materiology* (2008) they eagerly admit: "One of the main difficulties in understanding the concept of matter is

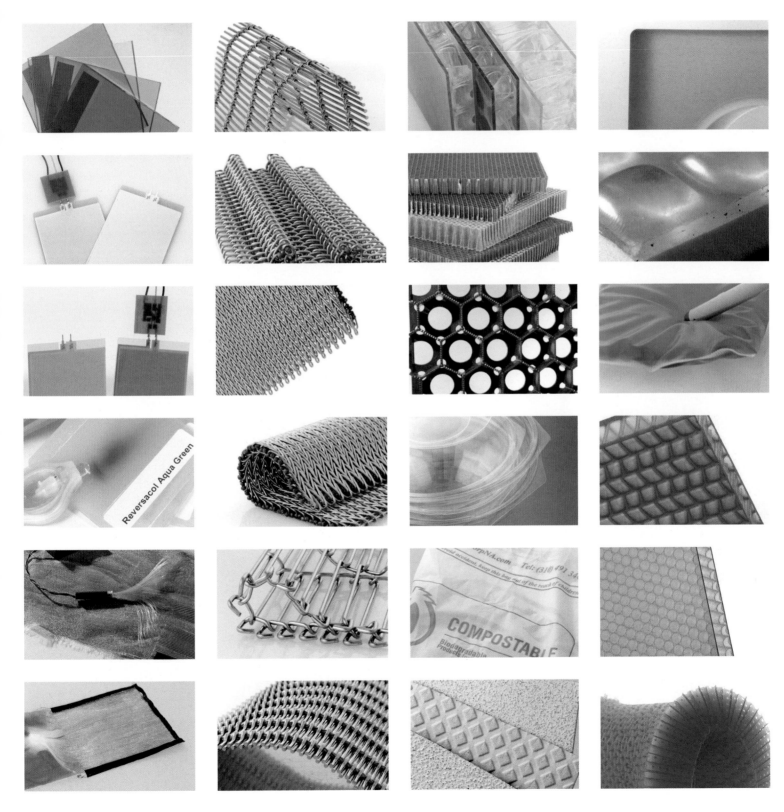

Harvard University Graduate School of Design,
Materials Collection online database search
options: by Form (Mesh) and by Properties
(Corrosion-Resistant), screenshots.

that it requires many tools which do not all employ the same level of language and approach… Matter can be experienced through sensory perception, technical description, scientific theory, or a philosophical approach – so many possibilities which inextricably overlap elements of different definition."[6]

In the context of this book's title, *Material Design*, "material" is similarly predicated on the notion that it is simultaneously matter – an alchemy of the periodical table; and meaning – that which accrues behavioral descriptors according to their ever-changing empirical or theoretical contexts. Therefore, "materiality" is not only synonymous with structural and aesthetic categories, but is also aligned with evolving theoretical positions on the perceived or potential role of materials in contemporary culture. Whether sensorial, ideological (e.g. sustainability), structural, performative (e.g. bioremediation, self-repair), economically viable, new or outmoded, material meaning is mutable. Consequently, the format of the contemporary material collections has been structured to facilitate ongoing feedback loops between the inauguration of new materials and the redefinition of design forms, processes, and culture.

This techno-cultural feedback loop can be identified, for instance, in Kula and Ternaux's description of the concurrent development of polymeric elasticity alongside the fascination with softness: "Often defined as an opposite, being soft ('not hard') has become a sought-after quality. Soft-to-the-touch keyboards and other ergonomically designed controls, shoes, and even automotive interiors, use flexible and casual shapes, and reactive materials such as 'memory' foam or medical gel… An intermediary state *par excellence*, neither solid, nor liquid, 'soft' has never deserved much scientific attention before now. Scientists were always far too busy studying those states of matter deemed 'fundamentally noble'. New areas of exploration are now tentatively opening up, into this transition between phases, a more adapted-adaptive response. Is this perhaps a fourth state of matter? A highly ambiguous state, it provokes attraction and repulsion, sparks irresponsible tactile temptation and hides unexpected depths. Nasty or nice? Softness fascinates us because it is reminiscent of life".[7]

Material ConneXion, New York, New York,
USA, material archives and samples.

Material ConneXion, Cologne, Germany,
material archives and samples.

iMatter, Holon, Israel,
material archives and samples.

Implicit then in the advent of technological agility are contemporary policies and cultural intrigues such as softness, transparency, ultra-lightweight, optical elusiveness, and biodegradability, to name a few. Although scientists and engineers insist on the objectivity of material facts, it is evident that the reverse holds true; the mutability of material meaning and relevance lies in recontextualization.[8] With the widespread topic of sustainability, for instance, environmental testing and performance specifications have become more available, which in turn have made our environmental eloquence in design more explicit. Furthermore, it was the urgency of environmental concerns and policies in the last 20 years that has driven giant plastic manufacturers to materialize the polymerization of starch from beets and corn and the manufacturing of biodegradable plastics. Once we enable a deviation from architectural classifications, new considerations arise, new testing parameters and qualitative performances are identified, and design language expands. Recontextualization is the material collector's recipe to incite innovation.

Genre: Unclassifiable

The CSI MasterFormat has prevailed as the standard classification and specification system for over 50 years in the USA. It organizes materials hierarchically, according to firstly, generic materials groupings such as paint, laminate, and concrete, and secondly, according to components or systems. According to Michelle Addington and Daniel Schodek these categories are not material- or performance-specific – such that the category of windows, for instance, includes multiple materials (e.g. wood, vinyl, aluminum, or steel) – thus giving primacy to applications and common uses. Properties are solely considered in the context of codes and requirements for preconceived applications. For example, wood is discussed only according to its suitability for load-bearing roof structures or flooring; doors are organized according to their suitability for security, fire protection, egress, or by the distinction between commercial or residential use.[9]

The hierarchical and linear information structure limits the possibility of unexpected solutions. For instance, woven stainless steel conveyor belts would typically be categorized under Conveying Equipment; a category one may not think to explore for the purpose of building facades, doors, or wall structures. And yet, the widespread use of metal meshes that originate in the conveyor belt industry have enabled many important architectural projects, including those of Dominique Perrault at the Bibliothèque Nationale de France in Paris and the Olympic Velodrome and Swimming Pool in Berlin, as well as the work of Studio Morsa at the Comme des Garçons shop in New York. Instead, the material collection system lists the conveyor belts according to multiple searchable attributes including: material content (metal), form/structure (mesh), fabrication process (woven), and properties (flexible, corrosion-resistant).

Addington and Schodek assert that conventional architectural codes are not intended to engender innovation. Rather, they are practical templates for communication between architects, contractors, fabricators, and suppliers.[10] Hence materials are relegated strictly to specifications at the end of the design process rather than utilizing material investigations as an iterative and generative process to design development. The peripheral consequences of a specification-driven system generally are the exclusion of new and unusual material technologies due to an emphasis on liability and known entities. Addington and Schodek state: "For many uses, codes and standards explicitly or implicitly identify acceptable materials, leaving the architect only to select between brands."[11]

The departure from conventional classification systems began with Material ConneXion Inc. (MC), which in 1996 established an unprecedented material library and consulting service, after which a number of commercial and academic institutions followed suit to both leverage and alleviate the urgent demand for the latest developments in materials (ills. pp. 153, 154, 170). The context to MC was Ezio Manzini's 1986 book *The Material of Invention*, as well as two seminal exhibitions – "Mondo Materialis," organized by MC's founder George Beylerian for the Steelcase Design Partnership in 1990,[12] and "Mutant Materials," curated by MoMA's Paula Antonelli in 1994.

Both exhibitions set forth an unprecedented emphasis to materials and their mutable truths. *Mutant Materials*[13] in particular was first to curate projects according to material composition (e.g. glass, plastic, ceramic) and performance (e.g. photochromism, elasticity, shape-memory). For the first time featured on pedestals were items such as 3M Privacy Film (liquid crystal film) laminated onto glass, manufactured by Vitracon in 1991 and designed to change its opacity from transparent to opaque upon being exposed to an electric field. Also featured was "Mobil" Container Systems, designed by Antonio Citterio for Kartell S.p.a. in 1993, and made of thermoplastic polymer that was fabricated to look like sand-blasted glass. The focus of the exhibit was on the designers' material use as much as on their "material misuse."[14] And although the show included everything from chairs to lighting to medical devices, the unifying sensorial tactility gave proof to the time's technological material triumphs.

Material Collections

MC was the first attempt to break away from the standard CSI system and develop a new database model for material classification based in properties and processes. It positioned itself as the link between designers, material scientists, and the manufacturing industry, which then lacked a physical and digital forum in which to do so. The multi-disciplinary research platform was established intentionally to be relevant to many design fields ranging from architecture to fashion in order to promote a blurring of disciplinary boundaries. With a current collection of over 5,000 material samples, a gallery space, and a magazine called *Matter*, this modern-day *Wunderkammer*[15] has opened the floodgates for the cultural fetishism of material collection, and articulated the crossover of disciplines through a reconstituted classification system.

The curatorial aspect has been consistently rooted in the identification and acquisition of the techno-culturally "new and innovative." This premise consists of three main criteria: literally new; new to the design fields; and conceptually aligned with current thematic streams, such as the interest in cellular structures and biomorphic geometries as featured in the seminal publication *Emergence: Morphogenetic Design*

Lee-Su Huang and Gregory Thomas Spaw,
Osnap!, installation at the Harvard University
Graduate School of Design, Cambridge,
Massachusetts, USA, 2009,
assembly sequence.

Strategies,[16] or in *Praxis, Journal of Writing + Building* in the issue titled "Expanding Surface" about the works of Andrew Kudless of Matsys. In this context, MC typically identifies widespread or emerging dialogues in design and re-calibrates its acquisitions accordingly. In other cases, its content influences new explorations in design. For instance, cellular structures, ranging from honeycomb and multi-core panels to aluminum foam and reticulated polymer foams, have occupied the shelves of many collections since 1997. Inspired by such samples, both the material developers Panelite (whose work is described later on in this chapter) and OMA's material researcher Chris van Duijn explored a series of cellular wall structures based on the geometry of a sponge for flexible clothes display systems in the New York and Los Angeles Prada Stores.[17]

Another example for the departure from conventional material classification systems is the Materials Collection at Harvard University's Graduate School of Design (GSD) (ills. pp. 150-152, 162). Founded in 2003, it is largely based on the same approach. The principal difference to MC is its aim to curate materiality in conjunction with the pedagogy and current discourse at the GSD. Set forth is an objective to utilize material technology research as a forum for curricular developments, publications, conferences, seminars, and prototyping (ills. pp. 149, 156, 157, 160). Much like the Material ConneXion system, the Materials Collection's physical archive and online database are designed as a cross-referenced categorization system. Additionally, the research conducted within the school's design studios and seminars feeds back into the Collection, creating an institutional archive of material trends and critical thought.

Today, material collections can be found in many locations throughout the world: MC has locations in New York, Milan, Cologne, Bangkok, and Daegu. Since 2002 matériO has established locations in Paris, Antwerp, and Barcelona. Materia launched their material center in Holland; iMatter opened in 2007 in Holon, Israel (ill. p. 154); the Swiss equivalent Material Archiv was launched in 2008; all of these are based on the premise of providing a liaison between design, industry, and science through consulting services. Therefore, each physical

location is often affiliated with other commercial or cultural associations to leverage local networks and catalyze economic and cultural development. Many of these membership-based organizations are also affiliated with academic institutions. Most offer academic membership packages, which grant access to the entire student body within an academic institution, and in some cases a custom selection of the physical library, according to the school's curricular focus, is duplicated and installed onsite. Some schools, such as the GSD, the University of Texas in Austin, and the Parsons School of Design, have established their own physical sample libraries and in some cases have also developed their own databases, independent of their memberships, with some of the above-mentioned services.

What is unique about the new models of material collections is that their subscribers come from different fields, which effectively produces a natural cross-pollination through their design requirements and field-specific terminologies. As the Material Research Director at Material ConneXion, I conducted research for BMW's automotive design team, who investigated textile-embedded sensor technologies and responsive textiles as an alternative solution for the metal car body. In the same period, I consulted for Target, who was developing a new line of electronics with Philips Electronics and Motorola Corporation; and for the cosmetics company AVEDA, who mandated environmentally responsible materials for their cosmetic product packaging. Two years later, Target launched their Iridescent Evolution using ChromaFlair, an iridescent coating that is widely used in the automotive industry; AVEDA introduced a new line of cosmetics utilizing a composite plastic that contains 70% agricultural byproducts such as coconut fibers and wheat husk.

Another important aspect to the collections is the physical material archive, whose format is designed to allow for material adjacencies that are at times completely unexpected. For instance, on the same shelf at Harvard's Materials Collection in the polymer section, one may find a View Control Film that was developed for automatic teller machines, and ethylene tetrafluoro-ethylene (ETFE) film that was originally designed as a release film for semiconductor and aerospace coatings. Using conventional cataloguing systems that are application-

Lee-Su Huang and Gregory Thomas Spaw,
Osnap!

based, those two films would never sit adjacent, or appear on the same database search results. In fact, those films may never even be part of a conventional architecture material library. However, both those films have been shifted from the periphery of architectural applications to the very center of inquiry in the last ten years. For example, View Control Film, which changes its transparency upon the viewer's angle, was used for the storefront window of Issey Miyake's Pleats Please boutique in SoHo, New York, designed by Toshiko Mori Architect in 1998. ETFE film is now legendary for its application in the 4,000 cushion panels (100,000 m² of Texlon® ETFE produced by Vector-Foiltec) on the 2008 Beijing Olympic Swimming Center ("Water Cube"), designed by PTW Architects and Arup. Compared to glass, ETFE is 1% the weight, transmits more light, is a better insulator, and costs 24 to 70% less to install. It is also resilient (able to bear 400 times its own weight, with an estimated 50-year lifespan), recyclable, and, like Teflon®, it is non-stick, non-staining and therefore requires no cleaning. A search in a conventional architectural material database for cladding materials would result in the ubiquitous glass, wood, metal, while a chance encounter (via the physical or digital archives) with a film, such as photovoltaic, photochromic, light interference, view control, or electroluminescent films, may revolutionize the meaning of the basic categories of how we make sense of materiality.

Analogue

Three key attributes define the physical material collection. The first is its immersive tangibility; its visual and tactile actuality. A common critique, particularly by engineers is that the selection of materials is strictly based on sensorial characteristics.[18] I would argue, however, that sensorial immediacy, experimentation and testing, prototyping and juxtaposing palettes of materials are essential to the design process even if this reduces certain elements of utility or efficiency made possible with the CSI database. Similarly, analogue modeling is at times most effective for the development of a design idea, despite the accessibility of sophisticated parametric digital programs. For instance, the visual effect of a dichroic-coated glass – where the light spectrum is simultaneously transmitted and reflected – is much better understood when visually experienced, rather than strictly read as a text. Furthermore, one could even argue that if designers would encounter the term dichroic in the database they might possibly disregard it, because the term is unfamiliar. Conversely, the visual intrigue may pique designers' interest to further examine the benefits associated with dichroic glass and also to discover its prevalent use in projects by designers such as James Carpenter.

This leads to the second aspect of the material sample library, which lies in the concept of displaying materials out of their conventional context. This format allows the designer to decontextualize materials from their typical associations in order to derive new ideas from their physical attributes. For instance, originating in the aerospace industry, the super-insulating Aerogel technology is now frequently used for high-performance sportswear and architectural panels; gabion cages typically used to stabilize eroding slopes form the temperature- and light-regulating permeable *brise-soleil* walls of Herzog & de Meuron's Dominus Winery in Napa Valley, California; geotextiles and bioengineering are now commonly integral to greenroof structures, such as in the case of the California Academy of Sciences in San Francisco by Renzo Piano Building Workshop and SWA. In similar manner Kurt W. Forster writes about the work of Herzog & de Meuron: "The transcendent quality Herzog & de Meuron seek in materials must spring from within a project after those materials have been removed from where they normally occur or have been divested of the purpose for which they are customarily employed. Within the tight matrix of utility and convention, materials offer no resistance. Only when altered or removed from the field of conventional reference can materials assume a specifically architectural purpose. It is precisely, and solely, from the discrepancy between their familiar purpose and newly invented ones that materials acquire character."[19]

The evolution of the translucent honeycomb panels by Panelite is an outcome of decontextualization. While graduate students at Columbia University, company founders Emmanuelle Bourlier and Christian Mittman sought a translucent, structural yet ultra-lightweight panel material they could use as a pivoting wall for a residential pool house. At MC, they found honeycomb panels, which are typically used for the construction of the airplane wing. This composite honeycomb core interlayer, sandwiched between two metal sheets, answered their need for a high-strength-to-weight ratio, but did not comply with their vision of translucency. During the same search in the library, they also came across a translucent fiberglass panel and decided to "material design" their own panel by taking only the honeycomb core and developing a now patented adhesive technology to laminate translucent sheets. Shortly after, Panelite was formed not only as the manufacturer of honeycomb panels, but also as a material designer who works with architectural firms to research and develop new materials. For example, the honeycomb composites now clad the Student Center at the Illinois Institute of Technology by Rem Koolhaas/OMA (ills.).

The third assertion about material collections is that they should be driven and guided by the intellectual trajectories and experimental objectives of their subscribers, whether professional or pedagogical. Once again, it is crucial to distinguish material collections from specification systems, whose contents are based on industry advertisement, by their sheer autonomy to be shaped according to their distinct interests and cultural contexts, rather than by financial interdependence to industry. However, self-directing independence is not all that I refer to, but rather more importantly, the proficiency of the institution and its material curators' ability to evolve the content according to their dedicated identification of contemporaneous ideas and agenda. Perhaps not unlike the *Wunderkammer*, the frenzied and indiscriminate compilation of material specimens today necessitates a percipient curatorial process, whose expertise in discerning between the banal and the unusual to uncover today's "Age of Explorations" is on a par with with astute observations of trend-forecasting firms and design critics. At Material ConneXion, the curatorial method enlists a jury of various acclaimed designers each month to deliberate on the inclusion of recently acquired materials. It is because the objects of fascination speak of meaning and significance to current design dialogues that the material objects facilitate a forum of discussion.

In fact, this materialist discourse has persistently gained credibility in the last dozen years so that in 2007 MC began

Beatrice Saraga, Wileen Kao, VERTical,
installation at the Harvard Graduate School
of Design, Cambridge, Massachusetts, USA,
2007, fabrication, detail.

R&Sie, Lost in Paris House, Paris, France, 2008,
interior, detail.

its own excellence awards for material innovation in design (e.g. Kennedy & Violich Architecture) and materials (e.g. Concrete Canvas's Concrete Cloth, a cement-impregnated flexible fabric technology). MC then formed a partnership with McDonough Braungart Design Chemistry, LLC (MBDC), and the Environmental Protection Encouragement Agency (EPEA) in 2009 to offer the patented Cradle to Cradle^{SM} material development services to manufacturers in order to optimize closed-loop industrial cycles. Similar to the professional model, the GSD Materials Collection was conceived as a laboratory, a forum for experimentation and installations, curricular development, publications, exhibitions, independent studies, and thesis preparations. It is seen as an extension of the curricular activities, and as a hybrid structure of "library" and "lab," which is intentionally situated between the library and the wood/CAD-CAM/laser cutting workshops. An investigation of natural and polymeric geotextiles for erosion control, for example, resulted in a prototype of a vertical green wall to test containment systems for soil-less media such as coconut fibers, Hydrogel (super-absorbent) fabric, and expanded shale. Such a speculative platform presents the potential for further affiliations with engineering and material science faculties in order to perform proper testing and patent new products.

Digital

Sanford Kwinter writes in his introduction to Reiser Umamoto's *Atlas of Novel Tectonics*: "When a tree is configured to function as a wood column or beam, it is one set of properties of cellulose that is selected for expression; or more properly, it is the geometry of vascular bundling that selects the properties of cellulose and conveys their felicitous rigidities and flexibilities to the macroscopic scale of the building itself. On the other hand, when a tree is configured into a log for burning, it is the fire itself – that exists already inside of the wood, only dormant or infinitely slowed – that is selected for expression or release. These two forms of expression, chemical and tectonic, are of exactly the same order of physical reality. It is a testimony to the diagram's action that such diverse properties can be called up and released. And it is no small revolution in design to have apprehended this simple but critical fraternity."[20]

Within the database, the decoding of attributes includes lists of terms associated with material composition (e.g. metal, polymer, ceramic, glass); commodity form or structure (e.g. sheet, roll, liquid, textile); process by which the material was fabricated (e.g. extruded, CNC-routed, spun-bonded, thermoformed, woven 3D); and properties, behavioral characteristics and specific attributes (e.g. anti-static, magneto-rheological, nutrient-providing, UV-resistant). This allows for a compound search by any combination of the listed attributes. The selected terms are then hyper-linked to allow cross-navigation.

For example, a search that begins with the term "film" under the category of "form" may result a wide selection of film types, one of which is 3M™ Optical Lighting Film, a transparent polycarbonate prismatic film used to transport and distribute light uniformly in lighting. Its prismatic microstructure is associated with the term "reflective," under the category of "property," then hyper-linked. By clicking on the term "reflective," a new set of materials results, which includes a variety of reflective materials that are not necessarily films, one of which are retro-reflective glass micro-spheres that are used for crosswalk safety markings. While the effect of the white stripes as they retro-reflect upon interaction with car headlights is a commonly known effect, other than road engineers and installers, very few are familiar with the glass beads, or know about their unique process of fabrication.

The clinical (detailed yet detached) dissection of material properties allows for a focus on the specific singularities (properties) and idiosyncratic nature of materials, while at the same time allowing for a "de-specialization"[21] of matter in terms of its prescribed applications; the result of which produces unpredictable solutions. Seen from this perspective, all materials become exceptions to the rule, or in other words, new and innovative. In time, "new" becomes routine, fundamental, or sometimes archaic. In fact, I would argue that the chronological newness of materials is a relatively inconsequential factor of innovation against the process of taxonavigation across the rhizomatic network of data, which provides for infinite pathways of information access and endless sets of interrelation.

1:1

Alongside data decoding, the photographic display of each material specimen – zooming in to emphasize its grain and microstructure – allows for a scrutinizing of their evidence of formation beyond their totality as a ready-made product for application. In other words, in presenting materials as artifacts with inherent matrices, patterns, and behavioral principles we open up a potential scalar projection of their microstructure to formulate architectural space. The decontextualization of materials from an architectural scale formulates a 1:1 materialist praxis and pedagogy – a scale-lessness that provokes the abstraction of those principles, and likewise, the extrapolation to other scales, other materials, other contexts.

With that in mind, an equally important objective of the accretion of material taxonomy is the appropriation of terminology to generate metaphors for design operations. Publications such as The *Function of Ornament*[22] by Farshid Moussavi and Michael Kubo, and *Tooling*[23] by Aranda/Lasch are two of many examples where operations and structures serve as analytical methods of structural performance and visual effect, or as the articulation of order in computation-driven design. The *Function of Ornament* offers three systems of classification concerning depth, material, and effect. The building's organization is generated by the identified index of operations and fabrication techniques, which then defines the effect and function of facades and thus gives legitimacy to a new kinship of architectural typologies. Neither scientific, nor technologically accurate, the lexicon of material operations in this case is appropriated for a dismantling of the conventional reading of facades, and for the assertion of a functional order of material geometry.

Similarly, the categories of algorithmic techniques outlined within Aranda/Lasch's book *Tooling* – Spiraling, Packing, Weaving, Blending, Cracking, Flocking, and Tiling – address the moments where the formless matter (pre-material) enters the realm of substance and organization (material). The taxonomical indexing, to which they refer as a recipe for programmatic computer code, delineates a procedural thinking for the

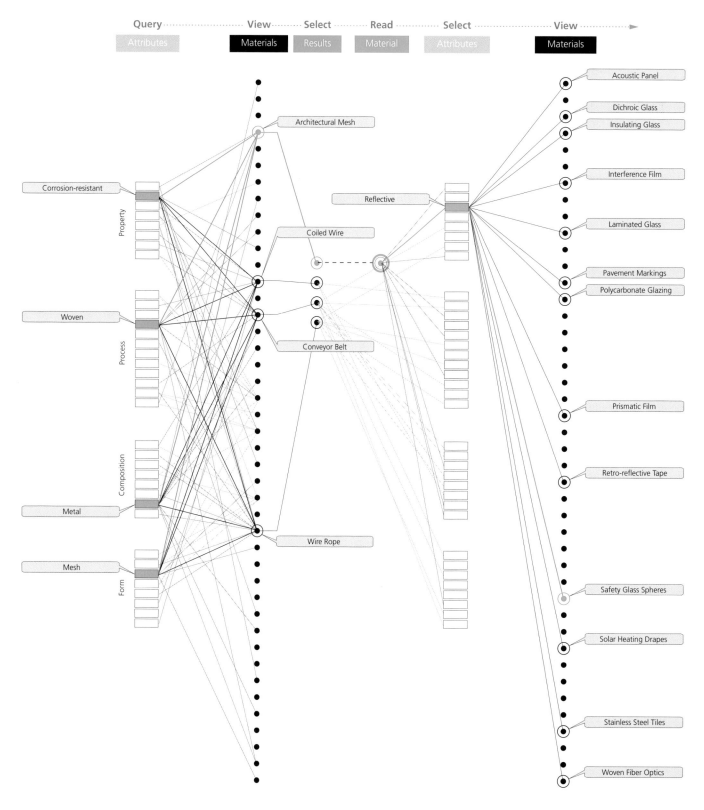

properties of their geometries. While the algorithm automates the emergence of shapes, the categorical articulation of the process generates design fodder. "Spiraling produces a shape unlike any other because it is seldom experienced as geometry, but rather as energy." The distinction of the form/shape of a spiral from its emergence – "the evidence of a shape in formation" – allows for yet another definition of materiality, a becoming of form onto itself through processes of fabrication.[24]

Taxonavigation suggests a model whereby the agency of materialism relies upon the premise of speculation rather than specification, in order to transcend the normative perception of material as a mere commodity product. The objective of the contemporary material collections is to give designers both the language and the means to dialogue with scientists and manufacturers and actively influence technological trajectories. Equally paramount is the ambition to generate distinct and prolific scholarship concerning materialism, such that it can interchange between its technical and theoretical constructs and consequently provoke invention. It is therefore essential to frame materialism as inherent to the design process, and as such employ open-ended tools that can elaborate upon this particular relationship and likewise, elicit latent ones.

Notes

1. Kula, Daniel, and Élodie Ternaux (matériO). "Reflections on Hyperchoice" and "De natura materiae" in *Materiology: The Creative's Guide to Materials and Technologies*. Amsterdam: Frame Publishers/Birkhäuser: Basel, Boston, Berlin, 2009. p. 313.
2. Daston, Lorraine. "Speechless" in *Things That Talk: Objects Lessons from Art and Science*. New York: Zone Books, 2008. p. 23.
3. Gausa, Manuel et al. *The Metapolis Dictionary of Advanced Architecture: City, Technology and Society in the Information Age*. Barcelona: Actar, 2003. p. 15.
4. *Ibid.* p. 14.
5. *Ibid.*
6. Kula, Daniel, and Élodie Ternaux (matériO). "Reflections …" p. 326.
7. *Ibid.* p. 313.
8. Daston, Lorraine. "Speechless" … p. 17.
9. Addington, Michelle, and Daniel Schodek. *Smart Materials and New Technologies for the Architecture and Design Professions*. Oxford: Architectural Press, 2005. pp. 25-26.
10. *Ibid.* p. 26.
11. *Ibid.* p. 25.
12. "Mondo Materialis" was subsequently featured in various venues including the Cooper-Hewitt National Design Museum.
13. "Mutant Materials": http://www. mutantmaterials. com/
14. Kennedy, Sheila, and Christoph Grunenberg (KVA). *Material Misuse*. London: Architectural Association, 2001.
15. The 17th-century Wunderkammer is described as a collection of wonders, of the new, rare, and unusual – an encyclopedic collection of all kinds of objects and materials of dissimilar and diverse origin. Such collections were the expression of the discovery of the New World, an Age of Exploration, "a period of rapidly expanding horizons of knowledge and the constant attempt to achieve the seemingly unachievable." These compilations were intended as "a microcosm of the Universe – a macrocosm;" a mirror of contemporary knowledge, "regardless of whether those objects were created by the genius of man or the caprice of nature. The rarer an item, the more attractive it appeared, be it a colossal 'giant's' bone or a precious find from a mineral vein turned into a sparkling jewel by a famous goldsmith." See Wolfram Koeppe, "Collecting for the Kunstkammer" in *Heilbrunn Timeline of Art History*, New York: The Metropolitan Museum of Art, 2000. – http:// www. metmuseum. org/toah/hd/kuns/hd_kuns. htm
16. Hensel, Michael; Menges, Achim, and Michael Weinstock, eds. *Emergence: Morphogenetic Design Strategies, Architectural Design*. London: Wiley-Academy, 2004.
17. Van Duijn, Chris. "Prada Bubble Mat Prototype" in Ferrer, Albert et al. *Verb matters: a survey of current formal and material possibilities in the context of the information age: built, active substance in the form of networks, at all scales from the biggest to the smallest*. Barcelona: Actar, 2004. pp. 80-91.
18. Addington, Michelle, and Daniel Schodek, *Smart Materials* … p. 29.
19. Forster, Kurt W. "Pieces for Four Hands and More Hands" in *Herzog & de Meuron: Natural History*. Ursprung, Philip, ed. Montreal: Canadian Centre for Architecture/Baden, Switzerland: Lars Müller Publishers, 2002. p. 54.
20. Kwinter, Sanford. "The Judo of Cold Combustion" in *Atlas of novel tectonics, Reiser + Umemoto*. New York: Princeton Architectural Press, 2006. p. 13.
21. Kula, Daniel, and Élodie Ternaux (matériO). "Reflections …" p. 313.
22. Moussavi, Farshid, and Michael Kubo, eds.; drawings by Hoffmann, J. Seth et al. *The function of ornament*. Barcelona: Actar, 2006.
23. Aranda, Benjamin, and Chris Lasch. *Tooling*. Foreword by Balmond, Cecil; afterword by Kwinter, Sanford. New York: Princeton Architectural Press, 2006.
24. *Ibid.* p. 10, 12.

The author would like to thank George Beylerian of Material ConneXion, Élodie Ternaux of matériO, Efrat Friedland of iMatter, Zaneta Hong of the University of Texas, Austin, as well as colleagues at the University of Toronto, Andrew Payne and Etienne Turpin, for their inspiration in issues of material technology, as well as their generosity in providing information and discussing the above ideas with her. She would also like to thank Hugh Wilburn, Jane Hutton, and Sophia Lau for their collaboration at the Harvard GSD Materials Collection, and Karen May of the University of Toronto for her assistance with visualization of the database.

The Future of Material Design

Thomas Schröpfer

Gramazio & Kohler, Architonic Concept Space, 2008, detail.

Over the past few decades, and continuing through today, the realm of material design has been undergoing a significant paradigm shift. Thanks to an influx of new technologies that allow new aesthetics and performance possibilities, the field is rapidly expanding, increasing the possibilities available to designers. An explosion of new materials and applications has been spurred by innovations at the very basic level of material composition. These advancements are fundamentally challenging the way we conceive of building materials, their applications and their environmental impacts. This is not to say that traditional materials – the familiar palette of wood, steel, concrete, glass, and plastics – upon which we have relied for so long, will be less important. Even as new materials emerge and consume our attention and interest, traditional materials will most likely remain the foundation of architecture's vocabulary. Their use has been honed over centuries, with discoveries of their behaviors and limits over long periods of time.[1]

Wood, for example, has been used as a building material ever since humans built shelters and boats. Over centuries, experiments had been made to give wood uniformity and stability as a building material. Evidence of lamination had been found in Egyptian tombs, and the Chinese were known to have used sheets of glued shaved wood for furniture. However, it was not until the early 20th century that engineered wood became easy enough to manufacture for widespread use. Such products as glue-laminated and laminated veneer beams are widely used in timber construction. Even today, the usage of wood continues to develop and expand with the emergence of new generations of material products, such as high-strength fabrics, and new lignin glue applications.

New materials are often used in conjunction with more established ones during their development, in ways entirely different than before. Concrete is another example of a material undergoing transformation; for example, material scientists have shown that adding phosphorescent inorganic pigments allows the surface of concrete to glow at night,[2] and recent uses of mesh reinforcement in place of reinforcement bars allow cast concrete to be extremely slender.[3] Even materials as straightforward as paints are enhanced with new properties,

such as infusions of fluorescent ink which allow it to glow in the dark.

Looking beyond traditional materials and their new variants, we see an expansive and emerging landscape of new materials. To bolster and enrich those materials already in use for generations, new technologies are facilitating unique solutions to increase building performance, efficiency, and sustainability. The new materials we are seeing now are unlike any development trends we have seen before. At the turn of the millennium, a series of developments in fields such as chemical engineering, manufacturing, and digital communications have allowed us to imagine a whole host of new possibilities. Today, glues that bond broken limbs, gene/DNA manipulation, laser-sealed seams on clothing, light-emitting fabrics, color-changing dinnerware, and personal mobile information devices are no longer flights of fancy. These advancements have continually surpassed all sorts of new frontiers; so the question is, why not in architecture as well?

It is about time that architecture drew inspirations from new kinds of technologies; for as automobiles, communications, and other technology-driven industries have made leaps and bounds over the last few decades, the fundamental concepts and material palette of architecture remain basically unchanged. To move forward, architecture would need a similar restructuring of its frameworks and foundations. Some of the most exciting developments in architecture occur at the elemental level of material design.

Material Technologies

With regard to material design and innovations, at least three groupings of new materials have emerged in recent times: composite materials provide greater efficiency, smart materials provide greater performance, and nanomaterials – among many other qualities – provide greater adaptability. Each of these groupings exploits new technologies in their development.

Composite Materials
The development of traditional materials in new and innovative ways is already far underway, through the realm of composite

Bohlin Cywinski Jackson (architects) with
Eckersley O'Callaghan (structural design),
Apple Store 5th Avenue, New York, New York,
USA, 2006, entrance view.

Bohlin Cywinski Jackson (architects) with
Eckersley O'Callaghan (structural design),
Glass Staircase Apple Store West 14th Street,
New York, New York, USA, 2007.

materials. For example, in concrete construction, new techniques of mesh-reinforcement instead of conventional bar-reinforcement allowed the firm of Anin Jeromin Fitilidis & Partner to achieve cast concrete structures unprecedented in slenderness (3.94 in / 10 cm) in the German office of LOOK UP.[4] In glass construction, a recent installation in Chicago's Sears Tower of large observation boxes allows visitors to be elevated 1,353 ft/ 412 m above street level and 4.2 ft/ 1.28 m out from the building envelope. Structural laminated glass, composed of three sheets of chemically tempered glass and layers of polymer film, is used for all five surfaces of the box and allows views unobstructed by structural members or opaque floors.[5] The entire fleet of Apple Stores built recently boasts similar structural applications, each with a custom all-glass monumental stair (ills.). The treads of the stair are composed of three-ply laminated glass, with each layer bonded to the next with an ionoplast interlayer. The treads are directly point-supported by the glass panels, while custom-made titanium connectors provide the tolerances required for the glass-to-glass connections. The aesthetic impact of this combination of technologies was thought to be so profound that Steve Jobs, founder and CEO of Apple Computers, and the structural engineer for the project, James O'Callaghan, felt the need to take a 14-year patent on the design. Another example for an exploration of the spatial and structural qualities of laminated glass is Laminata, an experimental prefabricated house made almost entirely from glass by the Dutch firm Kruunenberg Van der Erve Architects (ills. pp. 48, 54). To exaggerate the fact that the glass is only transparent when viewed at a 90-degree angle, thousands of identical glass sheets were arranged back to back to form an oblong, solid mass of glass, which was then cut lengthways. The construction of external and internal walls involved precutting 13,000 sheets of glass to size. The walls vary in thickness from 10 cm to an incredible 170 cm. Despite their massiveness, they still transmit light.[6]

Adaptive Materials, Smart Materials, Nanomaterials
Where composite materials can provide greater efficiency, smart materials expand the possibilities of material performance. As discussed in "Responsive Materials" by Sheila Kennedy, smart materials are the deployment of embodied chemical or mechanical devices within a material that make certain

behavioral characteristics possible. Smart materials are substances and products that have changeable properties and are able to reversibly change their shape or color in response to physical and/or chemical influences, e.g. light, temperature, or the application of an electrical field.[7] They can be categorized into semi-smart materials and smart materials. Smart materials are able to make calibrated changes in such characteristics as their density, opacity, kinetic movement, or state of deterioration. The primary distinction lies in the fact that smart material morphologies are repeatable and reversible, while those of semi-smart materials are limited over their lifecycle.

While adaptive and changing materials are not new to the discipline of architecture, the intentions and methodologies behind their recent use set them apart from previous generations. This has effected not only large paradigm shifts in building performance, ecological or otherwise, but has also opened the possibility of never-before seen visual phenomena and mutability. The use of adaptive materials in the past reflected the increasingly sophisticated understanding of their behaviors over time. For hundreds of years, carpenters have used soak-and-heat techniques to change the properties of wood so that it can be bent to form ribs for boats or violins, or components for furniture. But these and other techniques were applied to materials prior to their installation; the adaptive change achieved a static effect that was different than the initial state of the material. Today, it is the dynamism of change itself that designers seek.

Smart materials that require no human input in order to perform are (at this point) among the most sought-after. Photochromatic lenses, for example, are used not because of the particular degree to which they darken when worn in sunlight, but because they have the ability to reversibly change from being transparent to tinted and also because this happens autonomously. This example is also typical of smart materials in that the chemical change that occurs in the smart material is in itself relatively conventional and non-revolutionary. It is the simple reaction of silver chloride or silver halide molecules, changing shape when absorbing UV rays. Smart materials' significance comes from their application of change on a chemical level to a design solution appreciable by humans.

Certainly, there are surface-related applications with visual effects that only provide a sense of passing interest, such as the "appearing pattern wallpaper" that has been treated with photochromatic dye[8] or "heat" chairs coated with thermochromatic paint[9] that allow users to leave somewhat lasting impressions. These applications do not fundamentally change the performance of a building. As Ed van Hinte states in his book *Material World*, "a material without context is no more than a boring toy."[10] Our attention and efforts should be turned to applications such as thermochromatic cloth that help to reduce interior heat, or magneto-rheological fluids that change their direction of flow in milliseconds in response to a magnetic field, allowing unprecedented large-scale seismic dampers. In these dampers, magneto-rheological fluids (or MRFs) are stable suspensions of minute, magnetically polarisable particles in a non-magnetic carrier liquid. By applying a magnetic field, their viscosities can be varied and reversibly altered in milliseconds. In the MRFs, the particles are randomly distributed in the carrier liquid. When subjected to an electrical or magnetic field, they form long chains capable of carrying mechanical loads to a greater or lesser extent, which can then be deformed or broken by outside influences.[11]

Smart materials have also allowed greater efficiency in buildings, as well as a higher sensitivity to lifecycles of products used in building construction. Dye solar cells have advantages over their more conventional photovoltaic versions, in that they generate an electrical current with only a small amount of light. They can be used in low to medium temperatures, and have a relatively long lifespan.[12] Inorganically bonded natural composites use a non-toxic nanoscale binding agent in joining perennial plant fibers to form a lightweight, pressure- and bend-resistant, natural-sourced alternative to plastic honeycomb sandwich boards.[13] These performative and sustainable types of applications of smart materials are likely to have a lasting impact on material design and architecture.

As discussed in "Materializations of Nanotechnology in Architecture" by Peter Yeadon, properties at the nanoscale can give materials transformative properties, but typically the adaptability or changeability of nanomaterials occurs on such a minute level that the effect is almost imperceptible by humans. Even though the average building user may never register the mechanism behind these sophisticated technologies in their experience of the building, they are most likely to have a significant effect on the human experience of architecture.

While earlier material classifications divided each sector of the industry by elemental type – wood, glass, metal, concrete, plastics, etc. – each with their own research and advocacy groups, such nomenclature is no longer appropriate for the new generations of materials. Nanomaterials and smart materials, for instance, can be more easily divided along performative lines, such as property-changing materials, energy-exchanging materials, or matter-exchanging materials. Property-changing materials can be further divided into shape-changing smart materials, color- and optically-changing smart materials, and adhesion-changing smart materials, such as self-cleaning membranes treated with titanium dioxide (TiO_2). Titanium dioxide has emerged as popular nanotechnology that uses the hydrophilic properties of the molecules in conjunction with UV rays to expel non-water particles.[14] It was first used as a white pigment, but more recently, it has been used in conjunction with sunlight to purify water. A photocatalytic process allows only water to be absorbed into the titanium dioxide-treated surface, and other substances such as pesticides and pharmaceutical residues to be repelled. This characteristic can provide an easy-to-clean, hydrophilic surface, such as was used on the Chapel at the Osaka Hyatt Regency Hotel.[15]

Energy-exchanging materials can be subdivided into light-emitting smart materials, electricity-generating smart materials, and energy-exchanging smart materials. Dietrich Schwarz's Senior Citizens' Apartments building in Domat/Ems, Switzerland, is an interesting example of how new materials can be applied to improve the building performance. The glass facade is composed of latent heat-storing insulation glass. The triple-insulating glazing system uses a light-directing prism panel to deflect light in the summer, and permit light penetration in the winter. When the sun angle is low enough to pass through the prism in the winter months, it reaches salt hydrate-filled panels on the interior of the system. The sunlight is converted into solar radiation, and is stored by the melting of the salt hydrate, which in turn crystallizes when the room temperature cools, releasing its stored heat into the room. Heat retention is further aided by the opacity change of the salt hydrate in its different charged states; in their uncharged state the panels are opaque and in their charged state they are translucent.

Matter-exchanging smart materials are a smaller grouping of smart materials, and are currently mostly comprised of mineral ad- and absorbent materials and absorbent and super-absorbent polymer materials. Even though absorbent and super-absorbent polymers were not specifically developed for architectural uses, they can be used for applications that require sealing against rainwater (such as roof constructions) or groundwater under pressure.[16]

Experiments
Design manipulation has shifted, as earlier discussed, to the elemental scale. Nanotechnology now allows scientists to alter the very molecular structure of materials, resulting in astounding products. For other materials new interactions of elemental particles are being explored, while the material constituents remain the same. In transparent ceramics, for example, alumina particles are used as they are in normal ceramics, with the addition of Argon gas to compress the ceramic particles to roughly 500 nm, well below the wavelength of visible light (yet above the limit of 100 nm that defines the realm of nanotechnology). In normal polycrystalline materials, the grain size of the constituent particles – as well as the size of the spaces between the particles – scatters the light wavelengths in an incoherent manner as they pass through the material, so that, although the material is actually transparent, the human eye perceives it as opaque. When the particles are reduced to a size smaller than the light wavelength, the light is no longer scattered to a significant degree and the eye perceives the material as transparent. Ceramics treated in this way are extremely rigid and hard, scratch- and abrasion-proof and resistant to aggressive conditions; the new material has the transparency of glass and is three times harder than steel.[17] Transparent ceramics are already being applied in scientific sectors (in high-energy lasers, medical imaging, and space

exploration) and in military and security sectors (in armored and infrared products such as transparent armored windows and nose cones for heat-seeking missiles), and eventually they start being used in architecture and building construction. With their impact-resistant qualities, transparent ceramics could be used to combat earthquakes, wind loads, and other lateral forces. If transparent ceramics could take on much of the shear forces in a building, conventional treatment of architectural facades would become obsolete to a certain degree.

In other materials, scientists are experimenting with the well-established techniques and processes used to produce them. Porcelain foils are one example of re-engineering traditional techniques in order to achieve new products. Instead of forming the porcelain with molds and then setting the shape by firing it, porcelain foils use a technique usually employed "to transform ceramic powder into conductor plates or electric insulators." The resultant product is a thin sheet of porcelain, 200 µm to 1.5 mm in thickness, and can be further folded, cut, stamped, laminated, or embossed in ways previously unimaginable.[18] These foils can be used for sculptural ornamental applications in architecture, or to provide a finish surface that retains temperature and moisture in a different way than gypsum board and natural wood. Another example for this approach is the "welding" of wood, a recently developed technology that uses ultrasonic energy to connect porous materials together with thermoplastic elements. This enables furniture, window frames, and doors to be constructed without standard connecting elements, thus allowing the connections to take any form or shape.[19]

A third grouping of atomically re-configured materials are those in which the original recipe is completely abandoned for another that has less impact on the environment. Many of these types of materials have been reconstituted out of a different biodegradable medium in order to reduce the object's impact in landfills. Perhaps the most well-known and widespread examples are plastic water bottles and dining ware made from maize. Currently new plastics are produced from renewable resources that are fully compostable after use.[20] Products from these plastics may impact the building industry

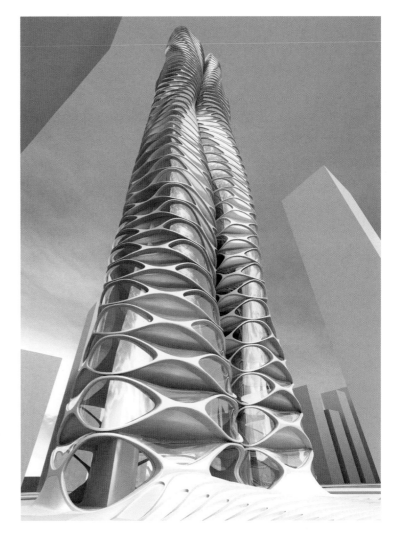

Material ConneXion, New York, New York,
USA, material archives and samples.

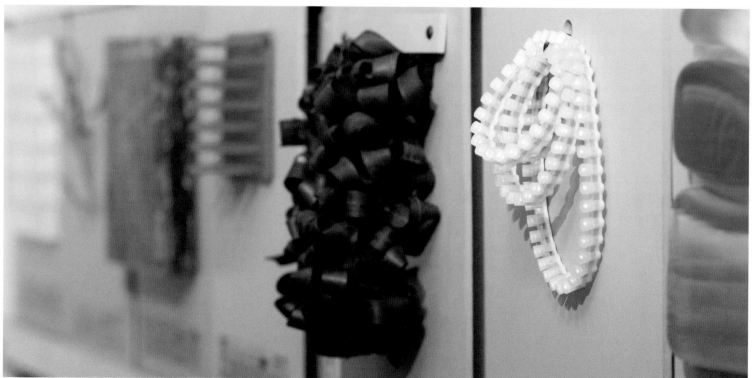

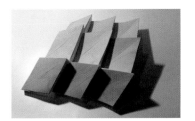

HfG Offenbach University for Art and Design,
Achim Menges (Instructor), Steffen Reichert,
Responsive Veneer Surface Structure, Germany,
2007, view and details.

at the implementation level, for example by allowing temporary fasteners and containers used at the building site to biodegrade in place after their use, rather than being shipped to a landfill, or remain on site as litter. Today biologically degradable raw materials such as saw dust or wood chippings can be bonded into pellets by using maize along with natural resins or biologically degradable plastics. The pellets are worked into extrudable shapes, resulting in architectural profiles that are biologically degradable, recyclable, very stable, structurally rigid, and non-flammable.

Research

To support and encourage these and other developments of materials, new research institutions have been set up. As discussed in "Encoding: Digital and Analogue Taxonavigation" by Liat Margolis, an expansive range of institutions are quickly emerging to make sense of the complicated new terrain that has emerged – for example the Center for Intelligent Material Systems and Structures at Virginia Polytechnic Institute and the Textiles Nanotechnology Laboratory at Cornell University. The California-based Institute for Molecular Manufacturing conducts and funds nanotechnology research, and in conjunction with its associated organization, the Foresight Institute, supports education efforts in nanotechnology. Material ConneXion, an institution with a large and comprehensive presence in the material design community, not only curates a library of advanced, innovative, sustainable materials and processes, but also brings together multi-disciplinary scientists and material specialists to produce innovative solutions to a wide array of problems (ills. pp. 153, 154, 170). The international group also conducts research to further materials innovation, the strategic value of materials, and sustainable material solutions.

Design Methods

Concurrent to the expansive numbers of new material technologies that are being developed, new methods of design have been for some time challenging the traditional methodologies. Computational design has impacted architectural design in multi-faceted ways, most noticeably through the rise of algorithmic and parametric-based forms. However, to a

large extent, computational design methodology has produced architecture that is materially generic.

In their critique of computational design that is generic in terms of the use of materials, the architects Achim Menges and Michael Hensel have argued for integrating aspects of formation and materialization. They criticize "the underlying impoverished notion of form generation, which refers to various digitally driven processes resulting in shapes that remain detached from material and construction logics." For them, material systems should be the generative drivers in the design process, leading to "an understanding of form, material, structure and behavior not as separate elements, but rather as complex interrelations."[21] This approach can be seen for example in Steffen Reichert's installation titled Responsive Surface Structure, where the hygroscopic characteristics of wood are investigated and deployed across a structural array (ills.). The project makes use of timber's inherent moisture-absorbing properties and the related differential surface expansion. This property is used to combine a humidity sensor, actuator, and regulating element into a singular component, a composite moisture-responsive veneer element that is attached to a load-bearing substructure. Once the veneer is exposed to a higher level of humidity, it swells and the subsequent surface expansion triggers a deformation that opens a gap between the substructure and the veneer element resulting in different degrees of porosity of the overall structure.[22]

Digital Fabrication Techniques

In conjunction with these advances in computational design, new rapid prototyping and fabrication techniques are making customizable components easily available and allow new languages of tectonics and form to be explored. Digital fabrication tools, such as CNC (computer numerically controlled) machinery (laser cutters, CNC mills, saws, and drills) and universal robots, make possible a proliferation of custom components that can be produced at a relatively low cost (ills. pp. 24, 40, 56). The phrase "mass customization" is increasingly being mentioned, in large part due to the proliferation of these advanced digital fabrication tools. Even though architects have been exploring the potentials of CNC machinery for a number of years now, cost and maintenance requirements have often limited intensive

SHoP Architects, Dunescape at P.S.1 MoMA,
Long Island City, New York, 2000, sections.

SHoP Architects, Dunescape at P.S.1 MoMA,
structure and surface details.

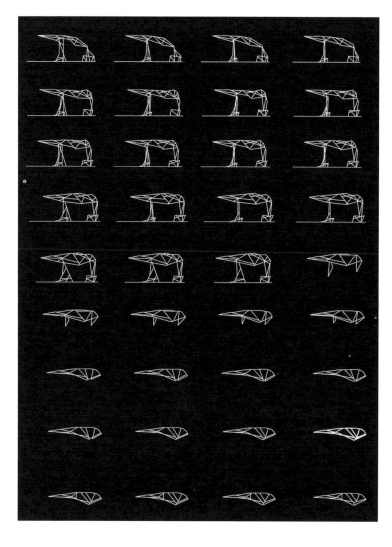

SHoP Architects, Dunescape at P.S.1 MoMA,
Long Island City, New York, 2000, sections.

explorations to the highly funded or academically associated practitioners. Universal robots are more economical as units can be purchased second-hand from manufacturers in other sectors, such as the automobile industry, who frequently update these systems. The explorations into the potential applications for these fabrication tools lag behind those of CNC machines, perhaps because of large space requirements for their operation.

The New York-based architecture firm SHoP has produced a series of projects that take advantage of these technologies, working with rather low-tech, easy-to-fabricate components that can be quickly assembled by a relatively small and unskilled labor force. Projects such as Dunescape at MoMA's P.S.1 (ills.), the Virgin Atlantic Clubhouse at John F. Kennedy Airport (ills. p. 173), and Mitchell Park Camera Obscura (ills. p. 179) all utilize some combination of such technologies, allowing entirely customized pieces to be fitted together with a minimal amount of instruction and relatively low fabrication costs. In the case of Dunescape, SHoP created a wood structure made of 6,000 unique cedar strips that are hinged to create various seating and enclosure conditions. Because the funding for the installation was very limited, construction was carried out largely by student volunteers. For the Virgin Atlantic Clubhouse at JFK Airport, in order to keep skilled labor costs to a minimum, a standardized assembly process was needed that nevertheless allowed for highly customized pieces. The fabrication of the screen components was automated off-site, using a CNC mill, and in order to avoid labor and construction regulations relating to interior structures, all dimensions were kept small enough to allow the individual components to be classified as furniture rather than structure. The elements were then numbered and fitted with spacer holes to allow for rapid on-site assembly. In the Camera Obscura project, a similar use of off-site custom CNC-milled components allowed assembly to occur with only two workers within a short time.

Another example similar to the Camera Obscura not only in terms of fabrication methods, but also for its exploration of the effect of the human eye's adjustment to tenebrous spaces is Voromuro (ills. cover, pp. 35, 175), created for the Institute of Contemporary Art in Boston by Office dA in 2007, that has

SHoP Architects, Virgin Atlantic Clubhouse,
New York, New York, 2004, materials template
and axonometric screen assembly.

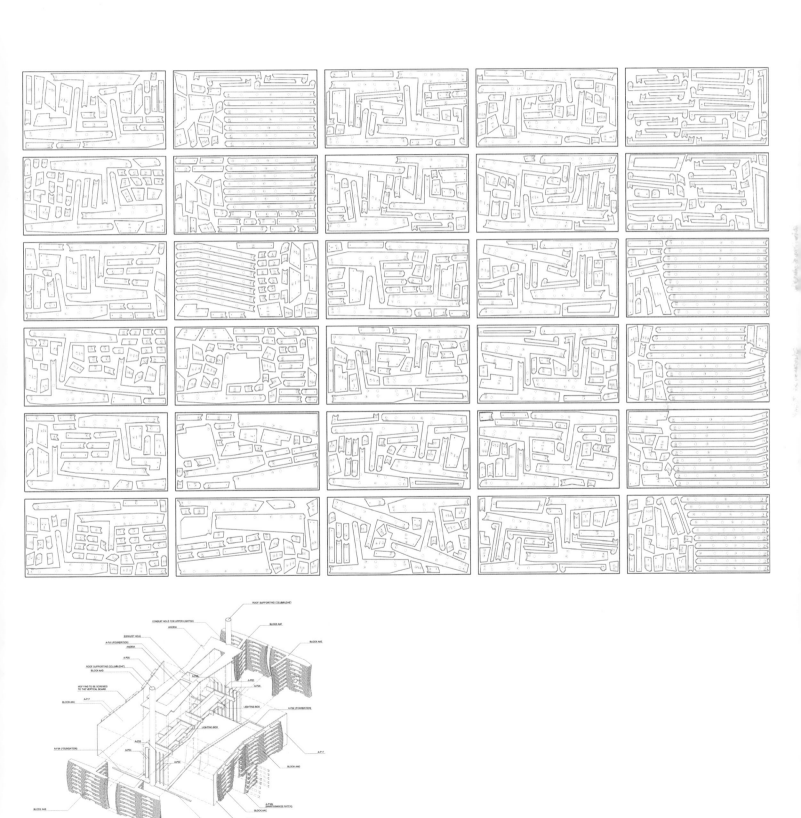

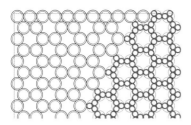

Schröpfer + Hee, Bamboo Oblique Pavilion,
material packing and partial axonometric.

been discussed in "Difficult Synthesis" by Nader Tehrani. In this
project, a Voronoi diagram, a special kind of decomposition of
a metric space determined by distances to a specified discrete
set of objects in space, was expanded into three dimensions
and torqued along a curve to produce a sinuous, cellular pattern
wherein the parametric and structural system were identical.
Flat milky-white glycolised polyethylene terephthalate (PETG)
plastic panels were CNC-milled into 600 unique profiles, then
bent into closed shells and riveted together.

The re-orientation of vernacular building materials into highly
precise arrangements is made possible through the use of
parametric design methods. Cellular patterns that occur in
nature are generators of the design of the Bamboo Oblique
Pavilion, created for the Gwangju Design Biennale in 2009
by Schröpfer + Hee, which uses digital technologies to
determine fractal tessellation patterns in aggregating bamboo
into a precise cubic arrangement (ills. pp. 174, 175). Material
optimization is achieved by an operation that ensures that rigid
packing is maintained with the most economical bundling of
sliced bamboo on each plane of the cube, introducing angled,
modulated light into the interior of the cube formation.
Each plane of the cube is uniquely customized for the desired
lighting orientation on the interior, yet the geometry is designed
to ensure that bundle-to-bundle connections are preserved.

Both advanced composite materials and digital fabrication
technologies were used for Lounge Landscape, a student
project from a class led by Achim Menges at the Hochschule
für Gestaltung (HfG) in Offenbach, Germany (ills. p. 176).
Based on a wave field that was generated by using digital design
tools, a modulated surface challenges normative typologies of
sitting, lying, and interactive boundaries. CNC mills were used
to fabricate a foam mold from which six geometrically unique
surfaces were derived. The master mold was sealed, coated,
and marked with the respective surface outlines, using a CNC
machine fitted with a marking pen. Two layers of fiberglass were
vacuum-formed over the mold and a 3D rubber spacer textile
was stretched in-between them.

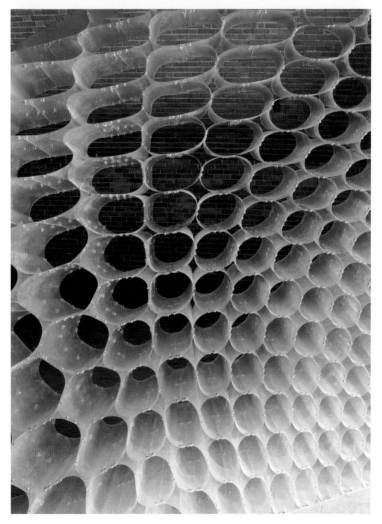

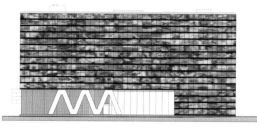

Neutelings Riedijk Architecten,
Netherlands Institute for Sound and Vision,
Hilversum, The Netherlands, 2006,
elevation.

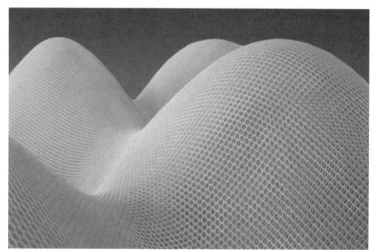

Today these new applications, however alluring and seductive, mostly remain on the level of installation art or interior design. It would be promising to see similar applications that develop out of digital fabrication tools but have a higher capacity for creating durable materials at the architectural scale. One such example is the glass facade developed by Neutelings Riedijk Architects for the Netherlands Institute for Sound and Vision (ills. pp. 176, 177). In order to produce an identity to the Institute, the architects selected still images from television archives that were translated into 748 unique, colored, high-relief glass panels. For each glass panel, a positive of the chosen image was CNC-milled into an MDF panel. This panel was coated with ceramic paste, laid on a sand mold, and oven-heated to 820°C. The high temperature allowed the glass to soften to a degree to take the shape of the mold and at the same time allowed the ceramic paste to burn the image into the glass. The resultant effect is of high tactility, allowing for the transmission of ephemeral light and creating a unique architectural experience.

In their facade for the Gantenbein Winery, the Swiss architects Fabio Gramazio and Matthias Kohler created a unique and technologically innovative design of undulating brickwork (ills. pp. 56, 57). Unlike the previously mentioned examples, Gramazio and Kohler experimented with architectural applications of digital construction through their use of a computer-controlled industrial robot. For the Gantenbein project, the program for a wine fermentation and reception building called for an innovative facade that would both act as a temperature buffer for the wine as well as prevent direct sunlight from entering and disrupting the fermentation process. The architects found masonry to be the most appropriate material, as its thermal mass would reduce heat and its pixel-like qualities would lend a dappled light effect. To exactly calibrate the light qualities within the fermentation room, robotic production was used to lay 20,000 bricks precisely according to programmed parameters – at the desired angle and at exact prescribed intervals. This allowed the architects to design and construct each wall to possess the desired light and air permeability, while creating a pattern that covers the entire building facades.[23]

Neutelings Riedijk Architecten,
Netherlands Institute for Sound and Vision,
view at night.

For both Gramazio & Kohler as well as Neutelings Riedijk, the new applications they have developed remain within the boundaries of established tectonic languages of architecture. They are facades and their advancements are mainly occurring as innovative ornament rather than transforming the way buildings and spaces are made or reflecting any sort of paradigm shift. The potentials of these recent advances in digital fabrication, while highly innovative, are still in their infancy. At the moment, tools such as industrial robots and laser cutters are still operating in a mimetic fashion, digitally reproducing analogue solutions to more or less conventional design problems. Achim Menges equates this idea to the usage of word-processing software as a digital "advance" that is actually only a mimetic optimization of an analogue typewriter. In his essay "Integral Formation and Materialization: Computational Form and Material Gestalt," Menges reiterates that even though CAD/CAM technologies "may lead occasionally to innovative structures and spatial qualities, it is important to recognize that the technology used in this way provides a mere extension of well-rehearsed and established design processes."[24]

Although it is a common criticism of the use of advanced digital techniques in architecture that they are ambivalent to materiality, material constraints and potentials are often the driving factors behind the development of digital relationships. Parametric digital tools allow us to accurately represent and manipulate forms while adding real-time feedback of embedded material information. The Zahner Company is a good example of this process. Zahner began over 100 years ago as a metal fabrication company. It has since evolved to become the industry's leading expert in custom architectural metal and cladding systems. As fabricators, they have a deep understanding of their material's potentials and have applied this knowledge while embracing BIM (Building Information Modeling) technology that allows them to achieve great complexity. They describe the future of the building industry as one in which digital technology is bridging the gaps between the construction vocations. In describing their excitement about BIM and CAD/CAM processes, Zahner states:

"Once the designer and the fabricator/constructor were much closer tied. The world was smaller, simpler then and one major project may have occupied much of a lifetime. Eventually, strict divisions of construction developed and risk transfer moved up there with quality and service as one of the primary focuses of the industry. All of a sudden we began building simple boxes out of rectangular components defined by these divisions. Complexity was risky. The structure was made of steel and bolted in straight lines by one division of labor. The cladding is attached to the structure in rectilinear components by yet another. Dignified guilds with apprentice inculcation disappeared and were replaced by semiskilled workers, lacking passion in what they were producing. It is hard to get passionate over a box. The connection between the designer and the fabricator today is being regenerated. The ability to model shape and form and then to transfer them to the manufacturing floor is introducing art back into fabrication process."[25]

Zahner highlights the potential for digital design processes to reconnect architects with fabrication techniques and to once again have a direct relationship with the materials that they are building with. With material information embedded into the digital design models, architects can directly engage conditions of material constraints within the design phase of the project.

Sustainability, Energy Efficiency and Material Lifecycles
Issues of sustainability, energy efficiency, and material lifecycles are increasingly prioritized in the discipline of material design. With buildings and their associated systems contributing, for example, an average of 32% of all greenhouse gases in the US, the green movement has impacted the building industry and its associated materials to an unprecedented extent.

Some architects turn to recombinant solutions to reduce energy requirements. Mitchell Joachim/Terreform ONE + Terrefuge's MATscape: A Material Mosaic Triplex project utilizes a complex combination of solar cells, wind quills, radiant floor heating, and rammed earth to reduce heating and cooling requirements (ills. p. 180). Situated in the commercial district of Munich, Germany, the Aviva MUNICH building operates its Venetian blinds and lighting systems through remote-controlled switches that use the piezoelectric effect instead of radio technology. Passive climatization can be achieved through phase-changing materials, or PCMs, such as paraffins and salt hydrate mixtures. When these compounds change their state from liquid to solid by means of crystallization, they release a quantity of heat energy previously taken in and stored at a higher temperature.[26] Available products range from gypsum plasterboard to aluminum foil bags with PCM. The increasing utilization of these new technologies indicates that physics is no longer the dominant field of science governing construction as thermodynamics, biology, and chemistry begin to play more important roles in facilitating comfort levels.

While the architects and clients of these signature projects have done much to pioneer the territory of green design, a more systematic (and affordable) way of encouraging sustainable building is needed to engage in an industry-wide reform. It is to this end that many governments and regulatory agencies have set up standards by which to rate and rank a building's impact on the environment. Certified environmental credentials encourage clients to invest more money up front and to insure the degree to which a building or product is sustainable. In the United States, the U.S. Green Building Council promotes the LEED (Leadership in Energy and Environmental Design) rating system. Striving to take a whole-building approach to environmental sensitivity, the LEED ratings are divided into five categories: sustainable site development, water savings, energy efficiency, material selection, and indoor environmental quality. The rankings have seen much success in the United States, with many projects changing their designs and substituting standard material components with their "green" counterparts, despite increased cost. Although LEED does not endorse any specific products or building components, companies that manufacture green materials have seen a growing market for their products. LEED takes into consideration many factors when awarding points for material selection, for instance the amount of recycled content in the component, whether or not the material is regional thereby reducing travel costs, whether it originates from a rapidly renewable resource, and whether or not it contains volatile organic compounds (VOCs). The system does not identify a building's "green-ness" merely by its operational cost in energy, it takes a more holistic view of the life to the

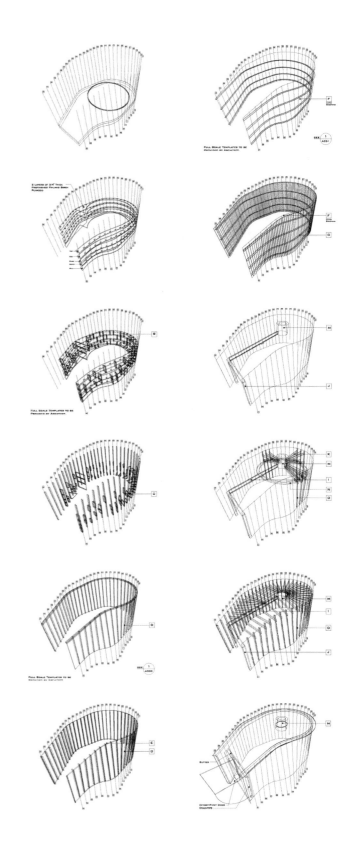

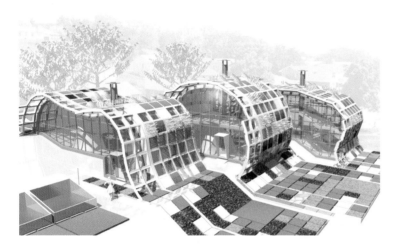

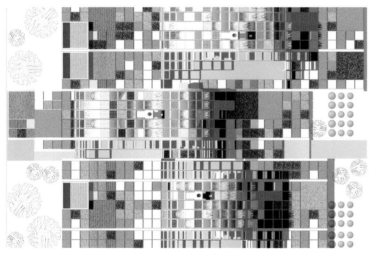

material before it arrives on the construction site, and its future after the life of the building.[27]

Germany has also begun to develop a rating system for green construction. The DGNB seal of the German Society for Sustainable Building is awarded based on a five-category catalogue with a total of 49 criteria. More stringent than the LEED system, the DGNB seal of quality also takes into account socio-cultural effects of construction. For example, a building may be evaluated on whether it is conducive to cyclists, or if it supports its occupants in recycling. Relatively few buildings and clients will be able to achieve the DGNB seal of quality, which thus serves to highlight projects that provide a high standard of construction as an attainable example.[28] Other ranking systems include the BRE Environmental Assessment Method in the UK, the HQE in France, and the Green Star in Australia.

The holistic approach attempted by these assessment methodologies brings an important issue of sustainability to the foreground. Known as "grey energy," the embodied energy of a building or a building component includes the amounts of energy used to make, transport, stock, market, and eventually dispose or re-purpose a material.[29] The environmental effects that the building industry can achieve depend much on how we manage the materials before and after construction. In trying to build more sustainable communities, understanding the nature and history of material components is as important, if not more so, than the new energy-harnessing technologies. To this end, it is important to ensure our timber comes from well-managed forests, and to promote the use of local materials that require less transportation and storage. A push is being made towards materials derived from renewable resources, such as the recyclable plastics mentioned above, foam made from sunflower seed oil,[30] or naturally-derived composites meant to replace fiber-reinforced plastic (or FRP). These composites are made from biopolymers (such as sugar beets, potatoes, maize, plant oils, or cellulose produced from waste paper) and natural fibers (such as flax, hemp, or ramie fiber), and can be burned or composted with zero CO_2 emissions.[31]

Of large concern are cradle-to-cradle lifecycles, a concept eluci-dated by William McDonough and Michael Braungart. They argue that the fundamental conflict between industrialism and environmentalism may be circumvented by making the currently open-loop industrial system of "take, make, and waste" into a closed circuit. Out of the waste of our current industries can come goods and services of ecological, social, and economic value.[32] This idea can be traced for example in foam wood products that are made of residual wood-processing materials. In these products, yeast and bacteria ferment with wood dust and chippings to produce a bread-dough-like foamed wood paste, which is then oven-dried to produce a hard, light, and porous board that can be used in place of gypsum board. Its disposal has no impact on the environment, taking up no room in landfills as the material is water-soluble.[33]

The new interest in understanding material histories has pushed biology and chemistry into the consciousness of architects. This has had an effect on the formal language of "green" architecture and it has inspired many new designs. Architect Philippe Rahm has begun to build architecture without the traditional palette of materials, instead using "meteorological" effects to define space (ills. pp. 44, 83). In a prototype for the Venice Biennale, he manipulates hot and cold elements to control a flow of air that defines programmatic spaces without walls by comfort levels (ills. p. 183).[34] The emphasis is on thermodynamics, more specifically convection, rather than on physical mechanics. Architect Sean Lally of WEATHERS proposes reimagining spatial boundaries as gradients of conditioned versus unconditioned space. In these designs he works with climatic conditions rather than material boundaries,[35] in a radical approach of building lightly as well as of atmospherically-based building. Other architects are using the tools for evaluating natural occurrences, such as heat flows, wind flows, and other fluid dynamics to help generate new forms. These points of departure may or may not result in sustainable projects, and are perhaps marked by a certain material ambivalence, but they indicate that the move toward sustainable architecture is not one that suppresses design in favor of technology. The pressures of sustainability have the potential to add new rigor and new inspiration in the search for contemporary architectural forms.

The Problem-Solving Approach: Pitfalls and Challenges

The very way in which designers conceive of materials and what is expected of them has expanded in range and been re-positioned. No longer are materials thought of as static, inert objects, but exhibit adaptive and changeable properties, as discussed for example in conjunction with smart materials in the previous sections. Adaptive, smart materials will not supplant traditional materials, but instead complement these in bolstering the performance capacities of tried-and-true systems. Beyond acting mimetically to the existing materials, the development has to add to the knowledge of the discipline of material design. Smart materials, for example, can be seen as a radical departure from the more normative building materials. Whereas standard building materials are static in that they are intended to withstand building forces, smart materials are dynamic in that they behave in response to energy fields. In this way, new generations of innovative materials and fabrication techniques are driving paradigm shifts embedded within the methodologies around which architectural designers operate.[36]

The conventional challenge of: "We have a given material – what can it do?" has been radically changed to: "What problem do we need to solve – how do we design a material to fulfill that need?" In projects related to the development of advanced materials, designers tended to keep an optimistic placeholder for a whole plethora of as-yet-unknown architectural devices offering innovative solutions. Smart materials were sometimes seen as the holy grail of such a search, and because the design need for these materials preceded their development, smart materials had huge expectations to fill, while the exact process of how they would operate was not of concern. Having specific requirements to fulfill has made the development of smart materials more constrictive, in some ways inhibiting the potentials of technological findings to guide the smart behavior. The scientific community has often lamented the opposite predicament, that of the "technology push," wherein the technology is available first and then must look for a problem for which it is the solution. This search for matching new technology to a problem can potentially lead to applications that might not have been developed in a problem-solving approach. Of course, architecture does not have short cycles of evolution and obsolescence, and new materials cannot easily be test-bedded and assimilated. Ideally, material design can bridge the gap between architects's desires and technology's limitations. In any case, architects can no longer assume that technology will one day conjure the correct solution.[37]

The way that these material trends will develop over time is, for now, unclear. But yet, there are still other, larger questions of how material design can be positioned in the field of architecture that need to be posed.

Will the enduring trend away from materials from local sources continue, as it has for the past 100 years or will it be reversed based on a growing concern for the environment? Since the beginning of the 20th century and the global explosion of the use of steel, concrete, and glass, the choice of materials has been separated from the concept of local availability. This is likely to continue, with the current proliferation of materials and processes being derived from some of the most sophisticated developments in science and engineering. There is an obvious conflict with the other goal being sought by designers of advanced materials, that of sustainability and ecologically-aware products. Advanced materials are likely to be produced by a small set of specialized manufacturers in limited locations, at least initially.

A scenario that seems most likely at this time is one wherein technology will be produced without geographic reference, but the applications of that technology will likely discriminate towards some kind of aesthetic expression, whether that be determined by the location or the designer's preferences.

What position alongside traditional materials will these new, performative materials take? Where in the course of architectural discourses will advanced material technologies align themselves? Will they follow ideas of honest and pure vocabularies of materials or will they support arguments for exuberance? There is a trend of using smart technologies as veneers, surfaces, or panels applied to more mundane substrates, like the heat-sensitive dyes or coatings, or the many different kinds of filters that may be applied to glass for aesthetic and/or performative effects. The struggle to fit new materials in architectural discourses is, of course, nothing new. This had been the case when the capabilities of innovation in architectural glass and steel at the beginning of the 20th century similarly preceded their effective and most elegant implementations. Even though their introduction radically changed approaches to design, they did not immediately achieve their own iconographic autonomy. Rather they were used initially to reproduce the iconography of other traditional materials.[38] We are now facing similar challenges, in that "most current attempts to implement smart materials in architectural design maintain the vocabulary of the two-dimensional surface or continuous entity and simply propose smart materials as replacements or substitutes for more conventional materials… The reconsideration of smart material implementation through another paradigm of material deployment has yet to fall under scrutiny."[39]

Assuming that the new generation of materials will become relevant beyond its contributions to visual experiences, will architects then no longer be "browsers" of materials, choosing them based on mostly aesthetic quality and a basic knowledge of their structural capacities? The current state of material specification in the architectural industry is typically that the selection of a particular finish has more to do with its appearance and profile dimension than its performative aspects. Obviously architects need to have a much deeper knowledge of chemistry, physics, and electrical engineering then before as this generation of materials is perhaps the most technologically advanced that has been developed as of yet. Much of the knowledge and many of the terms in these fields are a far cry from the sphere of knowledge that architects typically possess. But even though our vocabulary is different from the vocabulary of material science, we often act as referees and key decision-makers in the building-making process. Indeed, designers are faced with the challenge of assuming a high degree of expertise in an area in which they typically have no training at all. The question then is who should fill the technology gap – the architects or the scientists? If architects need to be proactive about learning chemistry and physics, why are scientists not providing simplified analyses of the products they produce? This market opportunity has already been identified, and material specialists have become

OCEAN/HfG Offenbach University for Art
and Design/Oslo School of Architecture,
Deichmanske Library Media Stations , Oslo,
Norway, 2008.

Philippe Rahm Architects, Convective Museum,
Wrocław, Poland 2008, interior rendering.

Philippe Rahm Architects, Interior Gulf Stream,
Paris, France, 2008, thermal diagram.

an emerging industry. To bridge the gap between scientist and architect, research and service centers that deal with innovative materials have become involved in the process. Private companies with commercial objectives first appeared in the mid-1990s and are now more widespread. Today, they act as mediators between designers, architects and manufacturers by collecting, organising, and systematising a vast amount of information, unfortunately categorized in a very disparate manner.[40]

Currently, developments in the applications of advanced material design span many different fields. On the one hand, there are highly scientific and technological applications, many of them in the aerospace and military technology industries. On the other hand, smart material applications are finding a niche in the realm of prototype objects, appearing in automobiles, furniture, textiles and art installations. One of the main questions that remains to be answered is how material design can be brought effectively to the level of mainstream design, where architecture can reap its benefits as well. While these applications must become easily accessible to the architectural designer, these technologies must also be easily understood as well as affordable, by building developers as well as clients. If there is no incentive or added value, be it monetary, ecological, or aesthetic, building clients will not pay top dollar for these emerging technologies, as they will be seen as being too extravagant or irrelevant.

Regardless of disciplinary boundaries, an optimized environment for accelerated research and design must prevail. Textiles, furniture, and art industries have proven to be successful incubators of advanced material design. These disciplines offer ideal laboratory conditions due to their quick concept-to-prototype-to-product timeline, as well as their smaller scale of operations and thus relatively low production costs in comparison to architecture. Ideal turnaround time and cashflow situations allow a wider range of experimental products to be developed, tested in the marketplace, and ultimately become a successful contribution to our disciplinary knowledge. Unfortunately for architecture in this respect, "buildings last for years – 30 years on average – and many last for a century or more. In spite of new construction, the yearly turnover in building stock is quite

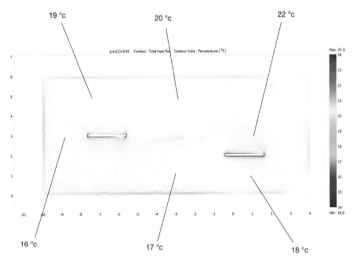

Gramazio & Kohler, Architonic Concept Space,
2008, detail and volumetric pixels or "voxels."

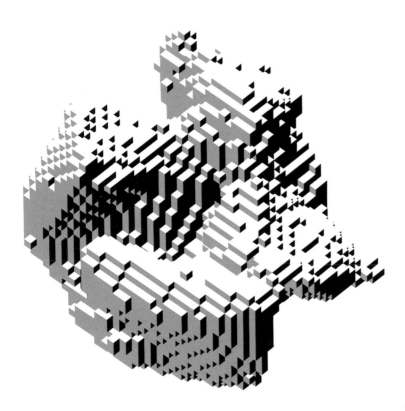

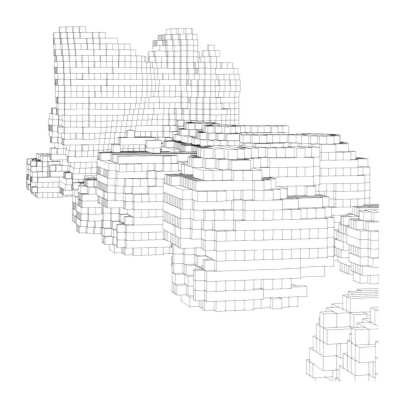

low. Anything new must be fully verified in some other industry before architects can pragmatically use it, and there must also be a match with a client who is willing to take the risk of investing in a technology that does not have a proven track record."[41] Some examples include experimentation in architectural interiors, such in as dECOi Architects' interactive kinetic wall, the Aegis Hyposurface (ills. pp. 122, 123), or Gramazio & Kohler's Architonic Concept Space (ills. pp. 165, 184). In the Aegis Hyposurface, wave movements and other natural simulations are created through diagonal tiles controlled by pneumatic reactive actuators. These actuators are mounted on a structural frame and controlled by software to spontaneously react to stimuli, including light, sound, and movement.[42] At the Architonic Concept Space, a series of sculptures named "The Eroded Cubes" were constructed out of bricks (volumetric pixels, or "voxels," as termed by the designers) using an industrial robot. The robot was programmed to use additive and subtractive operations to create interlocking conditions and functional cavities out of 0.5 m, 1 m and 2 m cubes. The resultant installations could be utilized as tables, chairs, and wall objects. These projects do help inspire and encourage further use of advanced materials, but it is not until these applications are subjected to the rigor of the building envelope and its associated complex systems, that their contribution to architecture and building becomes widely recognized.

Thus far, material experimentation has been mostly relegated to some of the most well-established architecture firms such as Herzog & de Meuron, Toyo Ito, Shigeru Ban, Kengo Kuma, and OMA with a history of innovative practices.[43] This has, in turn, led to the perception that material experimentation is an elitist pursuit, available only to those who have the most open-minded clients with deep pockets. It is a difficult proposition, for as had been discussed, the technologies behind most of the advanced material applications are highly complex, and usually involve a large amount of testing and experimentation by highly specialized scientists. Perhaps a segmentation of the industry, in which the basic technology is developed by scientists, then released into the marketplace in an "open-source" fashion, might engender the highest possibilities for a successful product. Or perhaps private research and development enterprises could bridge the knowledge gap between architects and scientists and make accessibility a high priority, allowing architects and designers to tap into the world of advanced materials.

The question, as discussed above, still remains of how these materials will have to be re-categorized in the light of their new properties. Additionally, it has yet to be seen how these new materials will be conveyed in our historically two-dimensional representational mediums. With this new generation of materials, how will designers represent time-change behaviors in a static 2D drawing? How will the new computational designs be represented? Two-dimensional mediums do not typically lend themselves well to the documentation of such things as tensile structures. Will sequences and animations form part of construction drawings? Will these limitations of representations strongly affect the types of materials that get developed?

After new materials become widely available and easily categorized, the question then becomes how to most optimally utilize them in an architectural context. As broached upon earlier in this chapter, these new materials do not simply replicate the properties already achievable with traditional materials. They do not simply reproduce the same materials structure, aesthetic palette, and ecological stance (or lack thereof); at least one – if not more— of these agendas must change in order for the materials to have long-term resonance. Nor can it be that advanced materials only add new territories in terms of ephemera and aesthetics, or they will become inconsequential as fads and gimmicks. New materials have the potential to actually impact the performance of a building, and as a bonus, impact the image of the building. Surface-only trends, such as thermochromatic surfaces or fluorescent paints, would have to develop deeper, more profound ways to impact spatial performance, or they may quickly become sidetracked in the rapidly developing field of material design.

There can be no doubt, however, that materials and materiality will continue to infuse architecture with poetry and grace through their transformative potential. Manfred Sack, the German architecture critic, once made a remark that, "again and again there is the sensuality of the material—how it feels, what it looks like: does it look dull, does it shimmer or sparkle? Its smell. Is it hard or soft, flexible, cold or warm, smooth or rough? What color is it and which structures does it reveal on its surface?"[44] In the context of material design today, this comment should be amended to include, "does it perform dynamically, and if so, how?" Through advanced material design, we are only now expanding the range of capabilities that materials hold.

Notes

1. Arroyo, Salvador Perez et al. (eds.). *Emerging Technologies and Housing Prototypes*. Rotterdam: Berlage Institute Postgraduate Laboratory of Architecture, 2007. p.29.
2. Ritter, Axel. *Smart Materials in Architecture, Interior Architecture and Design*. Basel, Boston, Berlin: Birkhäuser, 2007. p.121.
3. Bell Ballard, Victoria, and Patrick Rand. *Materials for Design*. New York: Princeton Architectural Press, 2006. p.74.
4. *Ibid.*, p.74.
5. Fountain, Henry. "As Unbreakable as ... Glass?" in *The New York Times*, 6 July 2009.
6. van Hinte, Ed. "The Great Disappearing Act" in: van Onna, Edwin. *Material World*, Basel, Boston, Berlin: Birkhäuser, 2003.
7. Ritter, p.26.
8. Ritter, p.79.
9. Addington, Michelle and Daniel Schodek. *Smart Materials and Technologies for the Architecture and Design Professions*, Boston: Architectural Press, 2005. p.4.
10. van Hinte, Preface.
11. Ritter, Axel. *Smart Materials* ... p.38.
12. *Ibid.* p.145.
13. Stattmann, Nicola. *Ultralight Superstrong: A New Generation of Design Materials*. Basel, Boston, Berlin: Birkhäuser, 2003. p.102.
14. van Hinte, Ed. "The Great Disappeating Act" ... Chapter 11.
15. Ritter, Axel. *Smart Materials* ... p.105.
16. *Ibid.* p.184.
17. Stattmann, Nicola. *Ultralight* ... p.26.
18. *Ibid.* p.32
19. *Ibid.* p.84.
20. *Ibid.* p.108.
21. Menges, Achim. "Inclusive Performance: Efficiency Versus Effectiveness – Towards a Morpho-Ecological Approach for Design" in *Architectural Design*, v. 78, n. 2 (2008). p.56.
22. Kolarevic, Branko, and Kevin R. Klinger, eds. *Manufacturing Material Effects: Rethinking Design and Making in Architecture*, New York: Routledge, 2008. p.204.
23. Gramazio, Fabio, and Matthias Kohler, *Digital Materiality in Architecture*, Basel: Lars Müller Publishers, 2008. p.95.
24. Kolarevic, Branko, and Kevin R. Klinger, eds. *Manufacturing...* p.196.
25. Zahner, L. William. "Zahner: Building Information Modeling (BIM)." Zahner webpage: http://www.azahner.com/building_information_modeling.cfm (accessed April 25, 2010).
26. Ritter, Axel. *Smart Materials* ... pp.160-165.
27. *Material and LEED: The architect's handbook of professional practice*. Joseph A. Demkin, ex. ed. Washington, DC: American Institute of Architects/Hoboken, NJ: John Wiley and Sons, 2008. 14th edition.
28. Jäger, Frank Peter. "DGNB Seal of Quality – Sustainable in Every Respect" in: *Detail Green* Special Edition, Jan. 2009.
29. *Ibid.*
30. *Ibid.* p.110.
31. Stattmann, Nicola. *Ultralight* ... p.100.
32. McDonough, William, and Michael Braungart. *Cradle to Cradle: Remaking the Way We Make Things*. New York: North Point Press, 2002.
33. Stattmann, Nicola. *Ultralight* ... p.96.
34. Rahm, Philippe. "Meteorological Architecture" in *AD*, v. 79, n. 3, pp.30-41.
35. Lally, Sean. "When Cold Air Sleeps" in *AD*, v. 79, no. 3, pp. 55-63.
36. Addington, Michelle, and Daniel Schodek. *Smart Materials* ... p. 4.
37. *Ibid.* p.viii.
38. Arroyo, Salvador Perez et al., eds. *Emerging Technologies* ... p.30.
39. Addington, Michelle, and Daniel Schodek. *Smart Materials* ... p.5.
40. Arroyo, Salvador Perez et al., eds. *Emerging Technologies* ... p.37.
41. Addington, Michelle, and Daniel Schodek. *Smart Materials* ... p.12.
42. Ritter, Axel. *Smart Materials* ... p.12.
43. Arroyo, Salvador Perez et al., eds. *Emerging Technologies* ... p.38.
44. Deplazes, Andrea. *Constructing Architecture: Materials, Processes, Structures*. Basel, Boston, Berlin: Birkhäuser, 2005. p.19.

On the Author and the Contributors

Thomas Schröpfer

Thomas Schröpfer is a co-founder and Principal of Schröpfer + Hee, an interdisciplinary architecture and design practice based in Cambridge, Massachusetts, and Associate Professor of Architecture at the Harvard University Graduate School of Design (GSD) where he teaches architecture design studios and courses on materials and construction. He had been practicing as an architect in Germany and leading research and development projects at Hochtief Group before he joined Harvard University as a faculty. Schröpfer's practice and research work focuses on issues of material performance, design strategies, and sustainability in architecture. He has published extensively including in *Journal of Architectural Education*, *Journal of Green Building*, and DETAIL *Green* and received many awards and recognitions, including from the Union Internationale des Architectes (UIA) and the Gwangju Design Biennale. He has lectured widely on his work that has been exhibited internationally.

Erwin Viray

Erwin Viray is the co-editor of the Tokyo-based architectural journal *A+U (Architecture and Urbanism)* and Professor and Chair in Architecture and Design at the Kyoto Institute of Technology Graduate School of Science and Technology. He was formerly Assistant Professor at the Department of Architecture of the National University of Singapore and Design Critic in Architecture at the Harvard University Graduate School of Design (GSD). He is the author of *Beauty of Materials: When Surfaces Start to Move* (Tokyo: Kyoritsu Publishing, 2002), curator for the "Exotic More or Less" exhibition at the AEDES Berlin architecture forum, 2006, and one of the ten critics for the publication *10x10_2* (London: Phaidon Press, 2006). Viray has participated as jury member in many international design awards.

Nader Tehrani

Nader Tehrani is the founding Principal of Boston-based Office dA, an architecture and design firm internationally recognized for its invention, precision, and advancement of new forms of knowledge. He is also a Professor and Head of the Department of Architecture at the Massachusetts Institute of Technology (MIT) School of Architecture and Planning. Working on interdisciplinary platforms, Tehrani's research has been focused on the transformation of the building industry, innovative material applications, and the development of new means and methods of construction. Office dA has received many awards and recognitions, including the AIA Institute Honor Award, the AIA/ALA Library Building Award, a Harleston Parker Award, and twelve Progressive Architecture Awards, and has been published and exhibited widely.

Justin Fowler

Justin Fowler is a Master of Architecture Candidate at the Harvard University Graduate School of Design (GSD).

Elizabeth Lovett

Elizabeth Lovett is a Graduate of the Master of Architecture Program at the Harvard University Graduate School of Design (GSD). She currently works as a designer for Zahner, an internationally active engineering and fabrication company, based in Kansas City, Missouri, which is best known for the use of metal in the fields of art and architecture.

Toshiko Mori

Toshiko Mori is the Principal of the New York City-based firm Toshiko Mori Architect, which has been noted for its intelligent approach to historical context, ecologically sensitive strategies, and innovative use of materials. Mori is also Professor in the Practice of Architecture at the Harvard University Graduate School of Design (GSD) and was Chair of the Department of Architecture from 2002 to 2008. Mori taught at the Cooper Union School of Architecture in New York City from 1983, until joining the Harvard GSD faculty in 1995. She has lectured and published widely and received many awards and recognitions, including the Cooper Union Inaugural John Hejduk Award, the Academy Award in Architecture from the American Academy of Arts and Letters, and the Medal of Honor from the New York City Chapter of the AIA.

James Carpenter

James Carpenter is the Principal of James Carpenter Design Associates (JCDA), a collaborative environment encouraging an exchange of ideas between architects, materials and structural engineers, environmental engineers and fabricators. The studio has developed architectural projects and structural designs employing glass, steel, wood, and composites for a variety of commissions, including museums, university buildings, commercial office towers and cultural facilities. Carpenter is the recipient of many awards and recognitions, including the National Environmental Design Award from the Smithsonian Institution, the American Institute of Architects Honor Award and a MacArthur Foundation Fellowship, and his work has been published and exhibited widely.

Sheila Kennedy

Sheila Kennedy is a founding Principal of Kennedy & Violich Architecture (KVA) in Boston and Professor of the Practice of Architecture at Massachusetts Institute of Technology (MIT). Kennedy has established a new model for an interdisciplinary design practice that explores architecture, digital technology, and emerging public needs. In 2000, Kennedy established MATx, a pioneering materials research unit at KVA which engages applied creative production across the fields of design, electronics, and architecture and material science. MATx works collaboratively with business leaders, manufacturers, cultural institutions, and public agencies to advance the widespread implementation of sustainable digital materials. Kennedy has received many awards and recognitions, including the US Congressional Award, the Energy Globe Award and the Tech Museum Laureate Award for technology that benefits humanity. Her work has been published and exhibited widely.

Peter Yeadon

Peter Yeadon is a founding Principal of Decker Yeadon, a research-based professional practice in New York City and Associate Professor at the Rhode Island School of Design (RISD). Yeadon's work explores how the use of new material technologies can address significant problems of our time. In particular, he is pursuing design applications for smart materials and nanotechnology that can offer innovative solutions to a variety of problems, including water conservation and quality, energy conservation, health and safety, and security. He has published and lectured widely and his work has received awards and recognitions including a nomination for the World Technology Award.

Liat Margolis

Liat Margolis is a Landscape Architect and Assistant Professor of Landscape Architecture at the University of Toronto, John H. Daniels Faculty of Architecture, Landscape and Design. Her research focuses on the knowledge transfer of multi-performance materials and technologies across disciplines. Margolis is a founder and former Director of Materials Research at the Harvard University Graduate School of Design (GSD), and was also the former Director of Material Research at Material ConneXion, where Margolis was instrumental in the development of a cross-disciplinary material database and archiving system, as well as research concerning the environmental impacts of industrial manufacturing. She has lectured and published widely, including *Living Systems. Innovative Materials and Technologies for Landscape Architecture* (with Alexander Robinson, Basel, Boston, Berlin: Birkhäuser, 2007).

Index of Names

of persons, projects, and locations

189

Subject Index

191

Illustration Credits